CHRISTMAS
TRUCE

Malcolm Brown and Shirley Seaton

CHRISTMAS TRUCE

The Western Front December 1914

MACMILLAN

First published 1984 by Leo Cooper Ltd
in association with Secker & Warburg Ltd

First published as an imprint of Pan Macmillan Ltd
in a revised and expanded edition 1994 by Papermac

This edition published 2014 by Macmillan
an imprint of Pan Macmillan, a division of Macmillan Publishers Limited
Pan Macmillan, 20 New Wharf Road, London N1 9RR
Basingstoke and Oxford
Associated companies throughout the world
www.panmacmillan.com

ISBN 978-1-4472-6427-9

1 3 5 7 9 8 6 4 2

A CIP catalogue record for this book is available from the British Library.

Typeset by Palimpsest Book Production Ltd, Falkirk, Stirlingshire
Printed and bound by CPI Group (UK) Ltd, Croydon, CR0 4YY

Visit www.panmacmillan.com to read more about all our books
and to buy them. You will also find features, author interviews and
news of any author events, and you can sign up for e-newsletters
so that you're always first to hear about our new releases.

Contents

Acknowledgements

When this book was first published we were pleased to pay tribute to a number of survivors of the Christmas truce whom we not only thanked as advisers and contributors, but also claimed as friends. Sadly, time has taken its toll on these splendid men, but we nevertheless wish to give them pride of place here; they brought the events of that remarkable Christmas alive for us in a very special manner and we salute their memory.

Additionally, we wish to acknowledge our debt to the many others, well over a hundred in number, whose accounts have made this book possible, and to thank most warmly those copyright holders who have given their permission for such accounts to be quoted. We also wish to acknowledge the use of Crown copyright material from the National Archives, which is reproduced by permission of Her Majesty's Stationery Office.

We are happy to record our gratitude once again to those who have helped us in other ways. There would have been no book at all had it not been for the persuasive encouragement of the late Roderick Suddaby, Keeper of the Department of Documents at the Imperial War Museum, and when acknowledging his role we must include the names of a number of his colleagues at that time, especially Clive Hughes and Philip Reed, and for the second edition Nigel Steel and Simon Robbins, and James Taylor of the Department of Printed Books.

Others who assisted in such matters as the checking of documents or translation from French or German were: Jill Dales (who also typed the original manuscript), Betty Brown, Peter Harris, Trudi Hoben and Moira Johnston, while help from overseas was provided by Mark Caldwell in Cologne, the late Barbara Breslove in New York, Roger Lampaert of Ypres-Zillebeke and Richard Baumgartner of Huntington, West Virginia, who provided us with some very useful German material and excellent advice for both editions.

Due acknowledgement must also be made to the BBC for providing the circumstances in which the authors first collaborated in telling the story of the truce, in their television documentary *Peace in No Man's Land*, originally shown in 1981 and since transmitted in a number of countries around the world.

List of Illustrations

Section One

Section Three

Explanatory Note

In referring to infantry battalions, we have followed the usage of the British Official History of the Great War, by adopting, for example, the formula '2/Grenadier Guards' as opposed to the formally correct but longer style '2nd Battalion, The Grenadier Guards'.

The complement of an infantry battalion was approximately 1000 men and 35 officers. In standard practice a brigade consisted of four infantry battalions, though in the early months of the war the number could rise to five, while from February 1918 it was reduced to three. A division, which at maximum strength consisted of 20,000 men of all ranks (though the figure was often much lower), was made up of three infantry brigades, plus artillery and other support forces. A Corps normally consisted of two or more divisions. Up to Christmas 1914 the British Expeditionary Force (BEF) in Europe consisted of five Corps, four British and one Indian, plus the Cavalry Corps and (from 18 December) the Indian Cavalry Corps. On 26 December the BEF was formed into two Armies, with General Sir Douglas Haig in command of First Army and General Sir Horace Smith-Dorrien in command of Second Army. Throughout this period the Commander-in-Chief was Field Marshal Sir John French, with headquarters at St Omer.

The BEF at first consisted of Regular Divisions only, but by Christmas there were numerous Territorial Force units serving at the front. The Territorials were originally weekend soldiers who had enlisted as a home defence force under the scheme launched by Lord Haldane in 1907; when asked to volunteer for overseas service in 1914 the majority had willingly agreed to do so. The 'New Army' units raised in response to the famous appeal of Lord Kitchener issued shortly after the outbreak of war were not involved in the first campaigns; however, numerous individual volunteers were present either because they had joined Territorial units which had accepted recruits following mobilization or as replacements in Regular units which had suffered heavily in the early battles. Additionally, Regular battalions had been topped up by members of their Special Regular Reserve, or by ex-Regulars who had volunteered to return to the colours on the outbreak of war.

Sources of quotations not ascribed in the text are given in 'Notes and References' or the 'Index of Soldiers' at the end of the book.

Maps

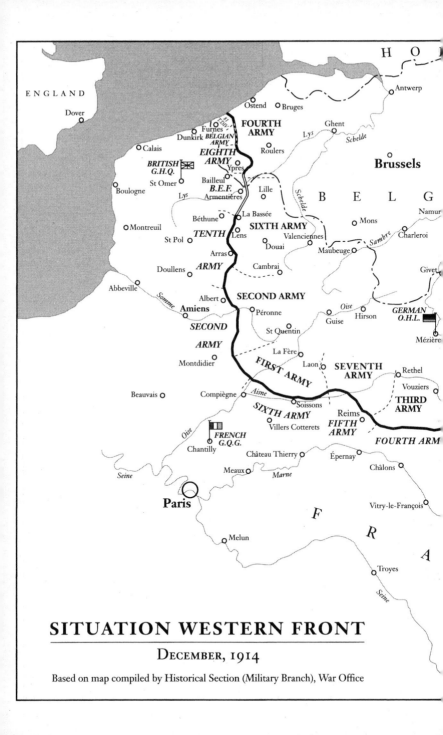

SITUATION WESTERN FRONT

December, 1914

Based on map compiled by Historical Section (Military Branch), War Office

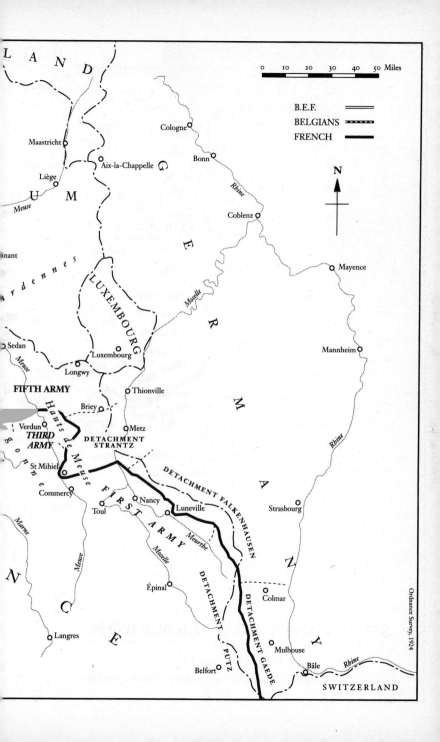

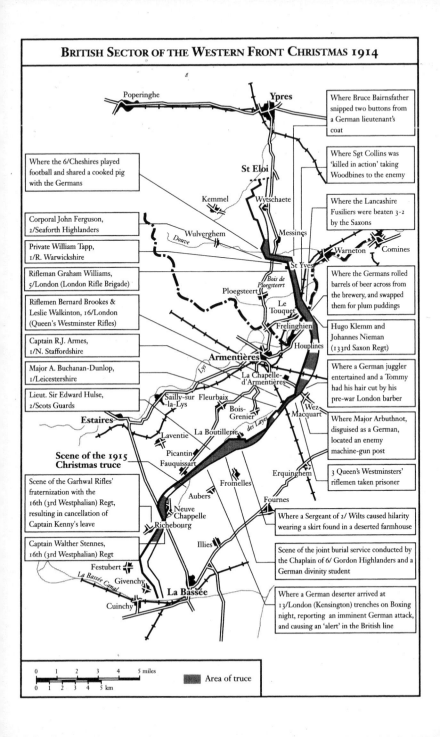

BRITISH SECTOR OF THE WESTERN FRONT CHRISTMAS 1914

Poperinghe

Ypres

St Eloi

Kemmel

Wytschaete

Wulverghem

Douve

Messines

Warneton   Comines

St Yves

Bois de
Ploegsteert

Ploegsteert

Le
Touquet

Frelinghien

Houplines

Armentières

La Chapelle-
d'Armentières

Lys

Sailly-sur-
la-Lys

Fleurbaix

Bois-
Grenier

Wez
Macquart

des Layes

Estaires

La Boutillerie

Laventie

Picantin

Fauquissart

**Scene of the 1915
Christmas truce**

Erquinghem

Fromelles

Fournes

Aubers

Neuve
Chappelle

Richebourg

Illies

Festubert

Givenchy

La Bassée Canal

La Bassée

Cuinchy

Where Bruce Bainsfather
snipped two buttons from
a German lieutenant's
coat

Where Sgt Collins was
'killed in action' taking
Woodbines to the enemy

Where the Lancashire
Fusiliers were beaten 3-2
by the Saxons

Where the Germans rolled
barrels of beer across from
the brewery, and swapped
them for plum puddings

Hugo Klemm and
Johannes Niemen
(133rd Saxon Regt)

Where a German juggler
entertained and a Tommy
had his hair cut by his
pre-war London barber

Where Major Arbuthnot,
disguised as a German,
located an enemy
machine-gun post

3 Queen's Westminsters'
riflemen taken prisoner

Where a Sergeant of 2/ Wilts caused hilarity
wearing a skirt found in a deserted farmhouse

Scene of the joint burial service conducted by
the Chaplain of 6/ Gordon Highlanders and a
German divinity student

Where a German deserter arrived at
13/London (Kensington) trenches on Boxing
night, reporting an imminent German attack,
and causing an 'alert' in the British line

Where the 6/Cheshires played
football and shared a cooked pig
with the Germans

Corporal John Ferguson,
2/Seaforth Highlanders

Private William Tapp,
1/R. Warwickshire

Rifleman Graham Williams,
5/London (London Rifle Brigade)

Riflemen Bernard Brookes &
Leslie Walkinton, 16/London
(Queen's Westminster Rifles)

Captain R.J. Armes,
1/N. Staffordshire

Major A. Buchanan-Dunlop,
1/Leicestershire

Lieut. Sir Edward Hulse,
2/Scots Guards

Scene of the Garhwal Rifles'
fraternization with the
16th (3rd Westphalian) Regt,
resulting in cancellation of
Captain Kenny's leave

Captain Walther Stennes,
16th (3rd Westphalian) Regt

| 0 | 1 | 2 | 3 | 4 | 5 miles |

| 0 | 1 | 2 | 3 | 4 | 5 km |

Area of truce

Preface

'One human episode amid all the atrocities . . .'

The Christmas truce really happened. It is as much part of the historical texture of the First World War as the gas clouds of Ypres or the Battle of the Somme or the Armistice of 1918. Yet it has often been dismissed as though it were merely a myth, a wartime yarn like the story of the Angels of Mons. Or, assuming anything of the kind occurred, it has been seen as a minor incident blown up out of all proportion, natural fodder for the sentimentalists and pacifists of later generations.

Veterans of the Western Front have been among the profoundest sceptics. In a letter to the authors in 1983 one former infantryman who was actually in France at the time dismissed the whole idea as a 'latrine rumour'. Similarly an ex-cavalryman, asked if he had been aware of the event, retorted with a typical Tommy's directness and, indeed, some heat: 'Christmas Truce? Eyewash!' But the truce *did* take place, and on a far greater scale than has generally been realized. It is verified, as this book shows, from a wide range of sources. Enemy really did meet enemy between the trenches. There was, for a time, genuine peace in No Man's Land. Though Germans and British were the main participants, French and Belgians took part as well. Most of those involved agreed it was a remarkable way to spend Christmas. 'Just you think,' wrote one British soldier, 'that while you were eating your turkey, etc., I was out talking and shaking hands with the very men I had been trying to kill a few hours before!! It was astounding!' Reversing the well-known quotation, a second lieutenant wrote, 'It was not war, but it was certainly magnificent!' 'It was a day of peace in war,' commented a German participant. 'It is only a pity that it was not a decisive peace.'

So the Christmas truce is no legend. It is not surprising, however, given the standard popular perception of the horrors of the First World War, that this supreme instance of 'All Quiet on the Western Front' has come to have something of a legendary quality. Young people who would normally dismiss that far-off conflict of their great-grandfathers in the century's teens as merely incomprehensible, find reassurance, even a kind of hope, in the Christmas truce. Brought to general notice largely by the stage and film versions of *Oh, What a Lovely War!* in the 1960s, it has been a useful, often moving, source of reference and inspiration for speech makers and cartoonists, for song writers, playwrights, film makers and poets. In 1993 an illustrated children's book based on the truce won a national prize. The event has, indeed, gained rather than lost in potency as time has gone by.

One thing must be said at the outset, however. This was not a unique occurrence in the history of war. Though it surprised people at the time – and continues to do so today – it was a resurgence of a long-established tradition. Informal truces and small armistices have often taken place during prolonged periods of fighting and the military history of the last two centuries in particular abounds with incidents of friendship between enemies. In the Peninsular War British and French troops at times visited each others' lines, drew water at the same wells, washed their muskets in the same stream, and even sat around the same campfire sharing their rations and playing cards. Indeed, there were so many cases of fraternization that Wellington realizing the implications issued the strictest orders, making it punishable by death to strike up friendly relations with the enemy. The Reverend Francis Kilvert, in his famous *Diary*, describes conversations with the old soldier Morgan, who recalled occasions in Spain on which British and French sentries laid down their arms, met in the middle space and drank together. In the Crimean War British, French and Russians at quiet times forgathered around the same fire, smoking and drinking. In the American Civil War Yankees and Rebels traded tobacco, coffee and newspapers (on one occasion pushing them across a river on improvised boats), fished peacefully on opposite sides of the same stream and even collected wild blackberries together. Similar stories are told of the Siege of Paris, where Germans once invited the French to join them in a massive share-out of wine-bottles; of the Boer War, in which on one occasion during a conference of commanders the rank and file of both sides engaged in a friendly game of football; and of the Russo-Japanese War, in which, among numerous other incidents, opposing officers entertained each other during an armistice for the burial of the dead, the Japanese bringing brandy, saké, beer and wine, the Russians bringing champagne, brandy and claret. Later wars too have their small crop of such stories, as is evident from the Postscript to this book; indeed, it is rare for a conflict at close quarters to continue very long without some generous gesture between enemies or an upsurge of the 'live and let live' spirit. So the Christmas truce of 1914 does not stand alone; on the other hand it is undoubtedly the greatest example of its kind.

Granted that the Christmas truce actually happened, there are certain misapprehensions regarding it which perhaps call for immediate comment. One widely held assumption is that only ordinary soldiers took part in it; that it was, as it were, essentially a protest of the cannon-fodder, Private Tommy and Musketier Fritz throwing aside the assumptions of conventional nationalism and thumbing their noses at those in authority over them. In fact, in many cases NCOs and officers joined in with equal readiness, while in others truces were initiated and the terms of armistice agreed at 'parleys' of officers between the trenches. Some of the best contemporary accounts occur in letters written by subalterns, captains, majors, even officers commanding who, while plainly realizing that this was not normal military conduct, participated nevertheless, recorded the event in as enthusiastic terms as their non-commissioned fellows, and were often equally eager for the truce to continue. There is also evidence that while some generals angrily opposed the truce, others tolerated it and indeed saw some advantage in allowing events to take their own course – while never for a moment doubting that eventually war would resume in full earnest.

Of course, in certain instances worried officers at the front *did* intervene to put a peremptory end to the spontaneous camaraderie of their subordinates. In other cases, the officers left the fraternizing to their men, partly from reluctance to participate but also from a shrewd idea that the Tommies left to themselves would find out more about the enemy's mood and dispositions. In yet other cases, offers of truce were so swiftly and decisively rebuffed that no one, officer or man, had occasion to step out into No Man's Land. Basically, however, people looking for any quasi-Marxist division by rank or class between those who took part and those who did not will not find particular satisfaction in this tale. The truth, we believe, makes a better story: officers and men of both sides mingling freely, in a mixture of attitudes from cautious acceptance to delighted, even emotional participation, the difference in nationality and rank for the moment all but forgotten.

One other misapprehension about the truce calls for rebuttal. There has grown up a belief, even among *aficionados* of the First World War, that the Christmas truce was considered by those in high circles to be so disgraceful an event, one so against the prevailing mood of the time, that all knowledge of it was withheld from the public at home until the war was safely over. This heresy – for it is no other – has not only lodged in the popular imagination but has also become the accepted wisdom of certain otherwise reliable historians. In fact, the truce was fully publicized from the moment news of it reached home and we found no trace of any censor's hand. Throughout January 1915 numerous national and local newspapers in Britain printed letter after letter from soldiers who took part; in addition they ran eye-catching headlines ('Extraordinary Unofficial Armistice', 'British, Indians and Germans Shake Hands', 'The Amazing Truce'), and even printed photographs of Britons and Germans together in No Man's Land. Similarly magazines like the *Illustrated London News*, *The Graphic* and *The Sphere* carried evocative drawings of particular incidents of the truce from material supplied by soldiers at the front. Germany also gave the event press publicity, though on a much smaller scale and for a shorter period.

True, the story was soon superseded by more sombre reports and headlines as 1915 went on, but it was by no means as dead as most events in yesterday's newspapers are normally thought to be. Contemporary histories of the war included it as a matter of course, and references to it occurred in some of the many books published during the war years whose aim was partly to chronicle the various campaigns and events, but also to inspire a suitably patriotic and ardent spirit. Hall Caine, a popular novelist of the time, included an approving section on the truce in his book *The Drama of 365 Days*, which came out in 1915. Publishing a year later, Sir Arthur Conan Doyle, in his history of 1914, called the Christmas truce 'an amazing spectacle' and, in a memorable description, saluted it as 'one human episode amid all the atrocities which have stained the memory of the war'.

Conan Doyle's phrase, indeed, sums up the attraction of the truce: it is the human dimension which means that this relatively obscure event in the fifth month of a fifty-two-month war is still remembered and will continue to catch the imagination. In a century in which our conception of war changed fundamentally, from the cavalry charge and the flash of sabres to the Exocet, the cruise missile and the Trident submarine, the fact that in 1914 some thousands of the fighting men of the belligerent nations met and shook hands between their trenches strikes a powerful and appealing note. It is perhaps the best and most heartening Christmas story of modern times.

Chapter One

A Background of Hatred

The Christmas truce was the culminating episode of a dramatic and tragic year. Nineteen fourteen, it is generally agreed, was one of the great watersheds of modern times. Commenting on it years later, Richard Aldington wrote: 'Pre-war seems like pre-history . . . One feels as if the period 1900–14 has to be treated archaeologically, painfully re-created by experts from slight vestiges.' Among those who recognized the cataclysm as it happened was Thomas Hardy; for him this was 'a time of "the breaking of nations"'. Old verities, old assumptions, old systems, old frontiers were never to be the same again. Much of the ideological turbulence of the world today can be directly traced to the great European upheavals which began in 1914. It was also the year in which the sacrifice of thousands of young men became an acceptable part of the international power-struggle: shocking in August, it was almost a ritual by December. For C. E. Montague 1916, the year when the volunteer armies were slaughtered on the Somme, was the time when 'a web was woven across the sky and a goblin made of the sun'. But the seeds of the Somme were sown when the nations declared war in 1914.

The Christmas truce was time off from that killing, a pause in the weaving of the web. But what gives it greater historical

interest and significance is that it happened so soon after a
violent explosion of nationalistic hatred, the result – and the
intention – of which was to inspire the peoples at war with
loathing and contempt for their opponents. In the case of the
small expeditionary force which Britain sent hurrying off to join
the affray on the outbreak of war contempt instantly became a
cachet: described by the Kaiser as a 'contemptible little army',
its members took the word as a badge of pride. Their choice
was an inspired one, for contempt, racial animus, the belief that
the enemy were capable of every kind of wickedness, was a
powerful ingredient of the atmosphere of 1914, a long-prepared
poison gas.

The explosion had been building up for years. That highly
nationalistic century, the nineteenth, had produced new rivals
to the long-established powers of Europe. In particular,
Germany's success with her land wars, and her overt determination to match the world's leading seapower, Britain, in the
element which the British thought peculiarly their own, sent
shockwaves of suspicion and anxiety across the whole continent.
The fact that Britain and Germany shared kinship, and a related
kingship, made no difference; if anything it added to rivalry a
dangerous whiff of betrayal. Concern at the new development
was, of course, natural in the older, more established nations;
this was a major change in the balance of power. But everywhere
there were those eager to exploit the new situation to their
advantage. In Britain, for example, pressure groups such as that
associated with Lord Roberts's campaign for compulsory military
service (Britain having always relied on the volunteer principle)
saw much profit to themselves in fuelling a mood of fierce
anti-Germanism, which the governing Liberal party deplored
but the opposition Conservative party largely supported. At
the same time, journalists like J. L. Garvin, first in the *Daily*

Telegraph and later as editor of *The Observer*, wrote in so antago-
nistic a fashion about Britain's Teutonic neighbour that the
German Emperor himself, Kaiser Wilhelm II, was driven to
complain at this 'continuing and systematic poisoning of the
wells'. Lord Northcliffe, who owned *The Observer*, also owned
the *Daily Mail*, which was the populist flag-carrier in a sustained
attempt to present Germany in the worst possible light. Novels,
stage plays and much bar and street-corner talk mined the same
seam. (The play *An Englishman's Home*, depicting resistance by
an English family during a German invasion, was so popular in
1909 as to beat all records by running at three London theatres
simultaneously.) Meanwhile in Germany the Kaiser's officer corps
took to drinking to *'Der Tag'* – the day of reckoning with
Germany's enemies. All this made acceptable the idea of some
kind of ultimate European conflagration. Looking back on the
pre-war situation from the perspective of 1919, H. G. Wells
wrote: 'Every intelligent person in the world felt that disaster
was impending and knew no way to avoid it.'

Yet part of the drama and the poignancy of 1914 stem from
the fact that there was a lull, almost with a hint of reprieve,
just before the final collapse. 'Few of us', wrote Wells, 'realized
in the earlier half of 1914 how near the crash was to us.' For
Harold Macmillan, then an undergraduate, there was no sense
of threat in those last months of peace. 'Certainly', he wrote,
many years later, 'had we been told, when we were enjoying
the carefree life of Oxford in the summer term of 1914, that
in a few weeks our little band of friends would abandon for
ever academic life and rush to take up arms, still more, that
only a few were destined to survive a four years' conflict, we
should have thought such prophecies the ravings of a maniac.'

Indeed, for Britain, such war clouds as there were in the
earlier months of the year loomed over Ireland, not Europe;

with a 'mutiny' by British officers at the Curragh, gunrunning to north and south and unofficial armies in open training, Ireland seemed to have all the ingredients of a major civil conflict. Meanwhile, ironically, relations between Britain and Germany had become, for the moment at least, almost genial.

In June 1914, as the crisis in Ireland continued to hold the headlines, there occurred an event which seemed to suggest that better times were ahead for these two great European powers. The Royal Navy was invited to attend Kiel Yachting Week. Two British squadrons rode at anchor alongside units of the Kaiser's High Seas Fleet. There was much mutual entertainment and no toasts to '*Der Tag*'. The officers of two German battleships, together with eighty of their bluejackets, were invited to witness a boxing contest on board HMS *Ajax*. The Kaiser's brother Henry was quoted as saying: 'This is what I have long hoped for, to see a portion of the British and German fleets lying side by side in friendship in Kiel harbour.' A British captain present was to say of the event years later: 'Never was a fairer prospect of peace and friendship between two sets of men bred to a profession of arms.' The Kaiser was in his most conciliatory mood and even appeared dressed as a British Admiral – 'proud', he said, 'to wear the uniform worn by Lord Nelson'. It was a highly successful fraternization.

On 28 June the imperial yacht was called in to be given an urgent message from Berlin. The Archduke Franz Ferdinand of Austria and his wife had been assassinated at Sarajevo. It was the falling of the first domino. The Kaiser returned to his capital. The Royal Navy squadrons sailed home. One month later the British Grand Fleet was steaming to its war station in Scapa Flow.

☆

So Armageddon, the war of wars, the ultimate conflict, came at last, and there began a campaign of hatred and vilification by both sides which made the propagandist tirades of the days of peace seem almost mild. 'The Prussian Junker', said Lloyd George in a speech in September, 'is the road-hog of Europe. Small nationalities in his way are flung to the roadside, bleeding and broken.' The Prime Minister Asquith, in a speech in October, accused Germany of 'devastation and destruction worthy of the blackest annals of the history of barbarism'. *Punch* portrayed the Kaiser as 'The Great Goth', but in popular parlance the German was 'the Hun', the Attila of modern times. In the same vein the French cartoonist, Jean Véber, portrayed the German soldier as an unleashed monster striding out to slaughter and destroy. Meanwhile such of the Kaiser's subjects as had taken up residence in Britain – there were many – felt the immediate impact of a fierce anti-Germanism which sprang up so swiftly as to leave no doubt that it came from well-established roots. Even before the declaration of war the process of ousting and ostracizing began. Bernard Brookes, a volunteer of the first week of the war, who was later to participate in the Christmas truce, had worked in the City of London for a Belgian firm which had a number of Germans in senior positions. On 3 August he wrote in his diary:

> As I write I am pleased to say that the office is now cleared of everything Germy, and it is resolved that none of the Germs will ever set foot in the office again if it is possible to avoid it.

The third of August was Bank Holiday Monday, and that day's holiday-makers, returning from their excursions to the East Coast, found themselves crossing paths with hundreds of Germans, many of them army reservists, hurrying home to the Fatherland. The exodus continued over the following days. For those who did not leave, either because they were over-age for military service or because they had been naturalized, there was a hard time to come as the host nation turned on German bandsmen, waiters, hairdressers and businessmen, and deprived them of their livelihoods, their premises and, frequently, their liberty. Concentration camps were opened, though it should be added that at this time they did not have the fearsome connotation they acquired a generation later. Catching the popular mood, the newspapers rejoiced as, that summer and autumn, Germans of all kinds, from suspect spies to plainly innocent old gentlemen, were hustled into custody. London hotels, such as the Ritz, the Carlton and the Savoy, published announcements to the effect that there was not a single person of German or Austrian birth, whether naturalized or not, employed in their establishments. The Hotel Cecil gave out that 'it had felt necessary to dispense with the services of German and Austrian employees'. The latter declarations are of particular relevance to the present story in that former waiters from British hotels seem to have been among the most prominent trucers during subsequent events in Flanders.

If the British acquired a talent for hating Germans, the Germans excelled themselves in hating the British – or, more specifically, England. England became the target of virulent German propaganda. Shortly after the war began, a minor Berlin-born German poet named Ernst Lissauer, serving as a private soldier in the army, wrote an anti-English poem. He called it *Hassgesang gegen England* – 'Hymn of Hate against England'. It so much caught the German mood that it became almost a second national anthem. First published in a Munich weekly newspaper in September, it was subsequently printed in leaflet form by the million, was taught to children in the classroom and was memorized by troops in the trenches. It won its author the award from the Kaiser of the fourth class of the Order of

the Red Eagle in January 1915. Translated by an American,
Barbara Henderson, for the *New York Times*, the 'Hymn of Hate'
became almost as well known in English as in German and was
much publicized – and derided – in the British press. The
following lines give its flavour.

> French and Russians they matter not;
> A blow for a blow, and a shot for a shot;
> We love them not, we hate them not . . .
> We have but one and only hate,
> We love as one, we hate as one,
> We have one foe and one alone.
> He is known to you all, he is known to you all!
> He crouches behind the dark gray flood,
> Full of envy, of rage, of craft, of gall,
> Cut off by waves that are thicker than blood . . .
> We will never forgo our hate,
> We have all but a single hate,
> We love as one, we hate as one.
> We have one foe, and one alone – England!

A less well-known but even more outspoken example of
anti-Englishness came to light early in 1915 when a copy of a
newspaper published by the Germans in occupied Lille was
discovered on a German soldier taken prisoner by the British.
Entitled 'Fire' and written by one Lieutenant-Colonel Kaden,
it was a bizarre but unambiguous concoction. These are a few
key sentences:

Let every German, man or woman, young or old, find in his
heart a Bismarck Column, a pillar of fire now in these days of
storm and stress. Let this fire, enkindled in every German
breast, be a fire of joy, of holiest enthusiasm. But let it be
terrible, unfettered, let it carry horror and destruction! Call it

HATE! Let no one come to you with 'Love thine enemy'! We all have but one enemy, *England*! How long we have wooed her almost to the point of our own self-abasement . . . She would have none of us . . . The time has passed when we would do homage to everything English – our cousins that were!

You men of Germany, from East and West, forced to shed your blood in the defence of your homeland through England's infamous envy and hatred of Germany's progress, feed the flame that burns in your souls. We have but one war-cry 'GOD PUNISH ENGLAND!' Hiss this to one another in the trenches, in the charge, hiss as it were the sound of licking flames . . .

Behold in every dead comrade a sacrifice forced from you by this accursed people. Take ten-fold vengeance for each hero's death!

You German people at home, feed this fire of hate!

You mothers, engrave this in the heart of the babe at your breast . . .

You fathers, proclaim it aloud over the billowing fields, that the toiling peasant may hear you, that the birds of the forest may fly away with the message: into all the land, that echoes from German cliffs send it reverberating like the clanging of bells from tower to abtower throughout the countryside: 'HATE, HATE, the accursed ENGLISH, HATE'!

It should be added that the British could express a fairly vigorous anti-Germanism and that their effusions too could be read on enemy soil. An Australian lady, Ethel Cooper, who lived in Germany throughout the war, wrote in February 1915 to her sister:

I loathe the newspapers, and yet what else is one to read! And I loathe most of all this policy of hatebreeding which is being followed everywhere. I must get you a copy of the so-called

'Song of Hate against England', which the Kaiser has ordered to be published among all the troops and learned in the schools! And in a *Daily Graphic* a little while ago, I found this:

> Down with the Germans, down with them all!
> O Army and Navy, be sure of their fall!
> Spare not one, the deceitful spies,
> Cut out their tongues, pull out their eyes!
> Down, down with them all.

And that is supposed to be a respectable London paper. I do assure you that when I read the words 'our sacred cause' now-a-days – in any paper – my stomach turns.

As if the falling-out of nations with a strong sense of relationship was not enough, strong fuel was added to the fire by the angry debate, the claims and counter-claims, relating to the treatment of the occupied territories of Belgium and France. Allied newspapers at that time were full of the appalling, inhuman atrocities allegedly committed by the invading Germans. Babies spiked on bayonets, hands or breasts cut off, priests hung as living clappers from bells – the worst examples from this gruesome catalogue have been convincingly discredited, but the fact remains that they did sack villages and towns, shoot hostages and show a thoroughly modern disregard for homes, churches and fine architecture generally in the pursuit of their objectives. The Germans for their part claimed that many of the civilians executed were guerrillas (or, to use the more precise terms, *francs-tireurs*) and that others were legitimately shot either to punish or deter resistance.

One other factor often overlooked is that the German newspapers also contained atrocity stories from Belgium – of horrors allegedly perpetrated by Belgians against Germans. A German

Reserve captain, Walter Bloem, in his account of his regiment's train journey to the front wrote:

> We brought the morning papers and read, amazed, of the experience of those of our troops already across the Belgian frontier – of priests, armed, at the head of marauding bands of Belgian civilians, committing every kind of atrocity, and putting the deeds of 1870 into the shade; of treacherous ambushes on patrols, and sentries found later with eyes pierced and tongues cut off, of poisoned wells and other horrors. Such was the first breath of war, full of venom, that, as it were, blew in our faces as we rolled on towards it.

☆

Caught between the hostile propaganda were the young men who would do the fighting. Regulars marched off to war, Reservists hurried to their depots, the recruiting offices opened. Britain's reliance on the volunteer principle proved itself well judged as thousands of would-be soldiers eagerly took the King's shilling. Bands played, jingoistic songs were sung, poets celebrated their response to the challenge of the hour and the first of many millions of war letters were written. One such was sent to his fiancée by a young Territorial, Dougan Chater, on the day that war was declared. Catching the sentiment of the moment, he wrote:

> It is awful, but one thing, it's got to happen some time, & best to have it while we are strong & have a good chance of whacking them.

'A good chance of whacking them.' The school bully must be punished, be given a sound thrashing and taught how to behave. Chater's phrase aptly evokes the simplistic values of the young at that time, as they went to war, in Rupert Brooke's phrase, like 'swimmers into cleanness leaping'. Few anticipated the long ordeal to come. Shared between soldiers and civilians alike was the assumption that the war would be short, successful and glorious. 'The general view', wrote Harold Macmillan, 'was that it would be over by Christmas. Our major anxiety was by hook or by crook not to miss it.'

Many of the enemy went to war with equal ardour. It was too readily assumed at the time – and has been too frequently assumed since – that because the Germans were in process of invading other nations' territories, including that of a guaranteed neutral, Belgium, they were an army of insensitive brutes blindly obeying the orders of tyrants and slave-drivers. Brutes there no doubt were – 'Frightful Fritzes' and 'Hateful Heinrichs', as Bruce Bairnsfather called them – but there were also thousands of eager patriots who believed as implicitly in their national cause as the British, the French or the Belgians believed in theirs. On 6 August a young student-soldier typical of many, Walter Limmer (who would in fact be killed before the end of September), wrote to his mother just before leaving for the front:

My dear ones, be proud that you live in such times and in such a nation, and that you have the privilege of sending several of those you love into this glorious struggle.

Summing up the mood in Germany of that time, Reserve Captain Walter Bloem commented:

The whole nation was in fact one immense united brotherhood.

No moment was more 'glorious' for the German soldier than the crossing of the sacred river Rhine while heading westwards to fight in the Fatherland's cause. As Captain Bloem described it, at the moment that the train reached the middle of the great river 'a mighty yell went up from the whole length of it' and

all on board began to sing 'the great chorus, the song of our
fathers, "The Watch on the Rhine"' – to the German the equivalent of 'Rule, Britannia' or the '*Marseillaise*'. This, for Bloem,
was an unforgettable experience: he was participating in his
country's bid to break out from the bonds imposed by encircling,
hostile neighbours.

> Was it real or was I living in a dream, in a fairy tale, in some
> heroic epic of the past? . . . As I realized the meaning of it
> all, my heart overflowed with that great joy of fulfilment, with
> the fullness of living.

Yet there were some who, even as they rushed to arms, were
aware of a worrying conflict of loyalties. One such was Willy
Berthold Paton Spencer (usually known as Wilbert), a Dulwich
College schoolboy whose enlistment in 1914 at the age of
seventeen gave rise to a special anxiety in his family. His mother
was a German, who was to find herself in the unhappy situation
of having three sons fighting on one side and a brother and
other relations fighting on the other. Among those relations was
the young aristocrat who would shortly become the most illus-
trious German air ace of the war, Baron Manfred von Richthofen
– the so-called 'Red Baron'. Wilbert Spencer's greatest fear was
that he might find himself in the appalling position of meeting
one of his German cousins face to face in battle.

Spencer would be among those who fraternized at Christmas
but before that he took part in a private truce of his own, while
still under training in England. His first weeks of soldiering
were spent as an officer cadet at the Royal Military Academy
Sandhurst, near which a large camp had been established for
German internees and prisoners of war. Having at this time few
hostile feelings towards his notional enemies, he asked for and

was granted permission to visit their camp one Sunday. He reported breezily to his family:

> So all yesterday I spent in amongst them – an awfully nice
> lot of fellows. I was awfully popular, having simply crowds
> around me listening to my excellent German pronunciation.
> I had long talks with them and promised to go over to Berlin
> after the war to drink a bottle of lager with them. I spoke to
> some of the famous Uhlans, bought an infantry helmet for a
> souvenir and also had one or two things given as well.

It was against the compatriots of these 'awfully nice fellows' that Spencer would soon find himself in action.

His story emphasizes an important truth, which was never to be apparent to the politicians, the propagandists and the civilians back home, that the fighting men of the belligerent nations had much more in common than most of them realized: their enthusiasm, their youth, their strong simplistic values, their commitment to what they saw as a worthy cause, their soldier's pride. They also shared their vulnerability to all the trials and dangers of a twentieth-century industrialized war. Inevitably they would largely ignore such common bonds in the years ahead, would not even recognize that they existed and, conditioned by the background of hatred against which the war was fought, would willingly do all they could to outwit, maim and annihilate each other. Yet from time to time there would be moments of comradeship and understanding, short episodes in which they – or at any rate a number of them – would opt out of the vicious killing-game in which they found themselves caught up, and would communicate not as soldier to soldier or enemy to enemy but as man to man. Some would even briefly acknowledge the inhumanity, the basic irrationality indeed, of what their nations required them to do. The greatest and most memorable of these episodes would take place at Christmas 1914. The war would not be over by Christmas as many people had hoped and expected, but there would be a Christmas peace of a kind, even though the slaughter would resume thereafter with an increased intensity and bitterness which would effectively guarantee that nothing on the same scale would ever happen again.

But for such an episode to take place, certain special circumstances were required. These were soon to be provided by the dramatic revolution in the style of warfare which took place in 1914 within weeks of the onset of hostilities.

Chapter Two

'Two huge armies sitting and watching each other'

It was ninety-nine years since Britain had sent an army to Western Europe. As the British Expeditionary Force marched towards the advancing enemy in 1914 some newspaper leader-writers optimistically anticipated another 1815, another Waterloo. But instead of one make-or-break encounter, there followed in swift succession the indecisive clash at Mons, followed by a long and exhausting retreat; the dramatic turning-of-the-tide on the Marne, and the first attritional battle of the war on the river Aisne. Indeed, it was as early as 15 September – barely six weeks after the declaration of war – that the French Commander-in-Chief, Joffre, ordered his armies to entrench. The British Commander, Sir John French, gave similar orders to the BEF the following day. So the troops of all three armies, digging in on the northern bank of the river Aisne, had their first taste of the kind of warfare that was to dominate the next four years. In a prophetic despatch to the King, French wrote: 'I think the battle of the Aisne is very typical of what battles in the future are most likely to resemble . . . The *spade* will be as great a necessity as the rifle.'

The change to trench warfare implied an awareness of the enemy quite different from that which pertained during the war of movement. The German was no longer a vague if dangerous threat beyond the horizon who might suddenly appear in sharp and menacing focus at the onset of battle: he was a near and, at times, visible neighbour – though at this stage not so close as in the days of cheek-by-jowl trenches yet to come. A captain of the 2/Grenadier Guards wrote on 23 September:

> The German line in one place is only about 750 yards from us and I was watching them yesterday moving about. You can see them quite plainly . . .

After dark they were, at times, audible too. The War Diary of the 16th Infantry Brigade recorded on 9 October:

> Afternoon quiet – At night much Singing and Shouting in German trenches and shooting of rifles apparently into the air.

But after three weeks the stalemate war was broken off and the armies briefly re-established a campaign of march and movement. The BEF transferred to the north-west to take up its position in the area which was to become – with significant additions – its more or less permanent battleground. New names began to appear in the official reports and the newspapers that were to become very familiar to the fighting soldiers of Britain and to their families back home – names like La Bassée, Neuve Chapelle, Armentières, Ypres. The First Battle of Ypres, fought in late October and early November, was a prolonged and bloody encounter in which the Germans sought desperately to break westwards towards the sea and the Allies fought with equal determination to contain them – and if possible strike eastwards on their own account. The casualty figures on both sides were very high. A British officer wrote of one attack which was repulsed with terrible German losses:

My right hand is one huge bruise from banging the bolt up and down. I don't think one could have missed at the distance and just for one short minute or two we poured the ammunition into them in boxfuls. My rifle was red hot at the finish . . .

In this battle thousands of those ardent young Germans who had responded with such unqualified patriotism to the Fatherland's call came to a very swift apotheosis. A German cavalry officer, Captain Rudolf Binding, wrote on 27 October:

These young fellows we have, only just trained, are too helpless, especially when their officers have been killed. Our light infantry battalion, almost all Marburg students . . . have suffered terribly from enemy shell-fire. In the next division, just such young souls, the intellectual flower of Germany, went singing into an attack on Langemarck, just as vain and just as costly.

The battles of 1914, in fact, cut swathes through many of the units, on both sides, which had gone so bravely to war just a few weeks before. Major Jeffreys of the 2/Grenadier Guards wrote in his diary in late November:

Our casualties since the beginning of the war have been:

17	officers killed
15	officers wounded
739	other ranks killed and wounded
188	other ranks missing

Total 959

Practically the strength of a whole battalion.

☆

After all this there had to be a lull: for all the armies involved, not only the men but also the options were played out. With so many battalions savagely hit, there was nothing for it but to wait for the arrival of new men from home depots to make up their sadly depleted numbers. More, the reinforcement units coming on to the stage required a period of acclimatization. There was also a growing feeling on all sides that no decisive blow would be possible before 1915, when new initiatives and a new season would spring the war back into top gear again. For the British, there was the additional awareness that they needed time to convert themselves from an expeditionary force into an army – the great hope at this period was the knowledge that under Kitchener's inspiration Britain was an armed camp of volunteer soldiers who were training enthusiastically on barrack squares and football grounds against the day of their being given the coveted passport to France and who, it was anticipated, would be marching to the front before long. So it was inevitable that there should be a cessation of hard fighting – a natural break, as it were – in the latter part of 1914, as the rival armies dug in where the last attacks and counter-attacks had left them. This, therefore, was the time when the trench lines which were to endure for so long and become so notorious appeared on the terrain of Belgium and France. This was the time too when the BEF established itself in the sector which it was to hold over Christmas 1914. For a brief while it relinquished its share of the Ypres Salient and regrouped along a front of some twenty-seven miles running from Kemmel, just south of Ypres, to the La Bassée Canal. Across the other side of No Man's Land, once again a neighbour, though a much nearer one now, was the enemy, in some places no more than seventy, fifty or even thirty yards distant. He was sometimes so close that you could hear him talk.

For those who had expected a swift outcome to the campaign all this was very frustrating. J. D. Wyatt, a second lieutenant of the Yorkshire Regiment, commented later that autumn in his diary:

> Something must happen soon. The situation seems absurd –
> 2 huge armies sitting & watching each other like this.

☆

The view from Kemmel Hill today is entirely peaceful; there are no reminders that this genial Belgian countryside was fought over in a four-year war or that the tower on the top of the hill was once a prime target for German artillery. To the north-west several miles off lies the walled city of Ypres, its towers and spires reconstructed exactly as they were up to October 1914: from a distance, indeed, one might almost be looking at a scene from the Middle Ages. Inevitably, as one approaches Ypres, the signs of war multiply, for there is no ignoring the numerous roadside memorials or the scatter of military cemeteries, many of them vast, in its neighbourhood. But if one turns southwards, towards the landscape associated with Christmas 1914, one could be forgiven for assuming that the fighting had scarcely touched it at all. There are far fewer cemeteries and almost no obvious relics of war. Well-tilled fields slope smoothly down to a shallow valley, then lift gently to the modest ridge on which sit the quiet, if drab-looking, villages of Wytschaete and Messines, which from a distance appear to consist merely of a cluster of ancient red roofs around a sturdy, brick-and-stone church tower. Only if one comes closer does one realize that the church and almost all the houses are relatively modern, since these places were in ruins for most of the war. The Germans had seized this ridge at the beginning of November, after fierce fighting, leaving the British holding the smaller valley villages such as Wulverghem and Neuve Eglise.

As one continues further south, the grey-green mass of Ploegsteert Wood appears – 'Plugstreet Wood' to the Tommies – a
crucial feature in the British line and, in fact, a focus of much
trucing and fraternization at Christmas 1914. There are several
war cemeteries here, but most of them are concealed within the
wood; fittingly enough, perhaps, for 'Plugstreet' was usually a
quiet or 'cushy' sector, unlike the terrible woods of the Ypres
Salient or the Somme, like Polygon, or Mametz, or Delville –
the 'Devil's Wood' to those who fought there. The diligent
searcher for signs of conflict in the wood will find a number of
old trench lines, most of them deep in the leaf-mould of so
many autumns or, less affected by time, an old concrete first-aid
post, with its evocative name, BLIGHTY HALL, still visible
in scratched letters on the lintel.

After Ploegsteert the undulations disappear and one enters
the totally flat countryside of the valley of the Lys – spacious
fields dotted with farmhouses edging a slow-flowing river a
hundred yards wide – where in 1914 the trenches ran right
down to the water's edge and where two neighbouring villages,
Frelinghien and Houplines, found themselves at Christmas one
in German and the other in British hands. It is at this point
that Belgium gives way to France. Behind Houplines, on what
was the British side, stands Armentières, towered and spired
like Ypres, but without Ypres's style and elegance; and, indeed,
more famous for its mademoiselle than its martyrdom, for it
was spared really heavy bombardment until 1918. The old front
line passes close to the town then heads south-westwards across
a further stretch of apparently endless Flanders plain, past a
number of tiny villages that are very much part of this story
– La Chapelle d'Armentières, Bois Grenier (between which two
places stride the concrete carriageways of the Dunkirk–Paris
autoroute), Fleurbaix, Laventie, Fauquissart, Neuve Chapelle,

Richebourg, Festubert, Givenchy. It is not a beautiful landscape, but it is a landscape of character, with long views across well-groomed fields of root crops or maize to distant barns and farmsteads, among which have sprung up in more recent years neat commuter houses custom-built for businessmen who drive daily in fast Renaults or Citroëns or Opels to Armentières or Lille. Copses darken the horizon, or little patterns of willow trees. Markedly different from Belgium, each village has its tall thin church spire. There are military cemeteries here too, but they are usually small or laid back unobtrusively from the main roads, part of the landscape now. Near Laventie there is one of the rare German cemeteries, its distinctive black crosses contrasting with the white Portland headstones which commemorate the British dead.

Here and there in this part of the line there are immediately recognizable reminders of the war. The most notable relics are screw-pickets, used by both sides – though not as early as 1914 – as stakes for their barbed-wire entanglements; now they support by the score the fences of the local farmers. There are concrete blockhouses too, also relics of later years than 1914; some of them have been converted into byres and storeplaces, though others are to be seen far out in the fields, derelict, ugly, with perhaps at closer view some recently dug-up shell propped against the crumbling doorway. Here and there too, in fields which the farmers have let lie, are obvious areas of former battleground, bearing the distortions of ancient shell-fire.

As one moves further down the line, Aubers Ridge lifts very slightly above the plain, on what was then the German side – scene, with Neuve Chapelle, of vicious and tragic fighting in 1915. Further on again, as one approaches the La Bassée Canal, the pit-heads and pyramid-like slag-heaps of the Loos–Lens industrial zone begin to appear, often under a plume of white or yellow smoke from some nearby chemical works. This area too was to see scenes of drama and gallantry in 1915, but was beyond the bounds of the British sector at Christmas 1914.

This then was the part of the Western Front in which the British established themselves as the First Battle of Ypres came to an end, and as the soldiers of all the armies concerned awaited the arrival of yet another belligerent: an enemy common to them all – the north European winter.

☆

Coincident with the decline in the weather was the arrival of many new men from Britain to reinforce and increase the hard-hit BEF. Now the last of the Regulars came out and the first of the Territorial battalions (see page 291), plus many of the early Kitchener volunteers, who found themselves sent to the front not in newly formed units but as replacements for badly depleted ones. In addition, after the longest journey of all, there was the Indian Corps, which had come five thousand miles from the heat of India to the cold of Flanders.

For the Indians the introduction to trench life was particu-larly severe. They arrived in October (their British officers being sent straight to the front without the benefit of even the briefest home leave) and found themselves holding a straggling line of fetid, waterlogged ditches and slimy streams from Port Arthur, just west of Neuve Chapelle, to Givenchy – a dismal sea of mud pitted with flooded shell-holes. They suffered acutely from the cold, were unable to get their accustomed special rations, and they lacked suitable clothing. Indeed, when the 2/39 Garhwal Rifles *did* receive some warm clothing in November during their first rest period after twenty days in trenches, all of it had to be returned as the chest measurements were too small. They also had certain problems which other units of the BEF did not have: no available depot from which to make good their losses and no reserve of officers who spoke their language. More, they were in a part of the line that was to see the heaviest fighting during the winter of 1914–15. Late November found them in a fierce local action at Festubert, with the Germans launching an initially successful attack and the 1/39 Garhwals subsequently counter-attacking to recapture their own lost trench. For the 2nd Battalion, which relieved them,

> the trench by this time was in a ghastly condition, with putrefying corpses in front and rear, and others merely put out of sight in the trench itself. The duty of disposing of these horrors was peculiarly repugnant to the Hindus.

But they had acquitted themselves well: a corporal (or *naik* to use the correct Indian terminology) won the VC, and two captains and several other men received decorations.

Elsewhere the principal battle at this stage was not so much with the enemy as with the conditions. Those who had been out in France for some months were sufficiently inured to the hardships of war to take these assaults of the weather more or less philosophically. But for the new arrivals it was often a difficult initiation. Lieutenant Sir Edward Hulse, 2/Scots Guards (an Old Etonian and Balliol man, aged twenty-five, whose account of the Christmas truce was to become the most widely publicized of all), wrote home in December about one Territorial battalion whose baptism had been more than usually rigorous:

> They have not quite shaken down yet, in fact the other day, when occupying the trenches next to us, they had given up the ghost complete; it had been pouring, and mud lay deep in the trenches; they were caked from head to foot, and I have never seen anything like their rifles! Not one would work, and they were just lying about the trenches getting stiff and cold.

One fellow had got both feet jammed in the clay, and when told to get up by an officer, had to get on all fours; he then got his hands stuck in too, and was caught like a fly on a flypaper; all he could do was look round and say to his pals, 'For Gawd's sake, shoot me!' I laughed till I cried. But they will shake down, directly they learn that the harder one works in the trenches, the drier and more comfortable one can keep both them and oneself.

Mud was the inevitable and much-hated by-product of shelled and fought-over land under more or less permanently falling rain. It became a torment, an impossible enemy, an inescapable adjunct to men's soaked and filthy uniform. Arthur Pelham-Burn, a second lieutenant of the 6/Gordon Highlanders, wrote in December to a schoolfriend:

I used to think I knew what mud was before I came out here but I was quite mistaken. The mud here varies from 6 inches to 3 & 4 feet, even 5 feet, and it is so sticky that, until we were all issued with boots, my men used to arrive in the trenches with bare feet.

It was a continuous struggle to keep the elements at bay. Sergeant William Williamson of the 2/Devons noted in his diary on 12 December:

During the day I improved my dugout. Made the top waterproof. The Company improved the trenches. I introduced sacks as overalls, to keep khaki a bit clean, the trenches being so muddy. During night it was very cold, & a continual rain. Get wet again as usual.

Nevertheless, despite the mud, the cold and the squalor, many of the new arrivals set to with a zest, determined to enjoy themselves. Major Archibald Buchanan-Dunlop of the

Leicestershire Regiment joined the 1st Battalion in trenches in late November. He summed up his first impressions in a letter to his wife:

> The Colonel is very cheery and jolly and we are all very well. The food is excellent, but is all brought in, of course, at night. No rest of course from bullets, but nobody minds them. Don't you worry a bit about me. I'm happy and well, and quite enjoying it as long as my Company is all right . . . I don't mind how much I rough it; it's good for me . . .

It was in a similar buoyant spirit that some of the new Territorial battalions adapted themselves to the life of the front-line soldier. Indeed, when the London Rifle Brigade arrived at 'Plugstreet' in November there was almost a holiday air among its members, as though their trip to France was merely an overseas extension of their annual summer camp. They had the advantage of better conditions, in that the wood, with its dense afforestation and numerous paths, gave reasonably safe access right up to the front line and the presence of so much timber allowed the construction of effective if primitive corduroy roads. But, though there was an atmosphere of excitement and adventure about their enterprise, with much joking and jollity and taking of photographs, they were all eager to prove themselves and have a crack at the enemy. When, during their first tour of the wood, a few stray bullets whizzed past them and one man was wounded in the head, they all felt, in the words of one of their number, Rifleman Graham Williams, 'most gratified to be actually under enemy fire'! Far from being a grim memory, this period for the London Rifle Brigade was a reasonably agreeable one. Williams wrote later:

> Altogether, life, and the war in general, during those Plugstreet days, was not at all unpleasant, when compared with later

experiences. Casualties were few and far between, usually 'Blighty' touches. When, occasionally, a member of the Battn had the misfortune to be killed, it was something to talk about through the Regiment.

Yet even when the initiation into trench life was considerably more arduous, there was a breezy spirit among the new arrivals indicative of an eagerness to prove themselves and make good. In December Leslie Walkinton, a seventeen-year-old rifleman of the Queen's Westminster Rifles, described his third visit to the front in a letter which his family – following a practice widespread at the time – promptly sent for publication to the local newspaper. He was aware as he wrote that the first Territorial battalion to see action, the London Scottish, had already distinguished itself in the field:

> It's pretty rough in the trenches this time. The water is 2 ft deep in places, but we are very cheery considering, and are resolved to stick it out. Our doings at the moment may not sound so glorious as those of the London Scottish, but as a test of endurance I am sure conditions could not be more severe.

☆

The rain which fell on the Allied trenches fell with equal relentlessness and similar results on the German ones. In mid-December the Commanding Officer of the 1/Grenadier Guards, Lieutenant-Colonel Laurence Fisher-Rowe, reported in a letter to his wife the experience of one of his officers:

> Jimmy went out last night and says he could hear the Huns sloshing about in their trenches & coughing as much as we do, so I expect they are equally uncomfortable.

Questions and suppositions about the other side of No Man's Land inevitably occurred to everyone in the trenches. Closeness bred curiosity and curiosity was to be a powerful motive in the initiation of the truces to come. What was he *really* like, this archetypal enemy with his spiked *pickelhaube* helmet, his barbaric record and his hymns of hate? Was he happy and content to be out there fighting for the Kaiser, or would he prefer, like all but the hardiest and most devoted professionals, to be back in the German equivalent of 'Blighty'? How did he cope with the rain, the mud, the lice, the rats, and all the other attractions of trench life? Imprecisely, by fits and starts, by no means universally, there began to appear the first signs of a fellow-feeling with the enemy, the first stirrings of that natural comradeship which springs up between men isolated from all normal experience and caught in the same extreme circumstances, which only *they*, and certainly no civilian, could properly understand. Looking back from the viewpoint of the 1980s, Leslie Walkinton summed up the general attitude to the German soldier at that time:

We hated their guts when they killed any of our friends; then we really did dislike them intensely. But otherwise we joked about them and I think they joked about us. And we thought, well, poor so-and-sos, they're in the same kind of muck as we are.

Chapter Three

'Pals by Xmas'

The Germans were indeed in 'the same kind of muck' as the British and felt precisely the same about it. In December Pioneer Friedrich Nickolaus, of the 53rd Reserve Pioneer Company, returned to his company after recovering from a wound. He described the conditions in which he found himself:

> Things have got very much worse: Flanders is just one great morass and all military operations have been brought to a standstill by the mud. Day and night we stand up to our knees in mud and water. We have to wrap our legs up to our thighs in sandbags just to survive. The rain pours incessantly from above, while beneath us the water-table has risen to just below ground level. The lookout positions have been raised up on stilts and the water is baled out of the trenches using pots and pans and any container to hand. If only there were such things as pumps in the trenches! In the communication trenches we have built raised walkways because it is simply impossible to drain them. On top of all this the mad gun-battle goes on across this forsaken plain, stretching out in front of us as flat as a table-top, where it is dangerous even to raise your head above ground during the day.

A month later, opposite British lines south of Armentières, a German student-soldier, Karl Aldag, wrote in a letter home:

I must confess this life of slime and mud often fills me with revulsion, also the never-ending wet, cold and futile work. These are hardships which no man would suffer in peacetime for the sake of any ordinary cause.

Only one thing keeps me calm, how one's strength grows with the demands made on it. I can feel more patience and perseverance in me than I have ever known before or would have thought possible. It is amazing how people come to terms with all this, how nobody gives in to tiredness or despair, even when the parapets collapse and night is spent building new ones.

Similar circumstances: similar reactions. Life was difficult but it and the war had to go on. And whatever curiosity or incipient fellow-feeling there might be as between one side and the other, everybody knew and accepted that they were there to fight. The lull had brought with it a certain inertia, which was greatly assisted by the general awareness that there would be no attempt at a decisive battle in the immediate future. Nevertheless this was war, not peace, so hostilities grumbled on, with occasional spasms of activity, frequent artillery fire (somewhat limited at least on the British side by a shortage of shells) and, an economical but singularly unpleasant way of harassment, sniping.

Major Buchanan-Dunlop of the 1/Leicesters was almost caught by a German sniper on his first arrival in the line. He wrote to his wife:

Last night, marching up here (you have to come up at night or you get picked off) I had a narrow shave. The enemy, who are only a couple of hundred yards from our trenches, fired, presumably at the sound of our marching, and just missed my head. The bullet went into the bank behind me.

Darkness, rain and mist were, in fact, no bar to the craft of a skilled sniper. Rifleman Bernard Brookes of the Queen's West-minsters felt extremely vulnerable when out digging a new trench on a particularly nasty night in early December some fifty yards in front of their former front line:

> In the previous party two men had been hit . . . We dug with feverish haste and were getting on well, when the man next to me was shot, and he died before the stretcher bearer had got him to the dressing station. This naturally made me dig harder than ever until I thought that my arms would drop out of their sockets.

The British snipers were also effective. On 20 October in trenches near Lille a German soldier, Willi Bohne, began a letter he did not live to complete:

> We are simply nothing but moles; for we are burrowing trenches so that the Herren Englander shan't break through here . . . We have constructed dugouts in which we can lay our weary heads at night and slip into to be out of the way of shrapnel.

It was not shrapnel but a sniper's bullet which killed him shortly afterwards. His letter was finished by a fellow soldier:

> I take the liberty of completing this letter begun by your son and brother, who is unable to finish it himself . . . Be prepared for the worst. The bullet which struck this hero was aimed only too well, for it killed him. Comfort yourselves with the knowledge that he died the finest of all deaths – a hero's death for the Fatherland.

As for shell-fire, the permanent unpredictable hazard of trench warfare, it could arrive at any time. In late November Private William Tapp of the 1/Royal Warwicks, summing up his first month's experience in Flanders, wrote in the opening entry of his diary:

> I am officer's servant so cook for him as well as myself, one day they were sending shells over at the rate of two per minute. I had chicken on a stove that I had made out of a biscuit tin that day, and I was very much afraid they would knock the lot over as the shells were knocking the top off my trench. Once or twice I had a glimpse of hell during that month, they attacked us one night when it was raining hard, a few inches of water under foot and shells bursting right in the trench, one of which stunned me and my officer for some minutes.

The British were giving as well as receiving at this time. Entrenchment inevitably led, under thrusting commanders, to the trench raid, that particularly demanding and risk-prone form of warfare in which losses were virtually guaranteed, which often seemed to produce only marginally valuable results and which, if successful, dealt death or injury without warning to unsuspecting, often sleeping, men in the enemy lines. The Garhwal Rifles of the Indian Corps mounted a raiding party on the German trenches on 9 November (arguably the first of the war), scaring the enemy with cheering and yelling at the signal to charge; but this technique worked much less well during a second attempt on the 13th, when they ran into heavy fire and both the assault party and the support party sent to give assistance suffered fifty per cent casualties. Later in November 'an exciting bit of work', as he called it, fell to the lot of Lieutenant Sir Edward Hulse, 2/Scots Guards, which he carried out with typical dash and bravado. The raid, fully chronicled by its leader, is perhaps worth noting here in some detail, partly as an example of the offensive side of the waiting war, but also because it helps to define the background of professional violence against

which the curious camaraderie of the truce took place, Hulse's
Scots Guards being not only doughty fighters but doughty
trucers as well.

Hulse had no difficulty in assembling his raiding party – 'I
got an NCO and eight men to volunteer with great ease', he
noted in his report – even though the allotted task was no
walk-over. They were to 'get right up to the enemy trenches,
peep over if not spotted, select our marks, fire two rounds rapid
and kill all we could, and then each man for himself'. One
factor, it was thought, was in their favour: the prevailing intelligence was that the enemy's front-line trenches were occupied
by only a smattering of sentries and snipers. The attack was
due to go in at 11 p.m., but there was a bright moon, so they
decided to wait. By 1.30 a.m. it was pitch dark and raining;
the order was given and Hulse and his nine comrades eased
themselves out into No Man's Land, crawling on hands and
knees over a field of turnips, moving four or five yards, lying
'doggo', listening, then crawling on again. The German sentries
were obviously on station for every now and then bullets sped
across the dead ground between the trenches, fortunately above
the heads of the slowly advancing raiders.

> When we had got halfway some firing opened away on the
> right, I think by the Border Regiment. This put the enemy
> on the alert, and by then I had satisfied myself that there were
> just as many of the enemy in their trenches as of us in our
> trenches, an unpleasant conclusion to arrive at, when we were
> supposed to be raiding a lightly held trench! A little further
> on I made certain of this, as I saw five fires, or rather the
> reflections of them . . . charcoal fires with a bit of wood burning
> probably . . . We were just advancing again when the swine
> called out in King's English, quite well pronounced, 'Halt,
> who goes there', and fired straight between the scout and

myself, he immediately fired where I had told him, and I fired at the flash of the rifle, and there was a high pitched groan; at the same time we all doubled up to the foot of the parapet, saw dim figures down in the trenches, bustling about, standing to arms and my NCO fired the trench bomb right into the little party by the fire. The other fellows all loosed off their two rounds rapid; there were various groans audible in the general hubbub, and we then ran like hares . . .

I found the bullets were all round me, so fell flat and waited another half-minute or so, until they seemed to alter the direction of their fire a bit. Then another run, and a heavy fall bang into our barbed wire, which was quite invisible and which I thought was further off. These short sprints were no easy matter, as one carried about an acre of wet clay and mud on each foot. I had to lie flat and disentangle myself, and at that moment their machine-gun swerved round and plastered away directly over my head no more than 2 or 3 feet. I waited again till it changed, and then ran like the devil for our trenches.

Hulse's assumption was that they had 'polished off' four or five of the Germans but, on the other side of the account, two of the Guardsmen were missing, 'having presumably overshot the mark in the dark and fallen into the German trenches'. The general opinion was that they were fortunate to have so few casualties. 'The CO and Adjutant', wrote Hulse to his mother, 'frankly told me that they did not expect many to get back.'

☆

Meanwhile, however, here and there along the line, as the weeks slipped by, enemies were – almost – becoming friends. A telegraphist of the Royal Engineers, Andrew Todd, described this

new development in a letter which eventually found its way
into the columns of *The Scotsman*:

> Perhaps it will surprise you to learn that the soldiers in both
> lines of trenches have become very 'pally' with each other.
> The trenches are only 60 yards apart at one place, and every
> morning about breakfast time one of the soldiers sticks a board
> in the air. As soon as this board goes up all firing ceases,
> and men from either side draw their water and rations. All
> through the breakfast hour, and so long as this board is up,
> silence reigns supreme, but whenever the board comes down
> the first unlucky devil who shows even so much as a hand
> gets a bullet through it.

Breakfast truces were in fact to become a virtually accepted
ritual on many parts of the Western Front throughout the war.
Captain B. H. Liddell Hart has written evocatively of 'the homely
smell of breakfast bacon that gained its conquest over the war
reek of chloride of lime, and in so doing not only brought a
tacit truce to the battle front, but helped in preserving sanity'.
The breakfast hour was also the usual time of the morning visit
to the latrine sap, an activity usually accorded due respect by
both sides. Ration parties too often enjoyed a mutually understood immunity and laughed and talked as they made their way
up to the trenches. But in the weeks before Christmas 1914
understandings with the enemy went well beyond the acceptance of certain daily routines. Proximity; curiosity; the sharing
of the same wretched conditions; the fact that so many Germans
spoke English and had lived in Britain; the general awareness
that, neither side being in a position to mount a major onslaught,
the war was not, as it were, as serious as it had been and would
again become; the natural instinct of the soldier to take advantage of any period of relative slackness and have a bit of fun

– all these factors worked together to produce a whole series of minor fraternizations and friendly acts up and down the line.

Albert Moren was a seventeen-year-old private in the 2/Queens in 1914. In places their front line was only a matter of yards from the Germans:

> We were so close, we threw tins of bully beef over to them or jam or biscuits and they threw things back. It wasn't done regularly, just an occasional sort of thing. We could hear the Germans at night, shouting and singing. They used to shout across 'Englander, Englander' and we used to say 'Good old Jerry', and things like that.

'Our chaps and the Germans often have a game with one another,' wrote Staff Sergeant Charles Sloan of the Royal Engineers, 'shouting at them and giving them the news.' Sometimes the news was given to them quite literally, as Sergeant Charles Johnson, of the 2/Royal Berkshires, described:

> On one occasion the Germans shouted over to our trenches for a *Daily Mirror* and guaranteed a safe passage to anyone who would bring the paper. Of course, no one risked it, but we managed to throw a *Mirror* weighted with a stone near enough for them to obtain it.

The 2/Royal Welch Fusiliers were to the north of Houplines, where the trench lines ran down into the river Lys. Their relations with their opponents were particularly friendly, though the Welshmen were not too surprised at the Germans' good humour since they had a brewery virtually in their front line. Captain C. I. Stockwell, one of the company commanders, noted in his diary:

> The Saxons opposite were quite human. One, who spoke excellent English, used to climb up in some eyrie in the brewery

and spend his time asking 'how London was getting on', 'how was Gertie Miller and the Gaiety', and so on. Lots of our men had blind shots at him in the dark, at which he laughed. One night I came out and called, 'Who the hell are you?' At once came back the answer, 'Ah, the officer – I expect I know you – I used to be the head-waiter at the Great Central Hotel.'

Ex-waiters and former members of other professions much associated with the German in Britain were the natural initiators of such inter-trench conversations. A trooper of the Scots Greys recounted the following story:

One day two of the Germans in the trench near ours asked if any of us came from Edinburgh and I shouted back that I did. They asked me if I knew a certain hairdresser's shop in Princes Street. They had worked there, they said. I replied that I had worked practically next door and had often been in the shop.

The tone of conversation between the trenches was brisk but amiable, as former Rifleman Leslie Walkinton of the Queen's Westminsters described:

We used to shout remarks to each other, sometimes rude ones, but generally with less venom than a couple of London cabbies after a mild collision.

Singing in the trenches was also a common phenomenon at that time. It was a great age of popular song and ready participation; camp concerts in which men sang ballads or played harmonicas and even officers walked unselfconsciously to the piano were an essential part of service life. It was therefore quite natural that, given a 'cushy' sector and a handful of enthusiasts, the relatively peaceful hours of the night should be improved from time to time with a little spontaneous entertainment.

That the 6/Gordon Highlanders participated in such singing bouts is admitted without compunction in their official history:

> During the winter [of 1914–15] it was not unusual for little groups of men to gather in the front trench, and there hold impromptu concerts, singing patriotic and sentimental songs. The Germans did much the same, and on calm evenings the songs from one line floated to the trenches on the other side, and were there received with applause and sometimes calls for an encore.

The Queen's Westminsters also took part in these nocturnal serenades:

> On a quiet night we used to sing to each other, sometimes alternate verses of the same tune like 'Hail thou once despised Jesus' and '*Deutschland, Deutschland über alles*'. They often sang their own words to the tune of 'God Save the King'. Then an officer of one side or the other would come and stop it by ordering a few rounds of fire. We used to be sporting and fire high with the first round – and so did Brother Boche.

The night was, of course, the natural time for such activities; more curious still were such episodes as took place during the day, when both sides were normally head-down in the trenches and, more often than not, there was not a movement to be seen or a sound to be heard in the area of the battle lines. Lieutenant D. O. Barnett of the Leinster Regiment, in a letter written in January 1915, described an incident which created a brief but dramatic sensation:

> Two lads in this regiment . . . got fed up with each other in the trenches. In broad daylight they got up on the parapet and fought. After ¼ hour one was knocked out, but all the time the Germans were cheering and firing their rifles in the

air to encourage the combatants! Who says the Germans are not sportsmen?

But the most bizarre daytime phenomenon of this phase of the war was, undoubtedly, the shooting match. In the part of the line held by Second Lieutenant Dougan Chater's 2/Gordon Highlanders things were extremely quiet. The Germans were only fifty to sixty yards off and there was much shouting between the trenches, the Germans speaking English, the Scotsmen responding with cries of 'waiter'. But there was better entertainment to be had:

> There was one fellow who had a fire with a chimney sticking up over the parapet & our men were having shots at it with their rifles. After each shot the Germans waved a stick or rang a bell according to whether we hit the chimney or not! There are lots of amusing incidents up there and altogether we have quite a cheery time.

There were numerous parallels to this story in the weeks before Christmas, with bottles or tins set up by opposing trenches and marksmen of both sides competing for bull's-eyes amid the plaudits of their comrades. Interestingly enough there seems to have been no attempt to conceal such essentially unmartial behaviour from the public. As early as 28 October *Punch* printed a cartoon clearly implying that it was an already accepted part of trench life. Later in the year – as it happens in its Boxing Day edition – the *Illustrated London News* included a double-page drawing of what its sub-editors described as an 'Anglo-German "Bisley" at the Front', based on details drawn from a participant's account. 'The friendly interlude went on', ran the accompanying caption, 'until a shell from far in the rear burst in the German trench and recalled both parties to a sense of the stern realities of the situation.'

Such activities should be seen as more than mere idle diversions. They clearly appealed to the sporting instincts of the participants, at a time when war was widely viewed *as* a form of sport, if one with dangerously high stakes. Indeed, the war itself was often referred to as the 'Great Game'; what is more, this concept survived all the rigours that followed so that it would not seem out of place for the comment to be made on Armistice Day 1918 that at last 'the great game was played out and the job done'. Significantly, references to the Germans 'playing the game' occur in some of the accounts of the Christmas truce. There seems little doubt that this sporting approach to war, with its strong emphasis on decency, fair play and respect for the other side, was one of that event's contributory causes.

☆

Instances of Franco-German fraternization had also been taking place for some time. A German soldier's letter which eventually found its way into the columns of *The Times* described a visit to the front on 28 November which surprised and amazed its writer. After being entertained by the officers of one company with a glass of Düsseldorf beer, he and his comrades went on to a second company, of which they had heard interesting things:

> They had exchanged papers with the French, who are lying just opposite. At first we couldn't believe it, but a corporal who had just come back from the *rendezvous* told us how it all came about. One of our scouting parties posted a placard with the proclamation of the 'Holy War' on a tree before the French outposts. This, of course, took place during the night. The next evening, when our scouts wanted to see if the poster had been removed, they found a letter written in good German,

in which the French proposed one hour's armistice at a certain time. In the letter was further found a couple of cigars.

Eventually it was agreed that a meeting would take place at 11 a.m. the following day German time. At the appointed hour a German corporal and a French sergeant, the latter being able to speak fluent German, advanced from their respective trenches. They saluted one another and shook hands; then the Frenchman was presented with the 'Order of the Day' from the German General Staff while the German was given a Paris newspaper:

> One final 'au revoir' and the cry was sounded 'Armistice expired' and they both got home in quick time. One wouldn't think it was possible, but it is true, every word of it. Our troops here are only 80 metres distant from the French, so that even our barbed-wire entanglements are joining those of the enemy.

The 'Germans' concerned in this minor armistice were from Schleswig-Holstein which, though part of Germany since 1864, had not forgotten its Danish origins, so that many such soldiers felt they were fighting for a cause not their own. But there was no hint of diluted nationalism among the Germans who regularly met the French at Drywege in Belgium in the bitter early days of December, when a common desire to make uncomfortable conditions a little more bearable brought them out into the open. Captain Rudolf Binding commented in his diary on 8 December on

> the fraternization that has been going on between our trenches and those of the enemy, when friend and foe alike go to fetch straw from the same rick to protect them from the cold and rain and to have some sort of bedding to lie on – and never a shot is fired.

For Binding, however, this was more than a curious incident, it was a revelation about the whole nature of war. 'Truly', he wrote, 'there is no longer any sense in this business.'

Sometime in this period, there was a particularly friendly gesture by some French troops on the Aisne to a German commander whom they had come to admire for his 'lion-like bravery'; he was, in fact, a Bavarian prince. They decided to honour the hero as he deserved:

> The French captain in command of the company was an excellent musician. He got together from his men an orchestra of trumpets and concertinas, and they even found a violin. After two days' practice he wrote a programme ornamented by one of his men, announcing that at 5 o'clock on the following afternoon a concert would take place in honour of the brave Bavarian prince. The programme was fastened to a stone and thrown into the German trench. At the appointed hour there was a blare of trumpets, and the captain appeared, armed only with a baton. The concert began, and the programme was played through. At the end the whole company sang the *'Marseillaise'*.
>
> There then appeared an officer from the German trench, who stood at attention and saluted. It was the Bavarian prince. The French captain returned the salute, while there was a thunder of applause and cheering from both trenches.

It was the French who were the perpetrators of the best practical joke at this time. With trenches cheek by jowl and the possibility of dialogue across the wire, there was always the opportunity to play tricks on the enemy. At one point the French and Germans were shouting to each other, and the Germans called out: 'Our Emperor has been down to see us.' The French replied, 'Yes, but he has not been down to the trenches – but our President is coming to visit us tomorrow.' Next day the

Germans heard a tremendous cheering and all the French troops
singing the '*Marseillaise*', and seeing a tall hat protruding above
the trench and moving along, they opened up with a vicious
fusillade.

The tall hat was on a stick, the French President was still
in Paris and the musical effects had been greatly assisted by a
gramophone record.

☆

Early in December news of certain curious happenings at the
front reached General Sir Horace Smith-Dorrien, the veteran
commander of the British II Corps. At fifty-six, Smith-Dorrien
had behind him years of experience in many campaigns. He was
one of the five officers who escaped from the disaster at Isand-
hlwana in the Zulu War in 1879; he had served in Egypt, spent
ten years in India, fought at Omdurman, distinguished himself
in the Boer War, and more recently made a considerable mark
as Commander at Aldershot. He had succeeded to the command
of II Corps on the sudden death – in the train while on his way
to the front – of Sir J. M. Grierson. He and Sir John French
had long held a violent dislike for each other and Smith-Dorrien's
career was to end suddenly the following May with his contro-
versial dismissal by French following the Second Battle of Ypres.
Smith-Dorrien also differed from his Field Marshal, in that he
was an infantryman, not a cavalryman. With his infantryman's
instincts and experience, he understood the reasons for these
bizarre trench tales but also saw the potential danger that lay
behind them.

On 2 December he wrote in his diary:

Weird stories come in from the trenches about fraternizing
with the Germans. They shout to each other and offer to

exchange certain articles and give certain information. In one
place, by arrangement, a bottle was put out between the
trenches and then they held a competition as to which could
break it first. There is a danger of opposing troops becoming
too friendly, but it is only too likely to happen and it happened
in the Peninsula. I therefore intend to issue instructions to my
Corps not to fraternize in any way whatever with the enemy
for fear one day they may be lulled into such a state of confidence as to be caught off their guard and rushed.

Three days later his 'instructions' went out, incorporated in
a remarkable document written by his Chief of Staff, Brigadier-
General Forestier-Walker, but expressing in forceful terms
Smith-Dorrien's shrewd analysis of the peculiar difficulties facing
an army in a state of relative quiescence, when the resumption
of the offensive was plainly some way ahead. In particular,
II Corps's Document G.507 is a penetrating and, in its way, a
historic statement of the causes and attractions of the concept
of 'live and let live' war and defines most of the elements that
were to result in the Christmas truce. These are some of the
key sentences:

It is during this period [of waiting] that the greatest danger
to the morale of the troops exists. Experience of this, and every
other war proves undoubtedly that troops in trenches in close
proximity to the enemy slide very easily, if permitted to do
so, into a 'live and let live' theory of life. Understandings –
amounting almost to unofficial armistices – grow up between
our troops and the enemy, with a view to making life easier,
until the sole object of war becomes obscured, and officers and
men sink into a military lethargy from which it is difficult to
arouse them when the moment for great sacrifices again
arises . . .

The attitude of our troops can be readily understood and

to a certain extent commands sympathy. So long as they know that no general advance is intended, they fail to see any object in undertaking small enterprises of no permanent utility, certain to result in some loss of life, and likely to provoke reprisals. Such an attitude is, however, most dangerous, for it discourages initiative in commanders, and destroys the offensive spirit in all ranks . . .

The Corps Commander, therefore, directs Divisional Commanders to impress on all subordinate commanders the absolute necessity of encouraging the offensive spirit of the troops, while on the defensive, by every means in their power.

Friendly intercourse with the enemy, unofficial armistices (e.g. 'we won't fire if you don't' etc.) and the exchange of tobacco and other comforts, however tempting and occasionally amusing they may be, are absolutely prohibited.

Thus, three weeks before Christmas, were the philosophy and practice which led to the most famous truce in military history roundly and specifically condemned. And indeed it is a fact that, though some units of II Corps were to take part in fraternization, the majority did not, so that it could be claimed that Smith-Dorrien's directive was reasonably effective. In the end, of course, much would depend on the response and initiative of local commanders; and there is no means of knowing whether they took Smith-Dorrien's instructions as a new and potent piece of military doctrine or merely a forthright restatement of what everybody knew in their bones was the inevitable attitude of high command.

Be that as it may, there appears to have been no falling-off generally in the instances of spontaneous *détente* and fraternization as Christmas approached. Private Tapp's 1/Royal Warwicks were at Ploegsteert, in the northernmost brigade of III Corps, just to the south of Smith-Dorrien's territory. On 8 December, he wrote in his diary:

Well the trenches have their bright side, for instance the Germans in their trenches have just sung our national anthem and then shouted 'hurrah' and then several boos so then we give them a song and *a cheer*, sometimes one of our fellows shouts 'waiter' 'sausages', and then send five rounds rapid over. The Germans seem to know who we are for they shout 'Good old Warwicks' and our officer always tells us to give them a song back, I think we shall be pals by Xmas.

Chapter Four

Pre-Christmas Initiatives

Early in December the idea of a truce of all the armies at Christmas time was mooted by the new Pope, Benedict XV. He beseeched the belligerent powers 'in the name of the Divinity . . . to cease the clang of arms while Christendom celebrates the Feast of the World's Redemption'. Germany accepted at once, though she made it clear that her agreement was conditional upon the acquiescence of the other nations involved. In fact his scheme had little chance from the outset. For one thing, Islamic Turkey would not easily respond to so specifically Christian a proposition; for another, the fact that the Orthodox Church celebrated Christmas thirteen days after the Western Churches added a further complication. Launched on the 7th, by the 13th the brief hope his idea had inspired was extinguished. The Pope commented sadly, 'Our Christmas initiative was not crowned with success' (see page 293).

Although he failed in this initiative, he later intervened successfully with the French and German governments over the exchange of prisoners of war.

Also at this time there was another, much less publicized, initiative from across the Atlantic. On 10 December in Washington Senator William S. Kenyon proposed a resolution requesting the belligerent nations of the world, including Japan and Turkey, to declare a truce of twenty days for the proper celebration of Christmas, 'with the hope also that such cessation of hostilities at such time may stimulate reflection upon the part of such nations as to the meaning and spirit of the Christmas time, to the end that there may come again on Earth peace, good will toward men'. This plea too fell on deaf ears, if it was heard at all; there being at that period no tradition of American involvement in world affairs, it seems to have had little impact in the councils of the warring powers.

But if there was to be no peace at Christmas, there was on all sides much goodwill towards the men who were to do the fighting – and a determination that they should have as enjoyable, indeed, as normal a time as possible when the festive season came.

In the weeks before Christmas the British newspapers and magazines carried scores of advertisements reminding the reader of the needs of the men in uniform and the opportunity provided by Christmas to satisfy them. Send him Oxo, send him Horlicks, send him Bovril, but above all send him things to wear. 'The added comfort and protection will mean much to men who are keeping watch, day and night, in trenches rimmed with ice – whose aim must be steady though their fingers shake with cold.'

An avalanche of mufflers, socks, scarves, gloves and other warm clothing (some all too soon to be lost in the mud), as well as cigarettes, tobacco and eatables, was to find its way to the front in parcels from loving relatives and friends and through the many 'gift funds' set up in Britain to which contributions came pouring in from corporations and kindergartens. On 5 December Sergeant William Williamson, of 2/Devons, noted in his diary:

> Received presentations as follows. Pipe & tobacco from the
> sick of Dartmoor, Packet of Gold Flake Cigarettes & box of

matches from Eccentric Club London, Woolen Belt from Princess Mary.

Princess Mary, later the Princess Royal, was the seventeen-
year-old daughter of King George V and Queen Mary; even as
Williamson was rejoicing over his belt, the special fund associated with her name was preparing the most memorable Christmas
surprise of all for the nation's service personnel.

Also eager to make its contribution at this time, the *Evening
News*'s 'Lonely Soldiers' Guild' was putting its readers in touch
with British and French soldiers, for 'an occasional reminder
through the medium of the penny post that, while he is at the
front, he is not forgotten by those in England'. And there were
gifts too for the solitary bachelor. On Christmas Day an artillery
officer wrote:

> The mail also brought us a parcel addressed, 'A Lonely Man'.
> Inside was a letter, pipes, tobacco, a tinder lighter, a pair
> of socks and a shirt – a nice present, a very nice thought. We
> tossed for it, and I got it for my section. The unmarried men
> then drew lots for it at stable time. The winner was greatly
> pleased, and has just brought me a nice letter of thanks to
> censor for the kind donor. I shall also send mine. How much
> such things cheer us all up!

The volume of mail to the front at Christmas 1914 was
phenomenal. According to contemporary newspaper reports, in
the six days preceding 12 December, which was assumed to be
the date for Christmas delivery, 250,000 parcels were addressed
to the troops and in the following week there were 200,000
more and two and a half million letters. Two thousand five
hundred letters were also being despatched daily to British
prisoners of war. Adding to the total in the last few days were
Christmas cards sent to every soldier, sailor or nurse by the King

and Queen and the special Christmas present from Princess Mary. This latter was a particularly generous and bulky gift, the transportation of which to the front caused some dislocation of the already overloaded railway system. Indeed, since the figures show that over 355,500 of them were delivered by Christmas, this was scarcely surprising. Not unnaturally, there were those who felt that this sudden obsession with Christmas and Christmas presents was in danger of deflecting the army away from its main purpose. On 18 December the 2nd in Command of the 2/Grenadier Guards, Major G. D. Jeffreys, wrote with some asperity in his diary:

> Everything seems hung up just now for all the Christmas parcels, which are becoming a positive nuisance. I am told that the rations of the army are to be held up for twenty-four hours to enable Princess Mary's presents to come up, and I have had reams of orders as to their distribution . . . It was the longest order I have had since I have been out, and it seems rather ridiculous to make such a tremendous business of it when, after all, our first business is to beat the Germans. Our enemy thinks of war, and nothing else, whilst we must mix it up with plum puddings.

☆

In fact, Major Jeffreys was quite wrong about the Germans. They too were thinking of the season to come. Indeed, as in Britain, the principal beneficiaries that year of Germany's deep affection for Christmas would be the men in uniform. She had cared for her troops from the moment they marched, by launching the idea of the love-gift, or *liebesgabe*: civilians were urged to prepare parcels of comforts, tobacco and other such items to be sent to the front for general distribution. Christmas turned this steady stream of giving into a vast flood.

As in Britain, the December editions of many popular German magazines carried numerous advertisements for Christmas parcels and gifts of all kinds for the soldiers in the field. Also, as in Britain, there was a considerable emphasis on warm clothing, along with watches of various kinds, cakes, liqueurs, cigarettes, and medicaments against colds and rheumatism. Scattered among the pages were artists'. impressions of soldiers in the field, warm, cheerful, healthy and relaxing contentedly by some appropriately decorated Christmas tree.

In fact, that the soldiers of the Fatherland should have a happy Christmas was a matter not merely of hope but, virtually, of instruction. A newspaper report stated:

> Notices were issued several days ago that the troops must do their best to enjoy the Yuletide. Hundreds and thousands of parcels have arrived from Germany – knitted articles, sweets, cakes and tobacco.

In addition, Christmas trees were despatched to the front in their thousands; these were to be crucial properties in the initiation of the Christmas truce. They were also sent to the ships and the U-boats of the High Seas Fleet. Their presence particularly angered the cavalry officer Captain Rudolf Binding, who wrote just before Christmas to his father:

> If I had my way some person in authority would proclaim that Christmas will not be celebrated this year . . . The simplicity of Christmas, with the laughter of children, the joy of giving little things; this is as it should be when it appears alone. But when it enters the list with a war it is out of place. Enemy, Death, and a Christmas tree – they cannot live so close together.

But Binding was an exception: the general attitude was different. Karl Aldag expressed the majority opinion when he commented with gratitude and delight on the mass of presents provided by the Fatherland:

> . . . Knitted comforts, tobacco, cake, chocolate, sausages – all 'love-gifts' – What Germany has done for us!

☆

At the front, however, other, more warlike initiatives were afoot. Shortly before Christmas, even as the train-loads of cards and comforts were beginning their slow journey towards the rail-heads, the British mounted a series of attacks on the German positions which were to cause many casualties. These were to be followed in one particular area by an episode which was, if to a limited extent, a rehearsal of the Christmas truce.

None of these attacks made any significant gains. They were carried out with bravery and fortitude, but they were ill-prepared, on too small a scale to be more than a gesture, and impeded by almost impossible ground. It was in angry comment on this small but sacrificial offensive that Winston Churchill, then First Lord of the Admiralty, wrote to the Prime Minister on 29 December: 'Are there not other alternatives than sending our armies to chew barbed wire in Flanders?'

Captain Billy Congreve, a highly professional Regular officer who was to win a posthumous VC on the Somme, now serving as ADC to Major-General J. A. L. Haldane, commanding 3rd Division, saw the first of these futile 'shows' on 14 December from a nearby vantage point, together with Sir John French, Sir Horace Smith-Dorrien, the Prince of Wales and 'many other lights of the Gilded Staff'. An impressive but ineffective bombardment was followed by an unsupported assault by two battalions, the 2/Royal Scots and the 1/Gordons, against well-fortified positions. 'The attack naturally failed,' Congreve noted in his diary the next day. 'We had about 400 casualties. It is most depressing.' The 2/Royal Scots *did* reach the enemy lines and captured two machine-guns and some prisoners, but were subsequently trapped by heavy fire from a German strong point whose existence, as Congreve wrote, 'could have been found out by a proper reconnaissance *before* the attack'. As for the 1/Gordons:

> Imagine sending a battalion alone to attack a strongly wired position up a hill and over mud a foot deep, under frontal and enfilade fire. It was a regular Valley of Death. The losses were, of course, very heavy. They were very, very gallant. Some almost reached the German trenches, where they were killed. One or two even got into the enemy trenches where they were killed or captured. A few lay in little depressions in the mud till darkness and then crawled back . . . They lost seven out of nine officers and 250 men.
>
> Such was the attack ordered by Sir John French. Next day, I read in the paper. 'British troops hurl back Germans at Wytschaete'. A beautiful epitaph for those poor Gordons who were little better than murdered.

In fact, Sir John French was less to blame than Congreve realized. This December offensive was the result of strong pressure from General Foch, and later from General Joffre, to mount supportive action for certain aggressive schemes devised by the French – schemes which in the end virtually came to nothing. The British yielded to these appeals for Allied solidarity with great reluctance. However, it is true that, having agreed that an offensive should be mounted, the Commander-in-Chief could have scarcely produced a more uninspiring plan. In the words of his biographer, Richard Holmes: 'He finished with the worst of both worlds, sporadic attacks which added to the butcher's bill to no real purpose.' As the pattern of useless and wasteful onslaughts continued over the following days, Congreve's father, Brigadier-General Walter Congreve VC, in command of 18th Brigade in the 6th Division further south, commented in his diary as angrily as his son:

> These small isolated attacks seem to me deadly . . . Horrid losses and nothing done with them.

It was the costly failure at Ploegsteert Wood on the afternoon of 18 December which moved Brigadier-General Congreve to write in this vein. Many men were hit by their own artillery fire before they got anywhere near the German lines.

Shortly after the Ploegsteert débâcle the 2/Royal Warwicks, supported by the companies of the 2/Queen's, went 'over the top' near the village of Bois Grenier. The attackers' progress to the front line was through muddy communicating trenches jammed by others trying to pass them on the way out. Adding a bizarre element to the scene was a flock of dead sheep in No Man's Land, killed when the British and the Germans first dug in. Here again scores of men were hit by British shell-fire, while many of those who managed to cross No Man's Land ended up hanging on the German barbed wire.

Witnessing all this from the British lines was Lieutenant Geoffrey Heinekey, who was in one of the two companies of the 2/Queen's not involved. In a letter to his mother three days later, in which he claimed that he had had 'the most exciting time of his life' since he last wrote, he described what he called 'the great attack on the German trenches':

> From 4 p.m. till 11 p.m. there was the most tremendous fusillade and gun firing which never ceased at all.
>   In the trenches we did not know what had happened but

slowly the Warwicks and Queens crawled back and then I
went out with some others to get in some of the wounded but
could not go far as the German trenches are only about 150
yards apart. The attack was not successful as the German
trenches were very strongly reinforced and it cost us very dear
– we lost 6 officers and 77 men and the Warwicks lost 300.

To the south-west in the region of Laventie, the 2/Scots
Guards and 2/Border went in at the latest zero hour of the day,
6 p.m. The following is taken from a diary account of the action
written by an anonymous Tommy of the Border Regiment:

> It was about 4.45 p.m. when the officer came down the trench
> and told us there was going to be an attack that night . . .
> And then you could hear men Praying to God to look after
> there wife and Children should any think happen to them.

The Borders left their trenches in some confusion, since in
the din and mêlée the whistle which was the signal to advance
was never heard; more, they were attacking with scant prepara-
tion and in darkness.

> Some how or other our left was too soon with the charge . . .
> and as soon as we went up . . . the Germans let us have it . . .
> and we were going down like rain drops. As our Trenches was
> only 70 yards apart we retired and then made the 2nd charge
> but received the same. We retired again and stopped in mid-
> field. And it was like being in a Blacksmith shop watching
> him swing a hammer on a red-hot shoe and the sparks flying
> all round you. But instead of them being sparks they were
> Bullets . . . It was a pitiful sight to see and hear our Comrades
> dying and could not get help to them as it ment serten death
> if we had moved . . . So we had to lay there from 6.30 to
> 8.15 a.m. the next morning. And as an Angel sent down from
> Heaven it came over verry misty and this being our only chance

we made good of it. So we crawl half-way and then make a run for it. We could not see where we were going so fell over our Comrades who were Dead. As we were making for our trenches and were about to drop in the Trench we were challenged for our Regt., Name, Platoon we belong to. So we got into our trench at 8.15 a.m. that morning after the Charge. And I must say I think it first time I said my Prayers in earness, which is nothing to my credit for when I looked round and saw my Chums I thanked God he had spared me there fate.

Meanwhile, there had been a hard-fought and relatively successful action further down the line, spearheaded by the 2/Devons. Some German trenches were captured and heavy casualties inflicted on the enemy. However, the following morning the Germans put in a vigorous counter-attack and bombed the Devons out of the ground gained.

There was one final attack in the small hours of the 19th. At 3.30 a.m. and 5.30 a.m. respectively the Meerut and Lahore Divisions of the Indian Corps went into action near Givenchy. There was a series of confused encounters which went on well into the hours of daylight and which were fought with much bravery and dash, but the casualties were heavy and the gains small.

☆

There was, however, to be a memorable postscript to this hard fighting on one sector of the British front. On 20 December Lieutenant Geoffrey Heinekey of 2/Queen's wrote to his mother:

The next morning a most extraordinary thing happened – I should think quite one of the most curious things in the war. Some Germans came out and held up their hands and began to take in some of our wounded and so we ourselves immediately got out of the trenches and began bringing in our wounded also. The Germans then beckoned to us and a lot of us went over and talked to them and they helped us to bury our dead. This lasted the whole morning and I talked to several of them and I must say they seemed extraordinarily fine men . . . It seemed too ironical for words. There, the night before we had been having a terrific battle and the morning after, there we were smoking their cigarettes and they smoking ours.

It was a foretaste of the great truce to come. Enemy talked with enemy in No Man's Land. Instead of the smell of cordite there was the relaxing tang of tobacco. But this brief armistice was not without its blemishes. A young lieutenant of the South Staffordshire Regiment came across to help with the wounded and was killed by a shot from a sniper, not from the fraternizing regiment but from the next regiment in line. A Tommy of the Queen's was similarly gunned down. More, two Queen's officers, Second Lieutenants Rought and Walmisley, and seven stretcher-bearers who approached too near to the German trenches were taken prisoner; their comrades believed they had been enticed. Unfortunately, it was not noticed that they were missing until the armistice was over. The end in fact came suddenly and not as expected by the participants when, without warning, from their positions behind the lines, the British artillery started shelling the enemy trenches.

There was a not dissimiliar gesture opposite the 2/Scots Guards, as Lieutenant Sir Edward Hulse recorded:

The morning after the attack, there was an almost tacit understanding as to no firing, and about 6.15 a.m. I saw eight or nine German shoulders and heads appear, and then three of them crawled out a few feet in front of their parapet and began dragging in some of our fellows who were either dead or unconscious . . . I passed down the order that none of my men were to fire and this seems to have been done all down the line. I helped one of our men in myself, and was not fired on, at all.

In fact, these chivalrous acts were well within the rules of war. Armistices, properly agreed, for the burials of the dead had long been part of the accepted military code. What makes the events of 19 December 1914 particularly notable is that they occurred in a conflict marked by so much structured animosity and mistrust. But they could only mollify, not change, the fact that several hundreds of lives had been wasted on an exercise which its instigators knew from the outset was of only marginal value. There would be many sad telegrams and letters of condolence that Christmas mingling with the festive mail.

Chapter Five

Christmas Eve

If the pre-Christmas period had its horrors at the front, it also – for the British – had its 'frightfulness' at home. On 16 December two German battlecruisers, *Derfflinger* and *Von der Tann*, emerged out of the morning mist to bombard Scarborough. Later they turned their attention with equally devastating effect to Whitby and the Hartlepools. Altogether 122 people were killed and 443 injured, and there was much damage to property. The German intention was to refute the British doctrine of the mastery of the seas. 'This attack will bring home to the English', wrote the *Kölnische Zeitung*, 'that their great fleet is unable to protect them.' There was an angry reaction among the British, the Germans being labelled with such descriptions as the 'assassin squadron' and the 'Scarborough bandits'. Churchill wrote of the 'stigma of the baby-killers of Scarborough' which would for ever brand officers and men of the German navy. At a time which ought to have been one of peace and goodwill, stated one commentator in the *Illustrated London News*, this had been a period of 'particular malignity as far as our German cousins were concerned'.

Malignity continued in Flanders where the end of the British offensive did not bring an end to the fighting. The Germans retaliated on the 20th by flinging themselves on the Indian

Corps, who were at the southern end of the British sector in the vicinity of Givenchy. The Indians were totally unable to withstand this counter-attack and, from the 22nd, were gradually withdrawn to be replaced by General Sir Douglas Haig's I Corps, which finally managed to re-establish the line. But it was a hard struggle with enormous casualties on both sides and the fighting continued until the 24th.

It was to be a dour Christmas on that part of the front, with few concessions to the season and business much as usual.

Elsewhere, however, along the greater part of the British front, the days before Christmas brought a period of relative calm. For once there was something pleasurable to look forward to: if nothing else Christmas would produce some variation in the normal routine. And for soldiers bored with the deadly monotony of a diet of corned beef (also known as bully beef or bully), Maconochie's stew (that combination of meat, potatoes, beans and other assorted vegetables to be eaten either cold or heated in its tins, which no Tommy could ever forget) and Tickler's jam (which only its makers believed was made of plum and apple) Christmas would provide a rare opportunity to dine and wine – or drink beer – in some sort of style.

Three days before Christmas Private William Tapp, of the Warwickshire Regiment, wrote in his diary:

22nd Dec and we ate at our old billet, a private house. I and 3 more servants have all received parcels from home and we are making this our Xmas day, we had bacon, one egg each, and chipped potatoes for Breakfast, eggs are a luxury now they are 3½d each and hard work to get any at all. Dinner roast beef, potatoes, brussels sprouts, which we had seen on the way down, also plum duff and mincepie and a couple of jugs of beer, cigarettes, for tea we are going to have a milk loaf which

has come from E[ngland], butter, cake, sweets, etc. I hope
every one in E[ngland] has as good food for their Xmas day.

Graham Williams and his fellow riflemen of the London
Rifle Brigade had booked a room in one of the several *estaminets*
of Ploegsteert for their Christmas celebration. A family with
whom they had become friendly while billeted in East Grinstead
had sent them a generous hamper. This was the foundation of
a thoroughly satisfactory feast which, complete with mince pies
and Christmas puddings, they enjoyed on the same day as Tapp
and his friends enjoyed theirs. The LRB men added to the
general gaiety by having a fully written out menu, complete
with (imaginary) musical programme. Later they were glad that,
even though they had expected to be in their billets over
Christmas, they had had their special meal on the 22nd, as the
next morning they were suddenly, and to their great disappointment, ordered back to the trenches.

They returned there lavishly supplied with presents from
home – indeed the LRB in particular received so many Christmas
parcels that they shared them out among the four other battalions of their brigade. However, no unit went short: puddings
and presents were to add their weight to many a pack as the
Tommies made their way to the line in the last days before
Christmas.

☆

But in the trenches, along many parts of the front, things were
not as they had been. The spirit of Christmas was in the air
and it was a most powerful and pervasive force. Added to the
other elements already present – the proximity, the sharing of
extreme conditions, the growing tendency towards a 'live and
let live' mentality, the eagerness of families, friends and even

authorities that the soldiers should share the pleasures of the season – that spirit became irresistible. Although many hardened Tommies were later to claim with pride that there was no lessening of warlike determination in their particular sector that Christmas, no concession to the calendar or the enemy, elsewhere even the most stalwart of professional soldiers were moved to respond to the increasingly relaxed and festive atmosphere. For Lieutenant Sir Edward Hulse of the Scots Guards, for example, Christmas provided two splendid opportunities, both to be seized with relish. One was to have a thoroughly good time, even in the troglodytic world of the trenches ('Germans or no Germans . . . we are going to have a 'ell of a bust, including plum puddings for the whole battalion'); and the other was to carry out a vocal assault, almost a vocal trench raid, on the enemy across the way. It was the duty of the alert and thrusting British officer to 'keep the Hun on his toes', constantly to maintain the spirit of the offensive. Hulse's Christmas adaptation of this concept was to attack the Germans with song and surprise them with a barrage of carols:

> I have got a select little party together who, led by my stentorian voice, are going to take up position in our trenches where we are closest to the enemy, about 80 yards, and from 10 p.m. onwards we are going to give the enemy every conceivable song in harmony, from carols to Tipperary . . . My fellows are most amused with the idea, and will make a rare noise when we get at it. Our object will be to drown the now toofamiliar strains of '*Deutschland über Alles*' and the '*Wacht am Rhein*' we hear from their trenches every evening.

The Germans, however, were now singing other songs than the patriotic and nationalistic ones which plainly irritated Lieutenant Hulse, while the British too, in some areas at least, were also adopting a seasonal repertoire. The German Karl Aldag wrote in his Christmas letter home:

> We were relieved on the evening of the 23rd about 10 o'clock. The English had been singing hymns, including a fine quartet. On our side too the beautiful old songs resounded, with only now and then a shot in between.

Meanwhile, the Christmas trees so heartily disapproved of by Captain Binding had reached the area of the German billet villages and some of them would soon be carried up, along with other symbols of the season, to the trenches. And the mood of Christmas was being powerfully evoked in special services attended *en masse* by the German troops. The Regimental History of the 16th (3rd Westphalian) Infantry Regiment records:

> In the little shell-riddled church of Illies homely Christmas trees were alight, and during a light frost white snowflakes fell through the damaged roof on to the ground and the priest preached a moving sermon – to soldiers of all denominations. The small organ and the regimental band under the direction of Bandmaster Beez, who had been with the regiment during the whole campaign, accompanied the various companies in the singing. Numerous gift parcels and letters had arrived from home, some by post, some by special lorries, and were taken up to the companies in the trenches by the ration parties.

☆

On some sectors the Christmas truce began on 23 December.

The 2/Cameronians relieved the 2/Royal Berks on the night of 20 December in the vicinity of Laventie. The trenches they took over were in poor condition due to the appalling weather, requiring a continuous effort to prevent them becoming water-logged. All seemed set for a particularly dreary stint in the line.

However, there were diversions afoot, as a lieutenant of the Cameronians, Malcolm Kennedy, described:

> On the morning of the 23rd, while my platoon was engaged in the never-ending task of baling water out of my trench, one of the men on sentry-duty called my attention to the fact that the German troops opposite were clambering out into the open, waving their arms in the air and making friendly gestures in our direction. As they were unarmed and showed no signs of hostile intention, I was wondering what to do when a message came along from the Company Commander saying, 'Don't shoot, but count them!' This was followed a minute or two later by the appearance of Ferrers himself [the Commanding Officer], who warned me against letting any Germans come too close as it might be only a ruse on their part to enable them to inspect our position at close quarters.
>
> Although the temporary truce that followed was apparently a purely spontaneous act of mutual friendship and goodwill, it was of so unique and surprising a nature that it was just as well to take no undue risks. The company on our left, however, allowed a couple of Germans to come across and a friendly exchange of cigars and verbal greetings took place, one of the two Germans jocularly remarking that he hoped the war would end soon, as he wanted to return to his former job as a taxi-driver in Birmingham.

At another part of the line, according to an account by Vize-Feldwebel Lange, a Saxon NCO (equivalent in rank to a staff sergeant in the British Army) of XIX Corps from Leipzig, after nightfall on the 23rd some Saxon soldiers put Christmas trees on the parapet of their trench, upon which a number of Tommies – who had had previous 'parleys' with the enemy in this sector and had grown accustomed to crawling across to exchange tinned meat and tobacco – came over to ask what the trees were for.

Told that it was the custom and that the Germans would be keeping Christmas on the night of the 24th, two of the Tommies hurried away, returning shortly to say that two of their officers were waiting beyond the wire anxious to speak to the major in charge. The officers proposed a private truce for Christmas Eve and Christmas Day. The idea was accepted.

After a relatively fine summer, 1914 had contrived to produce one of the wettest winters on record (see page 294). December had so far been a particularly miserable month, with almost every day having its visitation of rain. There was, however, a hint of change late on the 22nd. 'Last night was a jolly night,' wrote Major Buchanan-Dunlop of the 1/Leicesters the next afternoon, 'with bright stars and no rain, and my trenches were getting clean again; but this morning early snow began to fall and they are getting quite beastly again. However,' he added, with a touch of his characteristic cheery optimism, 'now, they have cleaned up a bit and the snow has stopped, so if only we could get a little frost we'd soon have them fairly passable . . .'

The frost Buchanan-Dunlop hoped for arrived on Christmas Eve. It transformed the scene. The mud hardened. The pools froze. The huddled shapes out in No Man's Land – dead sheep, or dead men – lay white with rime. Rime turned the copses into Christmas trees, and softened the hard outlines of ruined buildings. The air was sharp and bracing, anaesthetizing the usual trench smells of chloride of lime, soaked clothing, gunsmoke and decay. 'It was a beautiful sunny day and very clear,' Rifleman Bernard Brookes wrote in his diary. 'A Christmas-card Christmas Eve,' Albert Moren called it, remembering it nearly seventy years later. 'A really beautiful winter's day,' was Graham Williams's description, though his memory and that of his LRB comrades were not only of the sudden appropriate beauty of the weather:

Unfortunately, the day was marred at breakfast time, when a young and popular member of the original 'O' Coy, who was in the next bay to ours, was shot through the head by a sniper. This was the singer, Bassingham, who had been a regular performer at Company and Battalion concerts. Casualties still being comparatively rare, this cast a gloom over us all. His body having been placed outside the trench for removal by stretcher-bearers after dark, the normal routine was resumed.

It was, indeed, a good day for sniping; the clear weather gave good marksmen their chance and some took it with a will. 'Air very frosty,' Lieutenant William Tyrrell, Medical Officer attached to the 2/Lancashire Fusiliers, noted in his diary; 'makes the sniping very vicious to the ears – the swish of bullets resembles a cane swishing thro' water & the report of the rifles is peculiarly muffled.'

☆

At home the general expectation, encouraged by the newspapers, was that fighting would continue at Christmas. Certainly few anticipated the curious events to come. Yet there were those who saw that, in spite of all the hatred and the virulent propaganda, there might well be some friendly gesture between the two lines of trenches. A commentator in the *Illustrated London News* wrote that

> for Christmastide there will probably be something like a 'truce of God' (on the Western Front) – if not by mutual agreement, at least by common assent.

And on Christmas Eve the *Manchester Guardian* carried this remarkably prophetic statement:

It will be strange if one of those truces arranged tacitly by the men and winked at by the commanders does not occur tonight in order that, if possible, the Germans may find something to take the place of Christmas trees and the English something to take the place of holly in the trenches . . . Tomorrow, too, the boards which have been in use for signalling 'hits' on either side will very likely bear more or less chaffing greetings. For the longer [the] troops lie over against one another in trenches the more there grows up a certain friendly interest. This, however, does not interfere with the business of fighting.

Christmas Eve 1914 holds one other significant if minor distinction in twentieth-century history. It was the day on which the first bomb fell on the mainland of Britain. At 11 a.m. a solitary German aeroplane appeared over Dover and aimed a bomb at Dover Castle. The bomb missed its target and landed in the garden of Mr Thomas Terson JP, blowing a Mr John Banks out of a tree in the Rectory garden next door, in which he was cutting evergreens for the Christmas decorations in the parish church.

☆

In Flanders the Germans who had fraternized with the 2/Cameronians on the 23rd showed no inclination to resume normal hostilities on the 24th. The Scotsmen were due to leave the trenches that evening but, before their departure they were, as Lieutenant Kennedy put it, 'treated to further demonstrations of temporary friendliness and good will on the part of their opponents':

Time and again during the course of that day, the Eve of Christmas, there were wafted towards us from the trenches opposite the sounds of singing and merry-making, and occasionally the guttural tones of a German were to be heard shouting out lustily, 'A happy Christmas to you Englishmen!' Only too glad to show that the sentiments were reciprocated, back would go the response from a thick-set Clydesider, 'Same to you, Fritz, but dinna o'er eat yourself wi' they sausages!'

For the time being, all the horrors and discomforts of the War seemed to be forgotten. The Christmas spirit was in the air. As we filed out of the trenches that evening, we exchanged Christmas greetings with the Devons, who came to relieve us. We exchanged them too with the Middlesex, whom we passed on their way to relieve the West Yorks, whose trenches adjoined ours on our right flank, while ever and anon came the shouts from the German trenches conveying similar sentiments of friendship and goodwill to us all.

Signs of an unusual relaxation of tension were evident elsewhere. The 24th of December was 'very quiet' on the front occupied by the 2/Royal Welch Fusiliers on the banks of the river Lys. A pheasant, thought to be a refugee from 'Plugstreet' Wood, was shot through the head in No Man's Land and successfully retrieved; no doubt it would make a welcome contribution to the Christmas festivities. One of the battalion companies had a singsong in the trenches and, inspired by the festive mood, some of the Welshmen painted 'Merry Christmas' on a sheet of canvas in large letters, added a sketch of the Kaiser, and hoisted their curious creation on to the parapet. It was not shot down. Meanwhile, south of Armentières, a German band was playing hymns in or near the trenches all afternoon.

The weather was glorious. Several British aeroplanes were up, which were shot at in a desultory way by the Germans. A British battery was firing, though apparently with little serious purpose. Then, as an artillery officer wrote, 'about 6 o'clock things went positively dead; there was not a sound. Even our own pet sniper went off duty.' That evening there was to be no 'goodnight kiss' – as the Tommies called the sniper's farewell strike. But somewhere behind the lines an unusual and peculiar noise startled a group of RAMC men who were sitting in a field shelter which they had just constructed, eating a Christmas cake newly arrived from Blighty. Writing to his brother that same evening, one of their number, Lance-Corporal Laird, explained what it was:

> A party of twenty infantry marching along the road from the trenches singing, one man playing the bones, another two banging the cans, just as though such things as Germans did not exist.
>
> They turned into the field where we were, grouped round and sang carols, 'Tipperary', and several others we know, gave us three cheers for saving them at Mons, wished us a merry Christmas and safe New Year and return to England, and then marched out on the road again. Believe me, it was worth seeing.

At St Omer, twenty-seven miles behind the front line, the British High Command were concerned lest the enemy, far from seizing the chance to fraternize, should seize the chance to fight. On Christmas Eve GHQ issued a signal to be passed to all units:

> It is thought possible that the enemy may be contemplating an attack during Xmas or New Year. Special vigilance will be maintained during this period.

It was not until well after dark that this message was forwarded to the front-line battalions. By the time it reached them, in many sectors the preliminaries were over and the Christmas truce was well under way.

☆

The Germans had similar anxieties about British intentions. When Hugo Klemm and his comrades of the 133rd Saxon Infantry Regiment assembled that evening in front of the church in their billet village of Pont Rouge, preparatory to going into the line, they were given a strong warning by their company commander:

> He emphasized that for that day and the following days special alertness would be required, as it was expected that the English would perhaps take advantage of our good mood at Christmas by mounting a raid.

Vigilant or not, however, they were not going to be deprived of their Christmas celebrations:

> Several of my chums had been able to get hold of two small Christmas trees complete with candles, to be mounted on the parapet of the trenches, while others dragged planks, fascines etc with them, to be used in the battle against water and mud. As was usual at that time, having settled in the trenches, we fired the occasional shot from our outposts to let the enemy know we would not let ourselves be surprised.

These formalities over, they put their trees on the parapet and lit the candles. As they did so hundreds of their comrades were doing exactly the same; Klemm noted that as far as the eye could see lighted Christmas trees were appearing to right and left along the whole sector.

Johannes Niemann was a young lieutenant in the same Saxon Regiment:

> On Christmas Eve we got the order to go into the trenches. The day before we had celebrated Christmas in our rest quarters with the civilian people and children who were presented with chocolate, bonbons and cake. It was all in good humour.

Then at darkness we marched forward to the trenches like Father Christmas with parcels hanging from us. All was quiet. No shooting. Little snow. We posted a tiny Christmas tree in our dugout – the company commander, myself the lieutenant, and the two orderlies. We placed a second lighted tree on the breastwork.

Then we began to sing our old Christmas songs: '*Stille Nacht, Heilige Nacht*' and '*O du Fröhliche*' . . .

Klemm and his friends were also singing, and both he and Niemann remembered how from the other side of No Man's Land came the sound of applause and cheering. In fact, on perhaps as much as two-thirds of the British-held sector, Tommies were watching in fascinated amazement as the lighted Christmas trees, or in some cases lanterns or torches, appeared on the German parapets. In what was essentially a zone of ugliness and desolation they made a beautiful and incongruous sight. 'Like the footlights of a theatre,' was how one soldier put it in a letter home; and indeed there was something dramatic about the whole scene – the suddenness of it, the extent of it – though here and there were areas of normal darkness where no Christmas celebrations were taking place and where the only illuminations were the occasional spit of a sniper's rifle or the firework-like glow of a starshell. As striking as the sight presented by the German trenches was the sound coming from them, the distant, haunting sound of men singing, harmoniously and with deep emotion, the Christmas hymns which they had known since childhood. '*Stille Nacht*' – 'Silent Night', in its English form – stands out as being the carol most particularly and affectionately remembered by the listening Tommies, so much so that many of them could never hear that hymn in later life without being instantly transported back to the Western Front, Christmas Eve 1914. One such was Albert Moren, then in the front-line trenches held by 2/Queen's near the village of La Chapelle d'Armentières:

> It was a beautiful moonlit night, frost on the ground, white almost everywhere; and about seven or eight in the evening there was a lot of commotion in the German trenches and there were these lights – I don't know what they were. And then they sang 'Silent Night' – '*Stille Nacht*'. I shall never forget it, it was one of the highlights of my life. I thought, what a beautiful tune.

There were various reactions from the British side. One German soldier's letter records that during the singing of '*Stille Nacht*' those on guard duty kept a keen lookout through their observation slits, 'with rifles at the ready, as the enemy was only 80 metres away'. But their vigilance was not necessary:

> Suddenly a man from my company reported: 'The English are letting off fireworks.' And sure enough across the way from us the enemy trenches were lit up with fires and rockets and so on. We then made up a few banners reading 'Happy Christmas!' with a couple of candles behind and a couple on top.

In most cases, however, the British responded not with flares and fireworks, but with calls for more, and songs and carols of their own. According to Charles Brewer, a lieutenant in the 2/Bedfordshires, when the Germans struck up the famous German carol '*O Tannenbaum*', his men replied, 'less artistically but no less heartily', with 'We are Fred Karno's army' – sung to the tune of the well-known hymn 'The Church's One Foundation'. Johannes Niemann remembered the British on his front breaking into 'It's a long way to Tipperary' and 'Home Sweet Home'. The London Rifle Brigade on the other hand rose to the occasion with a performance of seasonal offerings as varied and vigorous as that of the German initiators. Proceedings did not begin in their part of the line until quite late in the evening when towards eleven o'clock (midnight according to German time) Rifleman Graham Williams was on sentry duty in the forward trenches:

> I was standing on the firestep, gazing towards the German lines and thinking what a very different sort of Christmas Eve this was from any I had experienced in the past. In the ordinary way of things, my father would be making Rum Punch from an old family recipe, which had been written out by his grandfather, and was kept, of all places, in the Family Bible! Earlier, after the evening meal, we would have decorated the living rooms and hall with the traditional greenery, and would now be looking forward to wishing one another a 'Happy Christmas', and toasting the occasion in the result of my father's labours. Instead of this, here was I, standing in a waterlogged trench, in a muddy Flemish field, and staring out over the flat, empty and desolate countryside, with no signs of life. There had been no shooting by either side since the sniper's shot that morning, which had killed young Bassingham. But this was not at all unusual.
>
> Then suddenly lights began to appear along the German parapet, which were evidently make-shift Christmas trees, adorned with lighted candles, which burnt steadily in the still, frosty air! Other sentries had, of course, seen the same thing, and quickly awoke those on duty, asleep in the shelters, to 'come and see this thing, which had come to pass'. Then our opponents began to sing 'Stille Nacht, Heilige Nacht'. This was actually the first time I heard this carol, which was not then so popular in this country as it has since become. They finished their carol and we thought that we ought to retaliate in some way, so we sang 'The First Nowell', and when we finished that they all began clapping; and then they struck up another

1. *The Prussian Monster Unleashed* by Jean Véber, September 1914.
A French cartoonist's vision of the predatory Hun

STUDY OF A PRUSSIAN HOUSEHOLD HAVING ITS MORNING HATE.

2. The British response by *Punch* to Germany's '*Hassgesang gegen England*'
(*Hymn of Hate against England*)

3. Ineffective pumping behind the British trench line at La Boutillerie,
December 1914

4. German trench, same period, photographed by Captain Josef Sewald

5. Ploegsteert Wood – to become known as one of the most peaceful sectors of the Western Front

6. A typical farm just behind the British front line – La Grande Flamengrie, near Bois Grenier. Snipers fired from the roof, and the cellars became a company headquarters

'A shooting test between British soldiers in their trench and Germans in a trench opposite: A German setting up a tin on a branch in the snow for our men to try their skill as "snipers" during a lull in the battle' (original caption)

7. First printed in the *Illustrated London News* on 26 December 1914, reprinted in Berlin and Dresden newspapers in January 1915

8. General Sir Horace Smith-Dorrien, Commander II Corps '. . . weird stories come in from the trenches about fraternizing with the Germans . . . I therefore intend to issue instructions to my Corps not to fraternize in any way whatever with the enemy . . .' (2 December 1914)

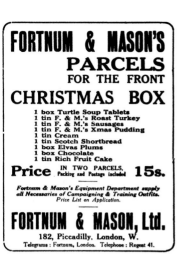

9, 10. December editions of British and German newspapers carried numerous advertisements for Christmas gifts to ease the hardships of trench life

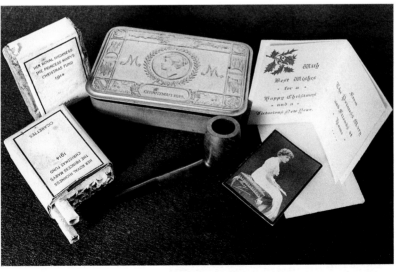

11. The gift box from Princess Mary's Fund. Over 355,000 found their way to front-line troops by Christmas, adding to the problems of the overloaded railway and postal systems

PREPARATIONS
FOR CHRISTMAS

12. British soldiers collecting
mistletoe

13. Germans decorating a
Christmas tree. The soldier
with raised right arm might
be thought to bear a striking
resemblance to the future
Führer. In fact Hitler was
with the 16/Bavarian Reserve
Infantry Regiment in the
Wytschaete area, north of
Messines, serving as a
Meldegänger (a runner).
He was out of the line over
the Christmas period

14. German soldiers singing carols around their candlelit Christmas tree, Christmas Eve 1914. This photograph was taken on the Eastern Front (on the banks of the river Angerap in East Prussia) but it parallels exactly what happened on the Western Front

THE ILLUSTRATED LONDON NEWS.

REGISTERED AS A NEWSPAPER FOR TRANSMISSION IN THE UNITED KINGDOM, AND TO CANADA AND NEWFOUNDLAND BY MAGAZINE POST.

No. 3951. — VOL. CXLVI.　　　SATURDAY, JANUARY 9, 1915.　　　SIXPENCE.

The Copyright of all the Editorial Matter, both Engravings and Letterpress, is Strictly Reserved in Great Britain, the Colonies, Europe, and the United States of America.

15. 'The Light of Peace in the trenches on Christmas Eve: A German soldier opens the spontaneous truce by approaching the British lines with a small Christmas tree'

(original caption)

favourite of theirs, 'O Tannenbaum'. And so it went on. First
the Germans would sing one of their carols and then we would
sing one of ours, until when we started up 'O Come All Ye
Faithful' the Germans immediately joined in singing the same
hymn to the Latin words 'Adeste Fideles'. And I thought, well,
this was really a most extraordinary thing – two nations both
singing the same carol in the middle of a war.

In the same trenches at Ploegsteert was Major Arthur Bates,
also of the London Rifle Brigade, watching the proceedings,
in spite of his relative seniority, with no disapproving eye.
Some time before midnight, while the impromptu concert was
still going on, he slipped away to write a brief letter to his
sister:

Dearest Dorothy,

Just a line from the trenches on Xmas Eve – a topping night
with not much firing going on & both sides singing. It will
be interesting to see what happens tomorrow. My orders to
the Coy are not to start firing unless the Germans do.

Best love from your loving brother. Arthur.

Williams also records that the Germans urged the British
to leave their trenches with shouts of, in English, 'Tommy, you
come over and see us!', to which someone on the British side
replied, 'No, you come here'. But neither side availed themselves
of the invitation and eventually the lights burned out and the
singing stopped, as everybody, apart from the sentries, attempted
to get some sleep. Elsewhere, however, men *did* leave their
trenches and there was active fraternization in No Man's Land.
In some instances only a few men were involved, in others little
groups of soldiers met and mingled, while their comrades peered
from their parapets, incredulously looking on, as the grey shapes

moved cautiously towards each other, talked, lit cigarettes, the whole scene lit by a bright, frosty moon.

It was the moon which worried Private Tapp of the 1/Royal Warwicks as his battalion, which had been in billets for several days, prepared to return to the line near Ploegsteert Wood:

> We go back to trenches tonight, it is going to be a moonlight night so I think we shall lose a few men while we are relieving the other regt. We get near the trenches but can't hear any firing, now we hear some singing from their trenches and ours.

Second Lieutenant Bruce Bairnsfather, who was to become the most famous soldier-cartoonist of the Great War, was the Machine-Gun Officer of the 1/Royal Warwicks. He had been out to a special trench dinner ('not quite so much bully and Maconochie about as usual, a bottle of red wine and a medley of tinned things from home deputizing in their absence') at a dugout a quarter of a mile away to the left, and returned to his lines to find several of his men 'listening to the burst of song floating across on the frosty air'. He noticed that the singing seemed to be loudest and most distinct some way to the right:

> 'Come on,' said I, 'let's go along the trench to the hedge there on the right – that's the nearest point to them, over there.'
>
> So we stumbled along our now hard, frosted ditch, and scrambled up on to the bank above, strode across the field to our next bit of trench on the right. Everyone was listening. An improvised Boche band was playing a precarious version of 'Deutschland, Deutschland, über Alles', at the conclusion of which some of our mouth-organ experts retaliated with snatches of ragtime songs and imitations of the German tune. Suddenly we heard a confused shouting from the other side. We all stopped to listen. The shout came again. A voice in the darkness shouted in English, with a strong German accent,

'Come over here!' A ripple of mirth swept along our trench, followed by a rude outburst of mouth organs and laughter. Presently in a lull, one of our sergeants repeated the request, 'Come over here!' . . .

After much suspicious shouting and jocular derision from both sides our sergeant went along the hedge which ran at right-angles to the two lines of trenches. He was quickly out of sight; but as we all listened in breathless silence, we soon heard a spasmodic conversation taking place out there in the darkness.

Tapp was also watching as the sergeant made his way into No Man's Land:

Our sergeant goes out, their man takes a lot of coaxing but comes at the finish and we find that they have sent two, we can hear them talking quite plain, they exchange cigarettes and the German shouts to wish us a Merry Xmas.

Another young officer of 1/Royal Warwicks, Lieutenant Frank Black, was there as this meeting took place. He could see sufficiently clearly to observe that when the sergeant met the two Germans they lit each other's cigarettes, at which there were cheers from both lines.

When the sergeant returned, he brought with him some cigars and cigarettes which he had received in exchange for the two tins of Maconochie's and the tin of Capstan tobacco which he had taken with him. He also brought with him an offer from the Germans not to fire until Boxing Day unless the British did, and a promise that if they received orders to fire they would fire high by way of warning. 'That evening', wrote Lieutenant Black, 'we were strolling about outside the trenches as though there was no war going on.' 'After months of vindictive sniping and shelling,' commented Bruce Bairnsfather, 'this little episode came as an invigorating tonic, and a welcome relief to the daily monotony of antagonism.' Having nothing to do and no wounded to carry, the battalion stretcher-bearers came down from headquarters and went round the companies carol-singing. 'They sing several in our trench before going,' wrote Tapp, 'the Gers give them a cheer for singing, this night I would not have missed for a lot, I don't go to sleep till 2.30 Xmas morning.'

A longer and more general fraternization took place on the front of the 2/Seaforth Highlanders, just to the north of Ploegsteert Wood. Here it was the Scotsmen who began singing carols and the Germans who applauded and replied. The latter were immediately recognized as being the better singers – 'I don't think we were so harmonious as the Germans,' commented Corporal John Ferguson, 'they had some fine voices amongst them' – and the Seaforths listened 'spellbound' as the sound floated over the turnip field to their trenches. Afterwards, there was the usual shouted conversation between the opposing lines. Ferguson's account continues:

> Someone calling us from the enemy's trenches 'Komradd, Onglees Komradd', I answered him, 'Hello! Fritz' (we call them all Fritz). 'Do you want any tobacco?' he asks. 'Yes.' 'Come halfways'; we shouted back and forward until Old Fritz clambered out of the trench, and accompanied by three others of my section we went out to meet him. We were walking between the trenches. At any other time this would have been suicide; even to show your head above the parapet would have been fatal, but tonight we go unarmed (but a little shaky) out to meet our enemies. 'Make for the light', he calls, and as we came nearer we saw he had his flash lamp in his hand, putting it in and out to guide us.
>
> We shook hands, wished each other a Merry Xmas, and were soon conversing as if we had known each other for years.

We were in front of their wire entanglements and surrounded by Germans – Fritz and I in the centre talking, and Fritz occasionally translating to his friends what I was saying. We stood inside the circle like streetcorner orators.

Soon most of our company ('A' company), hearing that I and some others had gone out, followed us; they called me 'Fergie' in the Regiment, and to find out where I was in the darkness they kept calling out 'Fergie'. The Germans, thinking that was an English greeting, answered 'Fergie'. What a sight – little groups of Germans and British extending almost the length of our front! Out of the darkness we could hear laughter and see lighted matches, a German lighting a Scotchman's cigarette and vice versa, exchanging cigarettes and souvenirs. Where they couldn't talk the language they were making themselves understood by signs, and everyone seemed to be getting on nicely. Here we were laughing and chatting to men whom only a few hours before we were trying to kill!

That the participants could scarcely believe what was happening – and scarcely expected their readers to believe them – comes through in numerous contemporary accounts. Sergeant A. Lovell of 3/Rifle Brigade described events on his battalion's front in a letter typical of many written on Christmas Day; it was published on the front page of the London *Evening News* in early January:

You will hardly credit what I am going to tell you: but thousands of our men will be writing home today telling the same strange and wonderful story. Listen.

Last night as I sat in my little dugout, writing, my chum came bursting in upon me with: 'Bob! Hark at 'em!' And I listened. From the German trenches came the sound of music and singing. My chum continued: 'They've got Christmas trees all along the top of their trenches! Never saw such a sight.'

I got up to investigate. Climbing the parapet, I saw a sight which I shall remember to my dying day. Right along the whole of the line were hung paper lanterns and illuminations of every description, many of them in such positions as to suggest that they were hung upon Christmas trees. And as I stood in wonder a rousing song came over to us; at first the words were indistinguishable, then, as the song was repeated again and again, we realized that we were listening to 'The Watch on the Rhine'. Our boys answered with a cheer, while a neighbouring regiment sang lustily the National Anthem. Some were for shooting the lights away, but almost at the first shot there came a shout in really good English, 'Stop shooting!' Then began a series of answering shouts from trench to trench. It was incredible. 'Hallo! Hallo! you English we wish to speak.' And everyone began to speak at once. Some were rational, others the reverse of complimentary. Eventually some sort of order obtained, and lo! a party of our men got out from the trenches and invited the Germans to meet them halfway and talk.

And there in the searchlight they stood, Englishman and German, chatting and smoking cigarettes together midway between the lines. A rousing cheer went up from friend and foe alike. The group was too far away from me to hear what was said, but presently we heard a cheery 'Good night. A Merry Christmas and a Happy New Year to you all', with which the parties returned to their respective trenches.

After this we remained the whole night through, singing with the enemy song for song.

Though good-humoured and friendly, the proceedings were generally somewhat more cautious and restrained than those described by Sergeant Lovell. The 2/Argyll and Sutherland Highlanders were at Houplines, near Armentières, in the same Infantry Brigade, the 19th, as the 2/Royal Welch Fusiliers. As elsewhere, candles appeared on the German parapets, '*Stille Nacht*' was sung together with a number of other carols and there followed the standard invitation to join the Germans in No Man's Land. Their spokesman could not have had better credentials: an ex-waiter who had worked in Glasgow and spoke good English. After some light-hearted banter it was finally agreed that two from each side should go out. All due precautions were taken and no one else, British or German, was allowed out of the trenches. A nineteen-year-old subaltern, Ian Stewart, asked permission to be one of those selected and his Company Commander agreed:

> I could talk some German and one of the German officers, some English. He was about my age. Our conversation was no different from that of meeting a friendly opponent at a football match. He . . . gave me a cigar to which I was unaccustomed and which nearly made me sick, and a photograph of his pre-War regimental football team of which he was very proud . . . My gift was a tin of bully beef from my emergency ration – the best thing available. After 10 minutes we said a friendly goodbye and returned to our lines and relative normality.

Some British battalions ignored the enemy's overtures, not because of any particular anti-German feeling but because they were bemused by what was happening and were uncertain as to how to respond. The following eyewitness account is included in the Regimental History of the 13/London Regiment, a Territorial battalion of the 8th Division, also known as 'Princess Louise's' and 'The Kensingtons'. They were to the south of Armentières, near Laventie:

> It was the first Christmas of the war and the enemy, no less than ourselves, felt very homesick. The Germans gave the first

sign. A tired sentry in the Battalion, looking out over the waste towards their lines spread the exciting news that the enemy's trenches were 'all alight'. He had hardly uttered the words before other sentries took up the cry and we all looked at the enemy's line, which was dotted here and there with clusters of lights. From behind the lines came voices crying 'English soldiers, English soldiers, Happy Christmas. Where are your Christmas trees?' and faint but clear, the songs of the season. We were a little embarrassed by this sudden comradeship and, as a lasting joke against us, let it be said that the order was given to stand to arms. But we did not fire, for the battalion on our right, The Royal Irish Rifles, with their national sense of humour, answered the enemy's salutations with songs and jokes and made appointments in No Man's Land for Christmas Day. We felt small and subdued and spent the remainder of Christmas Eve in watching the lights flicker and fade on the 'Christmas Trees' in their trenches and hearing the voices grow fainter and eventually cease.

The 1/Royal Irish Rifles did indeed fraternize, following a friendly invitation from the German trenches. The Germans, ignoring the Irish nationality of their opponents (on the assumption, as in the case of the Seaforths, that all British units were 'English'), called out to them, 'If you English come out and talk to us – we won't fire.' Their plea was successful: Irishmen emerged from their trenches and met the enemy halfway between the lines, the situation being eased by the fact that, in the words of the War Diary, 'a good many Germans spoke English well'. Even so the battalion command was sufficiently concerned about their response to the enemy's blandishments to decide that they must immediately inform Brigade Headquarters about what they called their 'soldier's truce'. At 8.30 p.m. they sent this signal:

Germans have illuminated their trenches, are singing songs, and are wishing us a Happy Xmas. Compliments are being exchanged but am nevertheless taking all military precautions . . .

The Queen's Westminster Rifles at La Chapelle d'Armentières were, like the Kensingtons, inclined to an initial suspicion when the Christmas Eve celebrations began on their sector. In his account, written three days later, Rifleman P. H. Jones described the process of events: first, the lighting of three large fires behind the enemy lines in an area where it would generally be madness to strike a match; next, the appearance of numerous small lights on the top of the enemy's trenches; then, the playing of 'weird tunes' on bugles or horns, after which they suddenly burst into songs of all kinds:

Our private opinion was that the enemy were priming themselves up for a big attack, so we commenced polishing up ammunition and rifles and getting all ready for speedy action. In fact we were about to loose off a few rounds at the biggest light when the following words were heard (probably through a megaphone) 'Englishman, Englishman, Don't shoot. You don't shoot we don't shoot.' Then followed a remark about Christmas. This was all very well, but we had heard so many yarns about German treachery that we kept a very sharp lookout.

How it all happened I don't know, but shortly after this our boys had lights out, and the enemy troops were busy singing each other songs, punctuated with terrific salvos of applause.

The scene from my sentry post was hardly creditable. Straight ahead were three large lights, with figures perfectly visible round them. The German trenches, which bent sharply and turned to the rear of our advanced positions, were illuminated with hundreds of little lights. Far away to the left, where our lines bent, a few lights showed our A Coy trenches, where the men were thundering out 'My Little Grey Home in the West'.

At the conclusion of this song the Saxons burst into loud cheers and obliged with some German tune. They also sang one of their national airs to the tune of 'God Save the King'. We replied with the Austrian hymn, at which the applause was terrific. The music then quietened down and some time was spent yelling facetious remarks across the trenches. After this some daredevils in E Coy actually went out, met and shook hands with some of the Germans and exchanged cake and biscuits. As the night went on this gradually grew quieter.

Jones does not say whether he observed his daredevil comrades' return; indeed, since a battalion's front covered quite a considerable area – roughly half a mile – there may well have been others heading towards the German line whom he did not see. However, the fact is that the following morning three men, Riflemen Byng, Goude and Pearce, were found to be missing. Rifleman Bernard Brookes was sent out on his bicycle to look for them. The obvious place was the dressing station at La Chapelle d'Armentières a mile or so away, but there was no sign of them there. The truth finally emerged during fraternization later in the day when the Germans informed the QWRs that the missing men had walked into the German trenches in a drunken state and had been taken prisoner. The British asked for their release, but the request was refused, since they had had the opportunity to see the German dispositions, in particular the location of their machine-guns. The one concession which the Germans offered was that the men would be interned in a civilian camp and would not be treated as prisoners of war and the British were forced to leave it at that (see page 295).

There were certain others to whom these Christmas celebrations were not, in the event, to be without their shadow. When the 2/Scots Guards were arranging an armistice with the 158th Saxon Regiment, a scout named Murker, who spoke German, was sent out to negotiate with a German patrol. He was given a glass of whisky, some cigars and a message to take back to the effect that the Germans would agree to a ceasefire if the British did likewise. All went smoothly that night but by the end of Christmas he too would find himself a prisoner of the enemy.

Shortly before Christmas a young schoolboy at Loretto School near Edinburgh sent to his father, Major Buchanan-Dunlop of the 1/Leicesters, a copy of the end-of-term carol concert programme. Major Buchanan-Dunlop was particularly pleased as he himself was an old boy of the school and, following his distinguished service in the Boer War, had been in charge of the Officers' Training Corps there. When the festivities at the front began, he organized, as he put it in a letter to his wife, a 'select band of officers and men' to sing carols to the Germans, and he took the programme with him – 'it was', he wrote, 'most useful to us'. He had a good voice, was an enthusiastic Christian and inevitably led the singing; as elsewhere, the Germans responded with carols of their own. The news of his exploits was to make headlines at home, where he would become briefly famous as the 'Major Who Sang Carols Between the Trenches' – a development which was to get him into some difficulty with the military authorities in the New Year. But on Christmas Eve, as the singing floated between the lines in an atmosphere of remarkable peace and goodwill, there was no hint of these troubles to come.

Not all officers, however, accepted the general change of atmosphere with the spirit of Christian charity shown by Buchanan-Dunlop, as the following letter – written by an

unnamed officer of the Rifle Brigade – clearly indicates; there
was too much bitterness standing in the way:

> When I got back to our trenches after dark on Christmas Eve
> I found the Boches' trenches looking like the Thames on Henley
> Regatta night! They had got little Christmas trees burning
> all along the parapet of their trench. No truce had been
> proclaimed, and I was all for not allowing the blighters to
> enjoy themselves, especially as they had killed one of our men
> that afternoon. But my captain (who hadn't seen our wounded
> going mad and slowly dying outside the German trenches on
> the Aisne) wouldn't let me shoot; however, I soon had an
> excuse as one of the Germans fired at us, so I quickly lined
> up my platoon and had those Christmas trees down and out.
>
> Meanwhile, unknown to us, two officers on our right,
> without saying a word to anybody, got out of their trench and
> walked halfway to the German trench and were met by two
> German officers and talked away quite civilly and actually
> shook hands! It was an awfully stupid thing to do as it might
> easily have had different results; but our captains are new and,
> not having seen the Germans in their true light yet, apparently
> won't believe the stories of their treachery and brutality.

On the other hand, Captain R. J. Armes, a thirty-eight-year-
old Regular officer of the 1/North Staffs, joined in gladly and,
indeed, was so excited by what he saw and heard that he hurried
away the moment the night's festivities were over to write
everything down in a long letter to his wife while it was still
fresh in his mind:

> I have just been through one of the most extraordinary scenes
> imaginable. Tonight is Xmas Eve and I came up into the
> trenches this evening for my tour of duty in them. Firing was
> going on all the time and the enemy's machine-guns were at
> it hard, firing at us. Then about seven the firing stopped.

I was in my dugout reading a paper and the mail was being dished out. It was reported that the Germans had lighted their trenches up all along our front. We had been calling to one another for some time Xmas wishes and other things. I went out and they shouted 'no shooting' and then somehow the scene became a peaceful one. All our men got out of the trenches and sat on the parapet, the Germans did the same, and they talked to one another in English and broken English. I got on the top of the trench and talked German and asked them to sing a German *Volkslied* [folk song], which they did, then our men sang quite well and each side clapped and cheered the other.

I asked a German who sang a solo to sing one of Schumann's songs, so he sang 'The Two Grenadiers' splendidly. Our men were a good audience and really enjoyed his singing.

Then Pope and I walked across and held a conversation with the German officer in command. One of his men introduced us properly, he asked my name and then presented me to his officer. I gave the latter permission to bury some German dead who were lying in between us, and we agreed to have no shooting until 12 midnight tomorrow. We talked together, 10 or more Germans gathered round. I was almost in their lines within a yard or so. We saluted each other, he thanked me for permission to bury his dead, and we fixed up how many men were to do it, and that otherwise both sides must remain in their trenches.

Then we wished one another good night and a good night's rest, and a happy Xmas and parted with a salute. I got back to the trench. The Germans sang '*Die Wacht am Rhein*', it sounded well. Then our men sang quite well 'Christians Awake', it sounded so well, and with a good night we all got back into our trenches. It was a curious scene, a lovely moon-light night, the German trenches with small lights on them, and the men on both sides gathered in groups on the parapets.

At times we heard the guns in the distance and an occasional rifle shot. I can hear them now, but about us is absolute quiet. I allowed one or two men to go out and meet a German or two halfway. They exchanged cigars, a smoke and talked. The officer I spoke to hopes we shall do the same on New Year's Day. I said, 'Yes, if I am here.' I felt I must sit down and write the story of this Xmas Eve before I went to lie down. Of course no precautions are relaxed, but I think they mean to play the game. All the same, I think I shall be awake all night so as to be on the safe side. It is weird to think that tomorrow night we shall be at it hard again. If one gets through this show it will be a Xmas time to live in one's memory. The German who sang had a really fine voice.

Am just off for a walk round the trenches to see all is well. Good night.

Captain Armes's letter emphasizes one very important contributory reason for the initiation of the Christmas truce – indeed, for some participants the *real* reason: Christmas was seen as a suitable time for the decent disposal of the dead bodies lying in No Man's Land, most of which were the victims of the previous week's attacks, though some had been out there since October. Opposite the 2/Bedfordshires behind the flickering Christmas trees a voice shouted across to the British lines at about 8 p.m.: 'I want to arrange to bury the dead. Will someone come out to me?' Second Lieutenant Harold de Buriatti went out with three men and met five Germans, whose leader, not an officer, spoke excellent English – a fact explained, as he told the Englishmen, by his having lived in Brighton and Canada. He said that they wanted to bury about twenty-four of their dead the following day. No specific arrangement was made at the time, but the Bedfordshires noted the request and returned to their lines. Before they parted the English-speaking German gave de Buriatti a signet ring which he retained for many years as a souvenir of this extraordinary occasion.

☆

As has already been described, the Indian Corps involved in the heavy fighting just before Christmas were being gradually withdrawn, but there were still some Indian units in the line at Christmas. How did they react when they suddenly found themselves surrounded by the sounds and trappings of a north European religious festival?

The 1/39 and 2/39 Royal Garhwal Rifles were in shallow, waterlogged trenches south-east of the village of Neuve Chapelle. They had not had a particularly pleasant Christmas Eve. Despite the hard frost, water continued to flow into their trenches; rumour had it that the Germans were using a hosepipe to pump the water from their lines into those of the lower-lying Indians. In fact, the Germans did not need a hosepipe; all the water they pumped out of their trenches ran naturally down a ditch alongside the main Estaires–La Bassée road into those of the unfortunate Garhwalis and the adjacent battalions of 24th Brigade.

Fifty to sixty yards away across No Man's Land was the 16th (3rd Westphalian, Freiherr von Sparr) Regiment of VII Corps, a distinguished regiment of the Prussian Army. Among their officers, in acting command of 6th Company, was Walther Stennes, who, though only nineteen, was known to his men as '*der Alte*' – 'the Old Man' – because of his reputation as a consistently brave and tenacious fighter, and despite his extremely boyish looks. In his account of Christmas Eve he wrote:

> The activities on both sides died down and after nightfall ceased completely. We had received mail, parcels and some

Xmas trees from home. The choir of my company tuned up
for some Xmas-songs. Temperature about freezing point . . .
I had inspected the sentries and warned them to be on guard.
In the dugouts the men were awake, gaily talking, eating,
reading and playing games.

Beyond the two lines of wire the Indians were watching and
listening. But what caught their attention more than anything
else were the lighted Christmas trees which, as elsewhere, the
Germans put in rows along their parapets. Far from seeming
exotic and strange, the flickering lights had a very familiar look.
The *Divali* or *Dipavali* festival is one of the most important of
the Hindu year. Originally a fertility festival, it is more generally dedicated to the goddess Lakshmi, giver of wealth. It lasts
five days, on the fourth of which little earthen bowls filled with
oil are lighted in the evening and set up in extended rows inside
and outside the houses. The word *Dipavali*, in fact, means 'a
row of lights'.

So the Germans celebrated and the Indians looked on and
were reminded of home.

☆

What of the French and Belgians on Christmas Eve?

The Belgians in December 1914 held only a small section
of the front, from just south of Nieuport on the Channel coast
to the northern end of the Ypres Salient. One Belgian soldier's
account which was quoted shortly afterwards in the British
newspapers spoke of 'a severe cannonade' on Christmas Eve, and
of confessions being heard and communion administered in the
dark and wretched cellar of a ruined house – there being nothing
left of the local church except part of the tower. 'We seemed to
be living again at the time of the catacombs,' he wrote. 'Never

shall I forget the touching ceremony, when amid the roar of the guns I took communion on Christmas Eve.' Thereafter he returned to the line to spend Christmas there.

> Christmas in the trenches! It must have been sad, do you say? Well, I am not sorry to have spent it there, and the recollection of it will ever be one of imperishable beauty. At midnight a baritone stood up and in a rich resonant voice sang '*Minuit, Chrétiens*'. The cannonade roared, and when the hymn finished applause broke out from our side and – from the German trenches! The Germans too, were celebrating Christmas, and we could hear them singing 200 yards away from us.

On the next day, in fact, there would be fraternization in this area.

There was much emotion at these midnight services, with their traditional and well-loved hymns. Robert de Wilde, Captain Commandant of the Belgian Artillery, described in his *Journal de Campagne* a mass held in an improvised sanctuary at Pervyse in the vicinity of the front line:

> It was freezing. The stars were shining superbly and the horizon was lit by multiple blue rockets launched from the German trenches.
>
> The floor of a barn, with its huge double doors for background, straw on every side, draughts everywhere – that was the chapel. A wooden table and two candles stuck in bottles – that was the altar.
>
> The soldiers were singing. It was unreal, sublime. They were singing: '*Minuit, Chrétiens*', '*Adeste fideles*', '*Les anges de nos campagnes*', all the songs we used to sing when we were little. The Christmases of long ago were coming to life again, all the things we had known in our childhood, the family, the countryside, the fireside, our eyes dazzled by the tree with its sparkling candles, all the things we now relive in our children.

The French held over four hundred miles of the front at this time and, indeed, were to hold by far the greater part of the line throughout the war – though there were long stretches where there was to be no serious fighting at all. In those there was no doubt Christmas as usual on 24 December, with the normal midnight services as though peace had never been disrupted; in the more active sectors, as in the case of the British, there were areas of tension and others of remarkable and poignant calm.

At one point, a French officer of the line, Capitaine Rimbault, sang carols with his lieutenants; then to cries of '*Vive la France!*', they drank champagne. Later, after dark, he gathered his men together in the middle of a wood, where they lit their few precious candles, keeping them low since the Boches were not far away:

> They are all there, around me, my brave soldiers! They have their drinking mugs in their hands, filled with the good wine of the Meuse. And I speak to them . . . I speak to them of Christmas, of the war, of their homes, of our hopes . . . There is no longer any difference of age or rank, there is only a brother speaking to his brothers, wishing them a good and gallant Christmas!
>
> At midnight, we held a mass, fifty metres from the Boches, in the trenches. A colour lieutenant [*lieutenant porte-drapeau*] said it for us. We had fixed up a sort of makeshift altar; from the nearby village, abandoned and in ruins, we had fetched a few candle-holders, a missal, a pyx, an altar-cloth. Debris from the forest supplied the rest. The men sang their carols, carols from their villages, from their childhood . . . carols of peace and gentleness which, coming from those rough lips, seemed more like songs of strife and battle.
>
> Throughout the whole ceremony, the Boches – Bavarian

Catholics – did not fire a single shot. For an instant the God of goodwill was once more master of this corner of earth.

The Württembergers of the 246th Reserve Regiment of Infantry were opposite the French at Polygon Wood near Ypres, scene of much hard fighting already and where there would be much hard fighting again. On the evening of 24 December they waited for the usual 'evening blessing' of artillery fire from the French. It did not come. Rifles at the ready, they prepared for a surprise attack. Nothing happened:

> Is it possible? Are the French really going to leave us in peace today, Christmas Eve? Then – listen – from across the way came the sound of a festive song. A Frenchman singing a Christmas carol with a marvellous tenor voice. Everyone lay still, listening in the quiet of the night. Is it our imagination or is it maybe meant to lull us into a false sense of security? Or is it in fact the victory of God's love over all human conflict? We all kept on our guard; only our thoughts flew home to our wives and children.

Where the German 212th Reserve Infantry Regiment were stationed to the north of Ypres, the singing was from their side and it was the turn of the French to listen. A French officer described what took place in an account which was later included in the German Regiment's official history. Here as at so many other points there were lighted Christmas trees and as the Germans began to sing the French officer felt a tremor of fear as he realized that the voices now ringing out with Christmas hymns had sung patriotic songs before the terrible attack at Bixschoote in October. 'One can imagine what coarse jibes and insults would have been hurled at the singers at any other time. But that is all changed.' The French deduced that one man, a soloist, was marching unseen along the whole German front, being answered whenever he stopped singing by hundreds of German voices taking up the chorus:

> I look at our side. Everyone is up and awake, they have all climbed up onto the parapet: some have even left the trench and gone into No Man's Land, just to be able to hear more clearly this unexpected concert! No one is angry and no one is poking fun. Rather there is a feeling of regret which shows itself in the faces and attitudes of those standing near me. And yet it would be so easy to put an end to this scene: one salvo from our sector and everything would go quiet, as quiet as any normal night here. But no one would commit the sacrilege of shooting at these soldiers at prayer. We feel that there are certain times when one can forget that one is here to kill. Not that that would stop us doing our duty a moment later.
>
> Bang! A shot has been fired.
>
> Oh the folly of that bullet which has torn the air apart and perhaps reached its target. All at once the singing stops. No cries, no curses, no complaints are heard. Someone down there thought he was doing good by aiming at that man. What a pity. We will have gained nothing by stopping them from celebrating Christmas in their own way. It would have been a more noble thing to have held our fire.

There are several accounts in which a striking solo voice, from one side or the other, is described as playing a memorable role. A correspondent of the British magazine *The Lady* told such a story in its edition of January 1915:

> I heard that in the French trenches in the Argonne Forest the cold was intense, and, whilst a spiritless fire was going on at intervals, a village church bell sounded the hour of midnght on Christmas Eve, whereupon a voice, clear and beautiful, was heard singing, *'Minuit, Chrétiens, c'est l'heure solennelle'*. And who do you think the singer was? *Granier*, of the Paris Opera.

The troops, French and German, forgot to fire whilst listening to that wonderful tenor voice lifted in harmonious sound above the snapping of the guns, and for a few moments all was peace.

A similar episode appears in the memoirs of Crown Prince Wilhelm of Prussia, the son of the Kaiser, then Commander of the German Fifth Army in the Argonne region, which had seen fierce fighting throughout this first winter of the war. On Christmas Eve he felt 'particularly drawn to my field-grey boys', and decided to visit them in the front line:

I spent the afternoon in the hutments of the Württembergers with the 120th and 124th Regiments. Thick snow lay on the hilltops above this Forest of the Dead. The shells howled their monotonous and hideous melody, and from time to time the sacred silence was rent by the burst of a machine-gun's fire. And in between, one could hear the dull drone of the trench mortar shells. Nevertheless, the spirits of the men were every-where very cheerful. Every dugout had its Christmas tree, and from all directions came the sound of rough men's voices singing our exquisite old Christmas songs.

Kirchhoff, the concert singer, who was attached to our Headquarters Staff for a while as orderly officer, sang his Christmas songs on that same sacred evening in the front-line trenches of the 130th Regiment. And on the following day he told me that some French soldiers who had climbed up their parapet had continued to applaud, until at last he gave them an encore. Thus, amid the bitter realities of trench warfare, with all its squalor, a Christmas song had worked a miracle and thrown a bridge from man to man.

But here and there the prevailing temper was distinctly violent, with minimal concession to the season of goodwill. A twenty-one-year-old student-soldier, Ludwig Finke, was in the German trenches to the west of Roulers in Belgium, where his

unit was pinned down by intensive artillery fire. He described
the experience in a letter written on 26 December:

> Two awful days came to an end on Christmas Eve. We had
> forty-eight hours of horror behind us. Many a time, with my
> hands folded round my rifle, I sent a prayer up to the starry
> sky. Nobody believed that we should ever get home again . . .
>
> I was sent off on the 23rd to fetch rations. When I got
> back I found that a direct hit had struck my dugout. Henn,
> the man with whom I shared it, was dead, lying up to the
> waist in rainwater, his skull smashed, and a splinter in his
> back. He was sitting just as he was when I left him a quarter
> of an hour before, his rifle on his arm . . . Altogether we lost
> eight killed and 37 wounded out of 85! . . .
>
> The whole of the 24th we lay in the dugout, the Sergeant
> Platoon Commander next to me. We smoked unceasingly and
> counted the shots . . .
>
> Then came the star-lit 'Holy Night', and our Christmas
> music was a horrible blending of the screams of the wounded,
> the whistling of rifle bullets and the bursting of shells. At
> last, at 2 o'clock, we were relieved. The new lot had not been
> up before and were upset by the awful rifle fire, so that every-
> thing got in a muddle. Thank God the scoundrels over there
> did not attack.

Nearby, just to the north of Ypres at Bixschoote, the German
205th Reserve Infantry Regiment went up to the front on
Christmas Eve after a somewhat basic Christmas service and a
handing out of Iron Crosses. At a rest point *en route* hundreds
of troops spontaneously broke into the singing of '*Stille Nacht*'.
Then there was a gruff 'to your rifles' and they marched off to
the trenches. Their Christmas 'present' was to be 'a continuous
hail of French grenades'. Their Regimental History commented:

'On both days of the Christmas festival the bloody game continued.'

Gotthold von Rohden, another student-soldier, aged nineteen, was out in No Man's Land on the night of Christmas Eve, in charge of a patrol, at Beaurains on the outskirts of Arras. The French were four hundred yards off and the Germans were more than usually wary, as there had been hints of a possible enemy attack. Taking advantage of a favourable fold of the ground, von Rohden and his six volunteer comrades succeeded in getting quite close to the French front line. In a letter home two days later recounting the event he reminded his family that

> while you were all sitting happily around the glittering Christmas tree and the children were excitedly awaiting the removal of the snow-white sheets from the tables stacked with presents . . . and while you later spent the evening in harmony side by side, just enjoying being together, I was busy crawling step by step, all senses alert, listening for the slightest sound, looking out for suspicious shadows, towards the enemy's trench.
>
> I was just thinking of making another move forward, when the French finally discovered us. The first sharp shots rang out in the 'Silent Night'.

The Germans decided to withdraw but they were pursued by a spate of French bullets. One of their number was shot in the thigh and incapacitated. As the others made their escape von Rohden stayed with him, 'cradling his head, trying to give him comfort and courage', and the two men lay crouched in No Man's Land as a French patrol came out to search for them. They felt discovery was certain, but, as von Rohden put it, 'God had other things in mind for us'. A sudden eruption of unlikely sound from the French trenches transformed the situation:

I think it was because of this night that we were saved, for the French had obviously attempted to celebrate the occasion with alcohol and now sang out loud into the night. They sang '*Marseillaise*', 'God Save the King', a Christmas hymn, soldier-songs. One of them shouted across: 'You wanted to get to Paris, you will not get to Paris.'

From the German line came the predictable reply. Huddled in No Man's Land, the two Germans listened to the impromptu singing-match:

On our side they sang Christmas songs in full harmony, then afterwards some national songs. If someone offered a solo, the other side applauded. The French kept as quiet as mice as they listened to the Christmas hymns which no doubt you were singing at home at the same time.

The French patrol lost interest and withdrew. Eventually a stretcher-bearer came out to help the two Germans back to their lines.

☆

As will have been realized, such acts of camaraderie as occurred on the French and Belgian sectors tended to take place at arm's length. Indeed, the French and Belgian troops did not mingle with the Germans on anything like the same scale as the British. The reasons are not hard to find. To allow the emotions associated with one of the two greatest religious festivals of the Christian year to impose their mood on the fighting zone was one thing; for Frenchmen – or Belgians – to walk out into No Man's Land to meet Germans face to face was quite another. A pause to commemorate Christmas was basically an aspect of the 'live and let live' approach to war at which the French in particular were already proving themselves adept over large stretches of the Western Front; to fraternize, to strike up a friendly, even jocular relationship, would be to grant recognition to an enemy who had brutally seized French and Belgian territory and was holding not only land but also people in thrall. Moreover, for the French the wound had not been there just for five months, it had been there for over forty years, since the annexation of Alsace-Lorraine following the Franco-Prussian war of 1870. To have dreamed of reconquest and revenge for so long and then, when the opportunity came, to have lost more territory still, was a particularly bitter blow to a nation which, a mere century or so before, had been the superpower of its time. So there was, on the whole, little temptation to think of the German as 'brother Boche'; by contrast, it was possible for an ardent French soldier to think of himself as, in a very special way, part of the sacred, wounded, embattled soil of his much-loved country. As one French officer expressed it: 'The frontier is myself. My breast is the living boundary of France. If I pull back, it is France into which the enemy will break. With every step I advance I am enlarging *la Patrie*.' For such men to make friends with the Germans would have been an act of ultimate betrayal.

Yet there were to be a number of acts of fraternization on Christmas Day, and some meetings between trenches did occur on Christmas Eve. A correspondent of the *Daily Telegraph* reported one such episode following a conversation with a wounded French soldier whom he met some days after Christmas in a Paris hospital:

> He said that on the night of December 24 the French and Germans came out of their respective trenches and met halfway between them. They not only talked, exchanged cigarettes &c, but also danced together in rings.

The wounded Frenchman also stated that the soldiers who had fraternized subsequently refused to fire on each other, and had to be removed from the trenches and replaced by other men.

For the British and the Germans, the special sanction imposed by the fact of *le pays envahi* – the homeland invaded – did not apply. Their sanctions were military and patriotic and, under the powerful impact of Christmas, to a substantial extent they had been temporarily withdrawn. Many men went to sleep on the cold, moonlit night of 24/25 December 1914 curious and excited as to what might happen on the morrow.

Chapter Six

Christmas Day

After the carol concerts, the cheers, applause and revelry of the previous night, Christmas Day dawned unnaturally quiet and still. An early morning fog hid the opposing trenches in some areas of the British sector, and everywhere a layer of white hoar frost etched the landscape while, as on Christmas Eve, hard ground gave temporary relief from the squelching mud.

Christmas Day hymns were sung in muted voices – unlike those of the night before. 'We started with a service at 8 a.m. in the barn,' wrote an officer in the Queen's Westminster Rifles, '3ft of straw underneath, half the roof off, and a great many holes in the walls from shells. Had to sing the hymn softly as, though the truce of the previous night was continued all day, we did not want the Deutschers to spot our headquarters.'

Rifleman Bernard Brookes of the same battalion had permission to go to 9 a.m. mass at a nearby church. It was very badly shelled and within range of enemy fire. No effort had been made to clear the wreckage, as this would have been fraught with danger. But a priest had come from Armentières to minister to the few people who were still living in the district. 'In this Church which would hold about three hundred', wrote Brookes, 'there were some thirty people, and I was the only soldier. It was indeed a unique service, and during a short address which the Priest gave I was about the only one who was not crying, and that because I did not understand much of what was being said.'

At a billet village at the northern end of the British sector, a service planned to be held in the school had to take place in the open air because of the unexpectedly large congregation. The Chaplain who was due to take it was late as the roads were 'like glass' and he had great difficulty in keeping his horse on its feet, so that the journey took twice as long as he had anticipated. As he approached the village he could hear 'a noise like thunder' as the waiting men stamped their boots on the stones of the schoolyard trying to keep warm:

> On my arrival the stamping ceased and we at once began the service – Scottish Borderers and Yorkshire Light Infantry, most of them were – and, in spite of the cold, both officers and men joined in the singing with a zest and heartiness which was most inspiring. My address was of necessity brief, but throughout the whole service there was that influence which it is the preacher's joy to feel.

At the front Second Lieutenant Bairnsfather awoke in a particularly thoughtful mood, much affected by the events of the night before. Hate, war and discomfort seemed entirely alien on this Christmas morning, and the spirit of Christmas seemed to be especially potent. For a moment he indulged in a typical soldier's fantasy:

> It was just the sort of day for peace to be declared. It would have made such a good finale. I should have liked to have suddenly heard an immense siren blowing. Everybody to stop and say 'What was that?' Siren blowing again: appearance of a small figure running across the frozen mud and waving something. He gets closer – a telegraph boy with a wire! He

hands it to me. With trembling fingers I open it: 'War off, return home – George, R. I.' Cheers! But no, it was a nice, fine day, that was all.

In fact it was more than that as he soon realized, for as he was walking through the trenches a little later he suddenly became aware of German heads showing over their parapet in a most reckless way and that some of his own Tommies were following suit:

> In less time than it takes to tell, half a dozen or so of each of the belligerents were outside their trenches and were advancing towards each other in No Man's Land.

Bairnsfather later congratulated himself on having been present at the point of the line where Christmas Day fraternization took place, evidently not realizing how widespread it was nor in how many other areas similar scenes were being enacted. Indeed, it was possible for a battalion to be completely unaware as to whether its near-neighbours were or were not taking part in a truce, so that what happened on Christmas Day was not, so to speak, a contagion of goodwill spreading along the line, but a series of individual initiatives at a very considerable number of places and times. That this is so is underlined by the great variety of ways in which friendly relations with the Germans were established – or re-established – on Christmas morning. Here a board would appear with 'Merry Christmas' written on it; elsewhere the message might be a more specific bid for a cease-fire, as in the case of the 2/Devons, who saw a board hoisted up with the words 'You no fight, we no fight'. Christmas greetings were shouted across in many areas, followed by offers of a cease-fire or invitations to come out or come over. Saxons hoping for a truce sometimes played on their presumed kinship with their British enemy: a 1/Leicester Tommy remembers a voice saying in clear English, 'Hello there, hello there, we are Saxons, you are Anglo-Saxons. If you don't fire, we won't fire.' Opposite the 2/Border Regiment the process started with a German officer emerging with a white flag. At other points friendly waves as the early fog lifted provided the first move. Some Queen's Westminsters, for example, tried the experiment of climbing out of the trench, waving, then jumping back in again; when no shots were fired they grew bolder and began to edge forward beyond their barbed wire. On the front held by the 2/Wiltshires, the fog cleared abruptly to reveal men on both sides running or walking in open ground trying to exercise or keep warm. 'They waved', wrote a junior officer who witnessed the scene, 'and our men waved back; after all it was Christmas Day . . . Soon the Germans opposite to us and our men were meeting in No Man's Land.' Another subaltern stated in his account that having received orders on Christmas morning not to shoot unless it was absolutely necessary, 'this injunction seemed to "wireless" itself to the Germans, for they stopped sniping altogether, and an unearthly stillness reigned over the scene'; in a short time the entire personnel of the rival trenches were standing on their respective parapets waving and shouting to each other. 'I need hardly tell you', the subaltern added, 'what a relief it was to everyone; it was not war, but it was certainly magnificent.' In the words of an Old Contemptible: 'It became evident that both sides had inexplicably decided to honour the Season of Goodwill.'

Most British accounts suggest that it was the Germans who made the first overtures on Christmas morning, just as the previous night they had led the way with the Christmas trees and carol-singing. On the other hand, some German reports give the honour to the British. One German soldier wrote in a contemporary letter:

> Suddenly from the enemy hurrahing was heard and, surprised, we came from our mouse-holes and saw the English advancing towards us . . . They had no rifles with them, and therefore we knew it could only be a greeting and that it was all right. We advanced towards them about halfway.

Another soldier's letter states quite unequivocally:

> At about 9 a.m. on Christmas day an English officer, accompanied by two of his men, came across and asked for a cease-fire until midnight to bury the dead. This was willingly granted.

In the case of the 133rd Saxon Regiment, however, according to Hugo Klemm, the initiative was definitely German, the prime mover being an NCO acting on a personal impulse. At dawn the Germans became aware of heads appearing everywhere along the parapets of the British lines, as the Tommies peered warily out into No Man's Land. Someone was needed to break the ice.

> A non-commissioned officer from our own company decided to take a Christmas tree into the area between the trenches. An Englishman came forwards towards him despite the shouts of warning from his friends, which did not prevent him from shaking hands with the enemy. After this had happened and the Englishman had returned safely to his lines, his comrades applauded the magnanimity of the Germans.

In this as in many instances, the first task following the establishing of friendly relations was to dispose of the decaying bodies of the dead, some of which were victims of the recent fighting while others had lain out in No Man's Land for weeks. Klemm's account continues:

It was then possible to take note of many fallen comrades, both German and English, who had lain between the two lines under a blanket of snow, the result of a battle of the previous November between Jäger from our Corps and the English. So in the grey light of dawn our platoon commander Lieutenant Grosse met an English officer and agreed to bury the dead behind the two lines if the higher authorities gave their assent.

The officer of the Rifle Brigade who had ordered the shooting down of Christmas trees the previous night and had thoroughly disapproved of his fellow officers going out to meet the enemy, now found himself not only conversing with the Germans but collaborating with them in the burial of the dead, though his suspicions were mainly allayed by his discovery that his opponents were not Prussians, for whom the British reserved their greatest animosity, but the more genial Saxons:

The Germans came out, and as soon as we saw they were Saxons I knew it was all right, because they're good fellows on the whole and play the game as far as they know it. The officer came out; we gravely saluted each other, and I then pointed to nine dead Germans lying in midfield and suggested burying them, which both sides proceeded to do. We gave them some wooden crosses for them, which completely won them over, and soon the men were on the best of terms and laughing.

It was a curious situation – enemies working together to sort out and bury the men they had jointly killed, men with whom they had marched side by side to war just a few weeks before. It was a grim business, too, as the freedom of No Man's Land revealed sights which had not been visible from the limited vision of the trenches. In front of the Queen's Westminster Rifles was a ploughed field, down the centre of which ran a large ditch, about four feet wide and four feet deep. When Rifleman P. H. Jones, going out to fraternize with the enemy, reached the ditch, he realized that it was 'simply packed with dead Germans. Their faces, brown and leather-like, with deep sunken cheeks, and eyebrows frozen stiff, stared up horribly through the clear water.' 'It was a ghastly sight,' wrote a subaltern, after scanning the 'dreadful ranks' of a group of dead Tommies laid out for burial, and fearing at every step to recognize someone he knew. 'They lay stiffly in contorted attitudes, dirty with frozen mud and powdered with rime.'

Up and down the lines the burials were carried out. As agreed with Captain Armes of the 1/North Staffs, the Germans opposite despatched a burial party from their trenches after reveille and some of the British went out to help. Opposite the 2/Bedfordshires, a German officer and two men, unarmed, emerged at 10 a.m. with a white flag to ask permission to bury their dead. This was agreed; and the Bedfordshires, who at this time were confined to their trenches, noted that many Germans sat on their parapets watching as the work went on. At Ploegsteert officers of the 1/Somerset Light Infantry met some German officers halfway between the trenches and it was arranged that the Somersets would bring in their dead for burial in their own battalion cemetery. The Somersets' War Diary noted: 'The bodies of Capt. Maud, Capt. Orr and 2/Lt Henson were brought in, also those of 18 NCOs and men. They were buried the same day.' The cemetery was a peaceful enclave some way back from the line in Ploegsteert Wood.

The 2/Wiltshires, at La Boutillerie, were another battalion which made arrangements with the Germans opposite for the burial of the dead. They had been joined shortly before Christmas by a newly commissioned subaltern, Wilbert Spencer, the young man of Anglo-German parentage who had won plaudits for his

linguistic skills from the German internees and prisoners of war
whom he had met at Camberley while he was undergoing officer
training at Sandhurst. He was now to find a more sombre use
for his talents, as is clear from the account of Christmas Day
he sent to his family on 28 December:

> There was no firing, so by degrees each side began gradually
> showing more of themselves, and then two of their men came
> halfway and called for an officer. I went out and found that
> they were willing to have an armistice for 4 hours, and to
> carry our dead men back halfway for us to bury. This I arranged
> and then – can you imagine it? – both sides came out, met
> in the middle, shook hands, wished each other compliments
> of the season, and had a chat. A strange sight between two
> hostile lines. Then they carried over the dead.

The grim procedures which followed seem to have seriously
eroded the friendly attitude which had come so easily to Spencer
in England. Indeed, whereas many found a sudden affection for
the enemy at Christmas 1914, for him the process worked the
other way. He was much changed from the enthusiastic young
cadet of three months earlier, eager to meet his opponents for
a postwar drink in Berlin:

> I won't describe the sights I saw, and which I shall never forget.
> We buried the dead as they were. Then back to the trenches
> with the feeling of hatred growing stronger after what we had
> just seen.

But the most memorable burials that day were those in
which men of both sides took part and men of both nations
were interred.

One joint burial service which made a lasting impression on
the participants took place to the south-west of Fleurbaix, in a

waterlogged cabbage patch near the Sailly–Fromelles road – at the scene of the attack by the 2/Scots Guards and 2/Border of 20th Brigade on the night of 18/19 December.

Early on Christmas Day, Revd J. Esslemont Adams, Chaplain of the Gordon Highlanders in the same Brigade and Minister of the West United Free Church, Aberdeen, carried out a burial service behind the lines for one of the 6/Gordons who had been killed by sniper fire the previous day. Subsequently, he accompanied the commanding officer, Lieutenant-Colonel McLean, on his daily tour of inspection. As they made their way through the trenches, they saw some of their men clambering out and talking with the enemy. Colonel McLean ran along the front line and ordered the men to come down, but they ignored his instructions, pointing out that others further along were standing on the top and that 'a number of the enemy were out on their side and gazing peacefully across'. Swiftly taking in the situation, Esslemont Adams realized that this was an ideal opportunity to arrange for the burial of the dead who had been lying beyond the wire since the previous week's attack: the Gordons had not been involved but they were now in trenches occupied at that time by the Scots Guards. He told the CO his intention, then climbed on to the fire-step and strode out into No Man's Land. On reaching a small ditch, which ran along the middle of the field between the lines, he held up his hands and called out to a group of Germans, 'I want to speak to your Commanding Officer. Does anyone speak English?' Several German officers were standing together, and one of them said, 'Yes! Come over the ditch.' The Chaplain hurried forward, saluted the senior German present and began to put his proposal to him and his staff.

Almost at the same moment a hare, disturbed by the unaccustomed activity in the field, burst into view and raced along between the lines. Germans and Scots, the latter with kilts flying, gave furious chase and it was finally captured by the Germans.

Adams and the German commander then resumed their 'parley' and the latter agreed to the burial of the dead and that subsequently Adams should conduct a short religious service: the 23rd Psalm would be read and a prayer offered in both English and German.

Throughout the morning the task of collecting the dead went on. The bodies were intermingled and lay dotted over the sixty yards separating the lines. They were carefully sorted out; the British were carried to the British side of the halfway line, the Germans to the German side. Spades were brought and each side set to work to dig the graves.

The Adjutant of the 2/Scots Guards, Captain Giles Loder, had led his battalion's attack on 18 December. On Christmas morning he was in the front-line trenches away to the right, and observed the activity going on opposite the Gordon Highlanders as the bodies were collected and the graves dug. So he climbed over the parapet and walked over the half-mile of open farmland to talk to the Germans and arrange burial for the Scots Guards killed in the same attack. He spoke with 'an extremely pleasant and superior brand of German officer, who arranged to bring all our dead to the halfway line'. There were twenty-nine in all, most of them lying close to the enemy wire. Loder sorted through the bodies, collecting the personal effects, paybooks and identity discs. 'It was heartrending', he wrote later that day in the battalion War Diary, 'to see some of the chaps one knew so well, and who had started out in such good spirits on December 18th, lying there dead, some with horrible wounds due to the explosive action of the high-velocity bullet at short range.' He detailed some men to bring in the rifles of his comrades but the Germans demurred at this; indeed, all rifles lying on their side of the halfway line they kept as spoils of war.

From his conversations with the Germans, he was also able to find out what had happened to his fellow officers who had been found missing after the attack. Very severely wounded, they had been among those seen by Lieutenant Hulse being dragged into the German trenches. One, Lieutenant The Hon. F. Hanbury-Tracy, had died after two days in the local hospital and had been buried in the German cemetery at Fromelles. Another officer whom the Germans had been unable to name had also died and been buried: from his description the Scotsmen were able to identify him as Lieutenant Nugent. Most of this information came from a French-speaking officer, who kept on pointing to the British dead and saying, '*Les Braves, c'est bien dommage.*' Loder gained the impression that they were treating their British prisoners well and had done all they could for the wounded.

Twenty years later to the day an article published in a German magazine under the title 'Christmas Peace 1914 at the Flanders Front' gave the view on these events as seen from the trenches opposite. The author was a Major Thomas, Instructor at the Infantry School, Dresden, and the article was written because Thomas had seen Hulse's account of the truce and had felt moved to reply, claiming he had taken a leading part in the negotiations with the Scots Guards. Presumably he was also the 'extremely pleasant and superior brand of officer' referred to by Loder:

The incident, looked at from the German side, was as follows:
The 2nd Battalion of the Westphalian Infantry Regiment 15, whose Adjutant I was at the time, occupied at Christmas

1914 a position in French Flanders beyond Le Meisnil and
Fromelles, about 10 miles to the West of Lille. On the 18th
December 1914 the British had suffered heavy losses during
an attack made in the evening towards our trenches. Their
dead had to remain unburied before our Front. As regards the
Christmas Armistice mentioned in the letter of the English
Officer (the initiative was not taken by us, but by the Englishman), it was a question of burying the German and English
heroes who were lying between the trenches on each side. On
Christmas Day, at about 11 o'clock, there was a continuous
waving of a white flag from the English trench which was
about 150 yards from our trench. Soon afterwards a number
of Englishmen climbed out of the trench and came towards
our front, making signs all the time. My Commander, Baron
von Blomberg (a cousin of the Reich Defence Minister), to
whom this had been reported, ordered me to find out what
the Englishman wanted. Accompanied by an English-speaking
war volunteer, I also went out of the trench to meet the
Englishman. The preliminary greetings exchanged under the
gaze of surprise of the men in the trenches on both sides were
of a rather embarrassing nature. We heard that it was the wish
of the Englishman to bury on the occasion of the Christmas
holiday their dead who were lying before the Front, and they
asked us to cease enemy action for an adequate period.

What were we to do? Time was short. We could not very
well conclude peace there, and there was no time for making
enquiries of the superior department, seeing that neither the
regiment nor the general command could assume responsibility
for a local armistice, but would probably have to consult first
the Chief Command. Major von B. therefore decided without
anything further that there should be a local armistice until
1 o'clock in the afternoon, telling the Englishman that their
dead must be buried by that time.

Altogether about a hundred bodies were gathered for burial, and there then took place what must surely have been one of the most moving and memorable services of the war. Nineteen-year-old Second Lieutenant Arthur Pelham-Burn, of the 6/Gordon Highlanders, who intended to train for the Anglican ministry, was among the participants. He described the event in a letter to an old Lancing schoolfriend. Burying the dead was 'awful, too awful to describe so I won't attempt it', but the ceremony that followed was different:

We then had a most wonderful joint burial service. Our Padre . . . arranged the prayers and psalm etc. and an interpreter wrote them out in German. They were read first in English by our Padre and then in German by a boy who was studying for the ministry. It was an extraordinary and most wonderful sight. The Germans formed up on one side, the English on the other, the officers standing in front, every head bared. Yes, I think it was a sight one will never see again.

Standing between the ranks of British and German officers, Chaplain Esslemont Adams spoke the familiar words of the 23rd Psalm, and in the cold, clear air they were echoed by the young Saxon divinity student by his side:

> The Lord is my shepherd: I shall not want.
> He maketh me to lie down in green pastures:
>> He leadeth me beside the still waters.

> Der Herr is mein Hirt: mir wird nichts mangeln.
> Er weidet mich auf einer grünen Aue:
>> und führt mich zum frischen Wasser.

As the service came to an end there was a moment of silence, then the Chaplain stepped forward and saluted the German commander, who shook hands with him and bade him farewell.

'It was an impressive sight,' the Regimental History of the 6/Gordons recorded, 'officers and men, bitter enemies as they were, uncovered, reverent, and for the moment united in offering for their dead the last offices of homage and honour.'

Reporting all this in his letter to his mother, Hulse commented:

> This episode was the sadder side of Xmas Day, but it was a great thing being able to collect [the dead], as their relations, to whom of course they had been reported missing, will be put out of suspense and hoping they are prisoners.

Hulse also remarked that the Germans they had been dealing with were mostly 158th Regiment and Jägers: 'the men we had attacked on the night of the 18th. Hence the feeling of temporary friendship, I suppose.' Summing up the episode in the battalion War Diary, Captain Loder wrote:

> Both sides have played the game and I know this Regiment anyhow has learnt to trust an Englishman's word.

But not all the participants took Loder's charitable view. Private Alexander Runcie of the 6/Gordon Highlanders, who had witnessed the joint burial and subsequently exchanged souvenirs with the Germans, recalled that

> one of our men on the way back from fraternizing showed me a dagger he had hidden and added 'I don't trust these bastards'.

☆

The joint burial service at Fleurbaix was the greatest occasion of its kind on Christmas Day; but at the other end of the scale there were some burial ceremonies no less moving because they concerned only one or two men. Captain Josef Sewald of the

17th Bavarian Regiment recalled being approached by a British officer with a special request:

> An English lieutenant said there was a comrade who had been killed the previous afternoon, and they wished to bury this man. I said 'Why not? – of course you can do it', and so they brought the dead man, laid him on the ground, and we all laid a handful of earth upon him and together prayed the Lord's Prayer: '*Vater unser, der du bist im Himmel, Geheiligt werde dein Name*'.

As at Fleurbaix German and British voices echoed each other, each man present speaking the familiar words of the 'Our Father' in his own language.

North of Ploegsteert Wood 'there were two dead Frenchmen between our lines,' wrote Corporal Robert Renton of the Seaforth Highlanders, 'and the Germans helped us to dig the grave. One of the officers held a service over one of the graves. It was a sight worth seeing, and one not easily forgotten, both Germans and British paying respects to the French dead.'

At Bois Grenier seven stretcher-bearers, all wearing Red Cross armlets, were allowed by the Germans to come out and bury some dead of the 2/West Yorks who had been lying behind the German lines. Taking advantage of the cease-fire, Sergeant Self of the same battalion, working entirely on his own, buried a comrade of his in a grave some four yards behind the front line:

> This in full view of the German front line – no mourners – no chaplain – just myself, a shallow grave, and a small wooden cross. The task finished I jumped down into our trench thankful that Fritz had kept faith to the truce.

Sergeant Self's particular memory of Christmas Day was of the unaccustomed silence – 'it was so quiet, it was uncanny'.

For once, natural sounds, normally drowned in the crackle and boom of guns, could be clearly heard:

> There were no planes overhead, no observation balloons, no bombs, no rifle fire, therefore no snipers, just an occasional lark overhead.

Lieutenant Hulse remarked on the same phenomenon:

> The silence seemed extraordinary after the usual din. From all sides birds seemed to arrive, and we hardly ever see a bird generally. Later in the day I fed about fifty sparrows outside my dugout, which shows how complete the silence and quiet was.

Private Tapp too was struck by the sudden absence of the cacophony of war:

> I miss the sounds of the shots flying over, it is like a clock which has stopped ticking.

But there were other sounds instead, and unfamiliar sights that were totally incompatible with the normal world of the trenches as, in the words of one participant, 'soldiers of both sides met in that strip of God-forsaken earth called No Man's Land, talking, gesticulating, and shaking hands'. For if, as Hulse put it, there was 'a sadder side' to Christmas Day in the burial of the dead, there was also its opposite, as men trained and committed to unremitting war met together in friendship and good humour to celebrate Christmas in their own highly individual fashion.

There is no doubt that many men who took part realized that they were doing something quite unusual and that they were sharing in an experience which they would only be able to describe in superlative terms. It was, wrote Sergeant A. Lovell of 3/Rifle Brigade, 'the most wonderful day on record'. 'On Christmas Day', wrote Corporal T. B. Watson of the Royal Scots Territorials, 'the greatest thing took place here.' 'The most extraordinary celebration of [Christmas] any of us will ever experience,' wrote a subaltern quoted in the *Daily Telegraph*. 'I had one of the greatest experiences of my life on Christmas Day,' Private C. Hunter of the 2/Monmouthshires told his parents. 'The funniest and most amusing Christmas I have ever spent,' was how it seemed to Rifleman Griffiths of the Queen's Westminster Rifles, and he added that it 'would have made a good chapter in Dickens's *Christmas Carol*'. Writing on Christmas Day itself, Second Lieutenant Dougan Chater of the 2/Gordon Highlanders told his mother: 'I think I have seen one of the most extraordinary sights that anyone has ever seen.' A German expressed his reaction with similar amazement: 'The way we spent Christmas in the trenches sounds almost like a fairy tale.'

Men were frequently struck by the sheer incongruity of what they were doing. 'Just you think', wrote Oswald Tilley of the London Rifle Brigade to his father and mother, 'that while you were eating your turkey etc., I was out talking and shaking hands with the very men I had been trying to kill a few hours before!! It was astounding!' 'You will hardly credit this, but it is the truth,' wrote Private Calder of the 6/Gordons. 'Fancy shooting at [the Germans] and going over to wish them a merry Christmas! I don't think it has happened in the world's history before. You would have thought that peace had been declared.' 'The whole thing is extraordinary,' wrote Captain Armes of the 1/North Staffs, as he continued the letter he had begun the previous night, 'the men were all so natural and friendly.' In his letter Oswald Tilley wrote: 'This experience has been the most practical demonstration I have seen of "Peace on earth and goodwill towards men".' A German soldier wrote: 'It was a

Christmas celebration in keeping with the command "Peace on earth" and a memory which will stay with us always.'

Indeed, the animosities which propagandists and politicians had sought to instil in their soldiers seem to have suddenly faded away – if only for the time being. 'We tried to explain', wrote Leslie Walkinton, 'that we bore no malice.' Bernard Brookes reported that 'the Germans have no bitter feelings towards us'. Bruce Bairnsfather stated that 'there was not an atom of hate on either side that day'. Dougan Chater, well aware of the context of international mistrust in which the truce was taking place, commented: 'It is really very extraordinary that this sort of thing should happen in a war in which there is so much bitterness and ill-feeling.' Describing the event many years afterwards, the German Josef Sewald recalled: 'There was laughter and joy as if there had never been any hostility between these thousands of young men.'

It would be wrong to imply that the crimes of which the German armies stood accused were entirely forgotten, but the blame was usually fixed elsewhere; in particular the Saxons were assumed to have had no hand in excesses blamed either on the Prussian soldiery or on the German leadership.

Indeed, predictably, propaganda had far outstripped reality and when enemies met face to face they found that they were not only human but also, on the whole, likeable. Lieutenant Hulse was scathing about some of the Germans whom he met – 'podgy fat bourgeois', was his description of two officers with whom he attempted to converse, 'looking very red and full of sausage and beer and wine, and . . . not very friendly', while Bairnsfather, perhaps with more wit than actual malice, referred to the Germans whom he encountered as 'sausage-eating wretches' and as 'faded, unimaginative products of perverse *kultur*'. But many other British soldiers found the Germans much more amiable than they would ever have imagined. 'They seem quite friendly and genuine,' was the opinion of Captain E. R. P. Berryman of the Royal Garhwal Rifles. 'I must say some of them are very nice fellows,' commented a piper of the Scots Guards, 'and did not show any hatred, which makes me think they are forced to fight.' 'We found them to be quite a gentlemanly lot of chaps,' wrote a soldier of the Rifle Brigade. 'They seem decent fellows,' wrote Private Tapp, but he later added: 'I cannot bring myself to shake hands with them, as I know I shouldn't if they were in our country, I have not forgotten Belgium and I never did like the word German.'

Yet whatever doubts and disclaimers there might have been, there was, in general, an amazing spirit of goodwill among the crowds of men swarming out from the trenches to fraternize. Barely ten minutes after the first approach from the German side, according to Dougan Chater, 'the ground between the two lines of trenches was swarming with men and officers of both sides, shaking hands and wishing each other a happy Christmas'. 'No Man's Land', wrote Graham Williams of the London Rifle Brigade, 'was full of parties of British and Germans laughing and talking together.' 'By breakfast time', wrote a junior officer of the 6/Cheshires, 'nearly all our men were on the ground between the trenches, and were the greatest pals.' A German soldier perhaps put it most pointedly of all: 'We achieved what the Pope himself could not do and in the middle of the war we had a merry Christmas.'

And all this was happening in the same seasonal weather as that of Christmas Eve. In most – though not all – areas the early morning fog dispersed quite quickly to reveal a cloudless blue sky. The ground was still hard and white. 'It was a perfect day,' wrote Bruce Bairnsfather. 'It was such a day as is invariably depicted by artists on Christmas cards – the ideal Christmas Day of fiction.'

☆

> When morning came everyone climbed out of their trenches. Both sides shook hands with each other, briefly made peace and exchanged gifts. We were given corned beef, tea and cigarettes, etc, which the English had a-plenty. They for their part were mad about our cigars.

So wrote the German soldier who described his Christmas in the trenches as seeming like a fairy tale. Up and down No Man's Land men were bearing gifts to the enemy, with bully beef, Maconochie's stew, Tickler's jams, cake, biscuits, chocolate, tea, cigarettes, rum and Christmas puddings offered by the British, and cigars, sweets, nuts, chocolates, sausages, sauerkraut, coffee, cognac, schnapps and even wine offered by the Germans. Not all the British recipients were as convinced as the German soldier quoted above of the excellence of German tobacco products: Lieutenant Hulse's encounter with two 'fat, bourgeois officers' was not improved by his being given what he described as 'a very nasty cigar'. Others, however, were more favourably impressed, while, according to Lieutenant Charles Brewer, the fact that every German whom he and his fellow Bedfordshires met seemed to be in possession of a well-filled cigar case produced a reaction of amazed respect among some of his men. 'Blimey,' exclaimed one of the Bedfordshire sergeants, 'it's a millionaires' battalion!'

The Bedfordshires, in fact, had no need to feel overawed: cigars featured prominently among the 'love-gifts' sent to the German front and the Kaiser himself had given a present of cigars to every German soldier.

There was much cheerful banter as all this went on, the proceedings being frequently assisted by the fact that not a few Germans spoke English. Hulse recorded an amusing moment:

> One of our fellows offered a German a cigarette: the German said, 'Virginian?' Our fellow said, 'Aye, straight-cut': the German said, 'No thanks, I only smoke Turkish'!. . . It gave us all a good laugh.

Many soldiers returned to their trenches later that day with their uniforms depleted of buttons, badges and other accoutrements. Indeed, according to Graham Williams of the London Rifle Brigade, this was an ideal opportunity to dispense with certain black metal shoulder-titles to which he and his friends had always taken great exception. For one thing they were very uncomfortable to wear when carrying the rifle on the shoulder; for another they bore the legend '5th City of London' (the battalion's wartime description) as opposed to the letters 'LRB' of which these young Territorials were so proud:

> I thought it would be a good idea to get rid of these things, so I swapped them for a very nice German leather equipment belt with brass buttons and the words *'Gott mit uns'* on it, and I used that all through the rest of the war to keep up my trousers.

Williams's account adds the amusing detail that the words *'Gott mit uns'* ('God with us') was taken by some Tommies as confirmation that the Germans really were 'Huns', as maintained by the popular press.

To the north of Ploegsteert Wood Private Tapp was also out giving and obtaining souvenirs: he did well, getting two buttons and a cap-badge in return for one button given away. Lieutenant

Bairnsfather, strolling the same piece of No Man's Land as Tapp, struck a more equal bargain.

> I spotted a German officer, some sort of lieutenant I should think and, being a bit of a collector, I intimated to him that I had taken a fancy to some of his buttons.
>
> We both then said things to each other which neither understood, and agreed to do a swap. I brought out my wire-clippers and, with a few deft snips, removed a couple of his buttons and put them in my pocket. I then gave him two of mine in exchange.

Some battalions forbade such lax treatment of regimental property. The Kensingtons, who had failed to respond to the German overtures the previous night, were now out in force in No Man's Land (though there had been a certain hesitation on the part of their officers until they saw the Royal Irish Rifles to their right greeting the enemy 'in the friendliest possible manner'). However, they were ordered 'to preserve the identity of the regiment by giving away no badges or buttons'. This somewhat restricted their capacity to barter, though in the end they managed to acquire some German insignia as well as a few odd bottles of schnapps.

One of the most prized souvenirs was the German spiked helmet, the *pickelhaube*. This had been much worn in the early part of the war but a recent order had substituted the much less picturesque pork-pie hat as the standard headgear of the German army. Among others an LRB man, bartering bully beef and 'Tickler's plum-and-apple so-called jam', managed to acquire one of these, though before it became officially his possession it was temporarily returned by special request to its former owner.

> The helmet achieved fame as on the following day a voice called out 'want to speak to officer' and being met in No Man's

Land continued, 'Yesterday I gave my hat for the Bullybif. I have grand inspection tomorrow. You lend me and I bring it back after.' The loan was made and the pact kept, sealed with some extra bully!

The Germans had their eyes on certain British items too. 'They greatly admired our equipment,' wrote Sergeant-Major Naden of the 6/Cheshires, 'and especially wanted us to give them our jack-knives.' Other souvenirs were of a sadder nature. 'An English soldier', wrote Hugo Klemm, 'gave me a cap badge belonging to a dead friend.'

☆

Some attempted 'parleys' were inevitably inhibited by the difficulties of language, but there were many English-speaking Germans on hand only too happy to engage in friendly conversation with their British opponents. Rifleman Graham Williams was one of the relatively few German speakers on the British side; he was inevitably in great demand and was deep in conversation with some Germans when he was suddenly accosted in the most English of accents:

As I was talking, a chap came up to me, and he actually greeted me with the words 'Watcha cock, how's London?' I said, 'Good Lord, you speak like a Londoner'; and he said, 'Well, I am a Londoner!' I said, 'Well, what on earth are you doing in the German army?' and he said, 'Well, I'm a German, I'm a German Londoner', and apparently he had been born in Germany, but had gone to England almost immediately afterwards with his parents, who had a small business in the East End of London somewhere, and he'd been brought up in England and gone to school in England. As by German law he was still a German national – he'd never been naturalized – he had been called up to go to Germany to do his national service: they did three years at that time. And afterwards he had come back to London, joined his parents and got a job as a porter at Victoria Station. He told me all this. He spoke absolute Cockney! It was most extraordinary . . .

In similar style Tommies at various places conversed with a waiter from the Ritz, a waiter from the Hotel Cecil, a waiter from De Keyser's Royal Hotel, Blackfriars, a former head waiter of the Trocadero, a hairdresser from the Strand and a chef from Birmingham who had left his wife and five children behind when he was recalled to the colours. Sergeant Philpotts of the 1/Royal Warwicks, who met the chef, added the following postscript to his account:

> . . . One day after hostilities had restarted a voice came from the German line, 'Are you the Warwicks? Any Brumagem lads there? I have a wife and five kids in Brumagem.' Our company wag who in civil life was a policeman called back 'Yes, mate, and if you don't get your head down there will be a widow and five orphans in Brumagem.'

A soldier from the same battalion found himself toasting a particularly demonstrative and friendly German:

> I had a drink of rum off one of the Saxons and then I drank his health. He nearly shook my hand off. He had worked in Birkenhead before the war.

For many men the shaking of an enemy hand was the most striking memory of the day.

Other Germans joined in the general talk not because they could offer any command of the language but because they wished to display their British connections. Private Field of the Buffs found himself approached by:

one small, grubby, and ill-shaven German, who had a few words of English. I asked him if he had ever been to England and he said 'no, but I am clerk; I business with England'. 'What is your business?' I asked, and I shrieked with joy as he gravely said 'exporters of mouth organs'.

The tone of conversation was usually peaceable and friendly, though sometimes there was a hint that one side or the other was using the occasion to squeeze a certain amount of military advantage. A British subaltern wrote:

> It was most amusing to observe the bland innocence with which they put questions, a truthful answer to which might have had unexpected consequences in the future. One charming lieutenant of artillery was most anxious to know just where my dugout, 'The Cormorants', was situated. No doubt he wanted to shoot his card, tied to a 'Whistling Willie'. I waved my hand airily over the next company's line, giving him the choice of various mangel-heaps in the rear. They spoke of a bottle of champagne. We raised our wistful eyes in hopeless longing. They expressed astonishment, and said how pleased they would have been, had they only known, to have sent to Lille for some. 'A charming town, Lille. Do you know it?' 'Not yet,' we assured them. Their laughter was quite frank that time.

Pleasantries suggesting that the other side was on the run usually found a good-humoured response. An officer of the Queen's Westminster Rifles told his family:

> One German NCO I spoke to said he went to America two months every year on business, and learnt his English there. He was to have been married on the 12th of last October to a lady in Chicago. I told him we would have them well licked by Easter, and he could get married then. He laughed.

Many men made a point of keeping away from serious arguments about the conduct or outcome of the war. 'Of course we didn't talk about who was going to win,' wrote Rifleman Leslie Walkinton, 'or anything touchy like that.' By contrast, Lieutenant Hulse found himself in a relatively animated exchange early on Christmas Day when he set off into No Man's Land to head off a group of four Germans who were advancing somewhat too purposefully towards the Scots Guards' lines. To begin with the conversation was amiable enough. The Germans explained that they had only come out 'to wish us a happy Christmas' and that they 'trusted us implicitly to keep the truce'. Their spokesman added that he came from Suffolk where he had left a girlfriend and a 3½ hp motorbike.

> He told me that he could not get a letter to the girl, and wanted to send one through me. I made him write out a postcard in front of me, in English, and I sent it off that night. I told him that she probably would not be a bit keen to see him again.

They then entered on a wide-ranging discussion, in the course of which they agreed that neither side should or did use the hated dum-dum bullet (see page 296), but they began to disagree markedly when they turned to the subject of the press:

> They howled with laughter at a D[*aily*] T[*elegraph*] of the 10th which they had seen the day before, and told me that we are being absolutely misguided by our papers, that France is *done*, Russia has received a series of very big blows, and will climb down shortly, and that the only thing which is keeping the war going at all is England! They firmly believe all this, I am sure. They think that our press is to blame in working up feeling against them by publishing false 'atrocity reports'. I told them of various sweet little cases which I have seen for

myself, and they told me of English prisoners whom they have
seen with soft-nosed bullets, and lead bullets with notches cut
in the nose; we had a heated, and at the same time, good-
natured argument, and ended by hinting to each other that
the other was lying!

'Newspapers' was the only answer another British officer
could give in reply to disapproval of the treatment of German
prisoners in concentration camps, which was voiced by one
extremely clean and smart *unteroffizier*. 'Another little fellow, a
private, who had let his beard grow and seemed on familiar
terms with all the higher NCOs, joined in, and said, "Yes, the
papers had been responsible for the whole war!"'

The most extraordinary 'news' was learnt by some astounded
Tommies. The 107th Saxons told the Queen's Westminster Rifles
'they were just outside Paris, having been brought up to the line
in closed railway carriages. They also believed that the Germans
were occupying London.' One of them told Leslie Walkinton that
they had seized Buckingham Palace, while some soldiers of 2/
Border were approached by a group of equally confident Germans:

> The first thing they asked us was when are you going to give
> in you are beat. So we asked them who had told them all this
> and they pointed to a paper they had in there [*sic*] hand. And
> they told me point blank that they had troop reviewing in Hyde
> Park and also troops in Calais. Well, me and my chum could
> not help laughing at them. And they looked at us and could
> not make it out. So I said to them, well, I must admit that you
> have got troops in London, but they are Prisoners of War. They
> would not take that, so my chum gave them the *News of the
> World*, and they thanked us and gave us a segar [*sic*] to smoke.

'London has been bombed by our Zepps,' a German told
A. W. Peel, of 1/Norfolk Regiment. 'I said don't talk rot – I've

got a paper only a few days old and that don't say anything about Zepps being over London. He said well you believe your paper and I'll believe mine.'

However, confidence in the accuracy of the official war news, already shaky among front-line soldiers, was all but destroyed for at least one rifleman of the Queen's Westminsters:

> After our talk I really think a lot of our newspaper reports must be horribly exaggerated. Of course these men were Saxons not Prussians.

There were Germans too who felt they had not been told the truth. In a letter to his parents Lance-Corporal Stephen Coy of the 6/Gordon Highlanders wrote:

> The Germans are 'fed up' with the war, and will not fire unless the British soldiers do. They admit they have been bluffed by the Kaiser, and say they were told the Germans had captured 160 guns from the Russians, but knew now that it was all lies. One fellow, who was a teacher in England, when asked what he thought of the war, said – 'The war is finished here. We don't want to shoot.'

Private C. Hunter of 2/Monmouthshires talked with a similarly disaffected German – 'a Nice chap who could speak English', with whom he conversed for two hours:

> He told me he wished it was all over, as he had had enough of it. He was a medical student who had been in England for two years and in France, and was coming to England last August only for the war. He asked me what we were at war for, and I told him he had better ask 'Willum'. He told me he had as many friends in England and France as he had in Germany and asked why should he be fighting his friends and his friends be fighting him. He would much rather be having a game of

football than this. He was only 20 years of age, but there were a lot of old men with them, and they were asking him so many questions to ask me. The first man I came to was an old man, and when we shook hands I thought he was not going to let my hand go. The tears came rolling down his cheeks, and I felt so sorry for him as he was so old, and wanted to go home.

Disillusioned soldiers on the British side were gratified to find German attitudes that coincided with their own. Second Lieutenant F. H. Black of 1/Royal Warwicks wrote in a letter of 31 December:

The Germans are just as tired of the war as we are, & said they should not fire again until we did.

☆

Inevitably it was a day of instant friendships with much exchanging of addresses and promises to write and meet again after the war. Photographs were brought out and duly admired. One sergeant was so struck by a photograph of three women which a German showed him that he professed himself in love with one of them and vowed that he would go to Germany after the war and marry her. Captain Armes of the 1/North Staffs met a German who was much taken by a photograph of Armes's two small daughters:

One fellow, a married man, wanted so much a photo of Betty and Nancy in bed, which I had, and I gave it him as I had two: it seems he showed it all round, as several Germans told me afterwards about it. He gave me a photograph of himself and family taken the other day which he had just got.

But here and there a few jokes were played. Captain Maurice Mascall of the Royal Garrison Artillery wrote in a letter dated Christmas Day:

Our gunners were wildly excited when they came back. Several
of them had acquired signed postcards, and one man had actually
promised to write to a Herr Kartoffel who lives in Chemnitz.

It is an amusing speculation that at some time in the following weeks or months the postal authorities in Saxony might
have found themselves puzzled at receiving a message from
a British soldier addressed to an alleged resident of Chemnitz
with the unlikely name of 'Mr Potato'.

☆

While these remarkable events were going on, there were other
parts of the British front where there was no fraternization and
no friendly communication of any kind between opposing lines.
Evidence assembled from many sources suggests that the Christmas
truce held – to a greater or lesser extent – over more than two-
thirds of the British-held sector; but elsewhere Christmas came
and went leaving little trace. In the confined and blinkered world
of the trenches, it was possible to be entirely unaware of what
was happening to the next brigade – even to the next battalion.
Thus many units not involved in the truce only came to hear
about it afterwards, or even never heard about it at all: hence the
number of old soldiers who tended to dismiss it as a piece of
romantic fiction. As late as 13 January 1915 Captain J. L. Jack
of 1/Cameronians, who kept a full diary throughout this whole
period, referred, with evident surprise, to what he called 'extraordinary stories of unofficial Christmas truces with the enemy',
adding the categorical statement: 'There was no truce on the front
of my battalion.' Yet his 1/Cameronians were in the same brigade
as the 2/Argyll and Sutherland Highlanders, the 2/Royal Welch
Fusiliers and the 5/Scottish Rifles, all of which fraternized to some
extent with the enemy. One highly relevant factor is that Jack

states that his battalion was opposite Prussians, whereas the others were opposite Saxons (see page 297). Certainly the Germans on his front made none of the friendly overtures which helped to launch the truce in so many other areas. As far as he was concerned 25 December was no different from any other date in the calendar, and he summed up Christmas 1914 with these grim words:

> So passes the first Christmas of the War, far away from the original 'Peace and Goodwill to all men' – or is the true message 'I came not to bring peace, but a sword'?

In some other areas, especially where there had been very recent hard fighting, overtures *were* made by the Germans only to be angrily rejected by the British. Towards the southern end of the line, the 2/Grenadier Guards had had a most unpleasant Christmas Eve, with considerable losses. On 25 December Major Jeffreys, second-in-command, noted in his diary:

> At Daybreak a few Germans put their heads up and shouted 'Merry Xmas'. Our men, after yesterday, were not feeling that way, and shot at them. They at once replied and a sniping match went on all day.

There was a similar rebuff at the northern end of the sector in the territory of 3rd Division, as recorded in the diary of Captain Billy Congreve:

> We have issued strict orders to the men not on any account to allow a 'truce', as we have heard that they will probably try to. The Germans did try. They came over towards us singing. So we opened rapid fire on to them, which is the only sort of truce they deserve.

Opposition to any offer of cease-fire or fraternization was not confined to certain hard-line, or hard-pressed, British troops.

On Christmas Day, for example, a German officer wrote a strongly argued letter (which was subsequently translated and published in *The Times*) in which he explained his reasons for rejecting a British initiative made the previous night. He was one who saw no reason to temporize or to divert from his purposes for some transient festival:

> Gentlemen – You asked us yesterday temporarily to suspend hostilities and to become friends during Christmas. Such a proposal in the past would have been accepted with pleasure, but at the present time, when we have clearly recognized England's real character, we refuse to make any such agreement. Although we do not doubt that you are men of honour, yet every feeling of ours revolts against any friendly intercourse towards the subjects of a nation which for years has, in under-hand ways, sought the friendship of all other nations, so that with their help they might annihilate us; a nation also which, while professing Christianity, is not ashamed to use dum-dum bullets; and whose greatest pleasure would be to see the polit-ical disappearance and social eclipse of Germany. Gentlemen, you are not, it is true, the responsible leaders of English poli-tics, and so you are not directly responsible for their baseness; but all the same you are Englishmen, whose annihilation we consider to be our most sacred duty. We therefore request you to take such action as will prevent your mercenaries, whom you call 'soldiers', from approaching our trenches in future. – Lieut. of Landwehr.

The *Landwehr* was the German equivalent of the British Territorial Force.

It is not surprising, in view of such attitudes, that at various points up and down the line the daily War Diaries suggest a continuance of almost normal hostilities. In the region of Festu-bert the 13th Infantry Brigade recorded 'a considerable amount of sniping along the whole front'. The southernmost battalion of all, 1/King's Royal Rifle Corps, reported seven men wounded, even though they left the trenches as early as 1.30 p.m.

Perhaps most tragically of all, some men were killed on Christmas Day, when they felt themselves to be secure, on fronts where cease-fires had been agreed and fraternizations were in progress.

The loss of two men of the 2/Monmouthshires in such circumstances left a particularly bitter memory. Private Ernest Palfrey, a former miner aged twenty-one, was shot while returning from the task of burying dead comrades. 'A truce was supposed to be prevailing,' ran the report in the *South Wales Echo*, 'but Private Palfrey received a bullet in the back of his neck which killed him instantly.' In similar fashion a sergeant was fatally hit. One of the dead man's comrades, Sergeant 'Blackwood' Jones, a former Pontypool footballer, who had himself led a group into No Man's Land carrying a newspaper on top of his rifle as a flag of truce, wrote angrily about the event in a letter which was published in the *South Wales Weekly Argus* under the headlines: 'SAD NEWS FROM THE FIRING LINE. SERGEANT TREACHEROUSLY SHOT.'

> I took some tobacco and jam to the Germans. But, never no more. Another sergeant, a pal of mine from Monmouth, did the same, but when he was coming back to the trench they shot him through the back and killed him. He fell down and said 'My God, I'm done.' They are dirty cowards, after giving them tobacco.

The sergeant in question was Frank Collins, a thirty-nine-year-old former postman, who left a widow and three children. His official notification of death described him as having been 'killed in action'. The action in which he was engaged was taking Woodbines to the enemy. The Germans opposite later sent over an apology.

Second Lieutenant Dougan Chater, 2/Gordon Highlanders, commented in a letter written on Christmas Day that 'the truce will probably go on until someone is foolish enough to let off his rifle. We nearly messed it up this afternoon, by one of our fellows letting off his rifle skywards by mistake, but they did not seem to notice it so it did not matter.' But on Christmas afternoon a shot fired by another battalion of 'Regulars' *did* have unhappy results, as described by Rifleman John Erskine of the Territorial 5/Scottish Rifles:

> We had a tragedy in the trenches during the time the hand shaking etc. was going on. One of the Regulars disobeyed our strict order not to fire and let off a shot. The Germans immediately replied and instead of firing on where the shot came from they evidently fired at the first person they saw. Unfortunately this happened to be one of our corporals, who was shot through the head . . . A most regrettable fact connected with the affair was that he has three brothers in this battalion, and it must have a most disheartening effect on them.

The Corporal in question was Walter Sinclair Smith, of 2 Company, 5/Scottish Rifles; he died without regaining consciousness. His Chaplain wrote later: 'He was in the trenches with his Company, so that you can feel he died fighting for his country in a just cause. He was buried side by side with many other soldiers who have fallen in this dreadful war.'

The Queen's Westminster Rifles heard of this as they arrived in billets at Houplines early the next morning. One of their officers wrote:

> The Scottish Rifles had a man shot at another place. Apparently someone loosed off by mistake, and hit a German officer

so they fired back. One of the German officers came over and apologized. It was a rotten mistake as the Rifleman died.

The 1/Leicesters also lost two men killed and three men wounded on Christmas Day while fraternization was in progress. According to Major Buchanan-Dunlop, they were somewhat awkwardly placed, with their centre and right opposite some non-trucing Germans whom he took to be Prussians ('very vicious indeed'), and their left opposite Saxons ('jolly cheery fellows for the most part, and it seems so silly in the circumstances to be fighting them'). Seeing that the next battalion was out in No Man's Land with the Saxons and aware that a ceasefire had been arranged, Buchanan-Dunlop decided to leave his trenches and meet the enemy face to face – a decision which was to cause him some difficulties at a later date. Writing the same day, he told his wife:

> I've spent an hour talking to the German officers and men who have drawn a line halfway between our left trenches and theirs and have all met our men and officers there. We exchanged cigars, cigarettes, and papers . . . Firing has practically stopped, and it's only when our men start repairing wire entanglements that they send along some warning shots.

In the course of Christmas Day, Buchanan-Dunlop led the men of his company in worship:

> I had to have three [services], one on the right, then move to the centre, then one on the left. I just had a few prayers, read them the Christmas story, and had some hymns. Mother sent me a lot of St John gospels for the pocket, and they have hymns at the end. Please tell her how useful they have been and how much the men liked it.
>
> The General happened to come round just as the last one was going on, and said it was awfully nice. He had come down

rather angry over the informal cessation of hostilities but seemed to be quite soothed by the hymns.

This was Brigadier-General E. C. Ingouville-Williams (known as 'Inky Bill'), in command of 16th Brigade. Buchanan-Dunlop's assumption that he had gone away 'soothed' was to prove somewhat ill-judged.

During the afternoon a second senior British officer paid a visit to the front and found fraternization in progress. This was Brigadier-General Walter Congreve VC, commanding 18th Brigade, father of Captain Billy Congreve, whose approval of the shooting down of Germans as they came singing out of their trenches that morning has already been noted. Congreve senior appears to have taken a much more indulgent view of events than his son: certainly his diary account of the day contains no angry criticism – indeed, if anything, it suggests a reasonable acquiescence in what was taking place, together with an awareness that such a situation could have its military advantage:

> After lunch went to Rue du Bois to take some presents mother had sent for the men and found an extraordinary state of affairs. The men had arranged a truce between themselves in a.m., and all day they have been walking about together singing and smoking. The officers also walked and smoked even to a colonel. At 4 p.m. it was arranged that all were to be back in their trenches and, at midnight, firing would commence. My friend said he had a cigar with the best shot in the German Army, who others said had killed more of us than any dozen others, 'but I know where his loophole is now and mean to down him tomorrow'.

A somewhat less charitable attitude was taken by a senior German officer visiting the line on Christmas Day, according to the Regimental History of the 139th (11th Royal Saxon) Infantry Regiment. The truce agreed at the front had not been reported to the higher command 'for the sake of caution', and when the Regimental commander came up to the line and found an English soldier out in the open digging he ordered the guard in the front-line trench to shoot the enemy down. The order was carried out but the marksman hit a ruined building. 'The Commander sneered at him,' says the Regimental History, 'but was astonished at the effect of the shot – the Englishman turned round and waved his spade. It is difficult to say whether in waving he was humorously giving the Germans a sign for "missed" or to remind us that we ought to keep truce and not fire till midday . . .'

One of the interesting aspects of the day, indeed, is the wide-ranging reaction of local commanders to fraternization. Corporal John Ferguson – 'Fergie' – and his fellow 2/Seaforths, having struck up the friendliest relations with the Germans opposite during the night, expected them to continue the next day, but it was not to be as they had planned:

As was arranged before saying 'Good-night', Fritz and his friends had to visit us this morning, and here they were coming. It was like an attacking force coming on to us in extended order, but all without 'arms'. Our Colonel, who had not heard about last night's occurrence, saw them coming, and also saw me up on the parapet and waving my hands as I called 'Here you are, Fritz.' Very soon he was in a rage. 'Who is that man waving the enemy over here? Send them back.' He called out to them in German, 'Go back or we'll fire', and everything he said in German was answered by our German friend Fritz in English. Our Major went out and spoke to Fritz. He told them that the only Germans we wanted near us were those who wished to give themselves up. Did he intend doing that? But

Fritz was ready for him. 'Respecting your rank, sir, but I am not here to talk "politics".' They were sent back to their trenches, and we were left at our loopholes with orders not to fire unless they left their trench, and then we could warn them back and fire high.

It was a very quiet day, but we had made friends with our enemy, and all day we kept calling and joking across to their trenches.

In complete contrast, the commanding officer of 2/Scots Guards, Captain George Paynter, strode out in mid-morning to where Hulse and others were fraternizing and arrived on the scene with a hearty 'Well, my lads, a Merry Christmas to you! This is d—d comic, isn't it?' (Paynter was indeed CO of the 2/Scots Guards while holding the comparatively junior substantive rank of Captain; an Etonian like Hulse, he had joined the Scots Guards in 1899, served with distinction in the Boer War and been awarded the DSO in October 1914.) Hulse wrote:

George told [the Germans] that he thought it only right that we should show that we could desist from hostilities on a day which was so important in both countries; and he then said, 'Well, my boys, I've brought you over something to celebrate this funny show with', and he produced from his pocket a large bottle of rum (not ration rum, but the proper stuff).

The bottle was passed from mouth to mouth and 'polished off before you could say knife'.

As the morning wore on – in that now thickly populated zone where normally no one dared set foot – fraternization began to take many curious forms. The hare which started up during the 'parley' of Chaplain Esslemont Adams was not the only one to be chased wildly across the cabbage patches and shell-holes that lay between the trenches. Rifleman Maskell of 3/Rifle Brigade saw two hares get up and found it 'laughable to see the Germans and ourselves helter-skelter after the Christmas dinner, which escaped'; while of five plump hares reported by Hulse, two were captured, and the spoils shared. The 6/Cheshires killed a pig which they found behind their lines and, according to their Regimental History, 'cooked it in No Man's Land and shared it with the Boche'. Captain Josef Sewald recalled seeing Germans kneeling down with their heads held up to be shaved by English soldiers; and Bruce Bairnsfather retained as one of his principal memories of the day

> a vision of one of my machine-gunners, who was a bit of an amateur hairdresser in civil life, cutting the unnaturally long hair of a docile Boche, who was patiently kneeling on the ground whilst the automatic clippers crept up the back of his neck.

One Tommy of 3/Rifle Brigade even had his hair cut by his former barber from High Holborn, who was now a Saxon soldier. All this provided much entertainment for those looking on; and a further sensation was created in this same area, where a German juggler who had performed in London before the war drew a large crowd of British and Germans.

Nor was there any lack of background music to these increasingly bizarre scenes. Bagpipes were played in Scottish trenches, mouth organs added to the cheerful din and there was much lively singing. Hulse as ever was at the centre of these activities:

> A German NCO with the Iron Cross – gained, he told me, for conspicuous skill in sniping – started his fellows off on some marching tune. When they had done I set the note for

'The Boys of Bonnie Scotland, where the heather and the bluebells grow', and so we went on, singing everything from 'Good King Wenceslas' down to the ordinary Tommies' songs, and ending up with 'Auld Lang Syne', which we all, English, Scots, Irish, Prussian, Württembergers, etc. joined in. It was absolutely astounding, and if I had seen it on a cinematograph film I should have sworn that it was faked!

Captain Armes had, like Hulse, enjoyed his forenoon, and in similar style:

All this morning we have been fraternizing, singing songs. I have been within a yard in front of their trenches, have spoken to and exchanged greetings with a colonel, staff officers and several company officers. All were very nice and friendly . . .

We have just knocked off for dinner, and have arranged to meet again afterwards.

Or, as Lieutenant Hulse put it, writing three days later:

We then retired to our respective trenches for dinners and plum puddings.

☆

There seems to have been a general exodus at this point in search of Christmas fare, as though this was an agreed luncheon interval at a sporting contest, with every intention of a resumption of play in the afternoon. For most there was a decent meal to look forward to: Christmas puddings were in ready supply – Lady Rawlinson, for example, had given a pudding to every member of her husband's IV Corps – and the mass of Christmas parcels from home ensured that few had to subsist on the basic trench diet. Indeed, it is arguable that as much corned beef and Maconochie's stew was consumed on the

German side that day as on the British, as the Germans enjoyed the novelty of what was to the Tommies dreary routine. Even so British standard foods featured in several of the recorded menus of that day, usually improved with festive variations. Lance-Corporal Bell of the London Rifle Brigade noted in his diary:

> For dinner we warmed two tins of Maconochie (M. and V. ration) and some Christmas pudding sent from home, with biscuits, butter, jam and coffee.

Rifleman Bernard Brookes of the Queen's Westminsters had to be content with 'bully' and 'spuds' as his basic Christmas dish, but 'vin rouge' and 'Xmas pudding' (the former found in the cellars of the farm the Queen's Westminsters were using as headquarters) gave the meal an appropriately seasonal flavour. And Rifleman A. E. Watts of the same battalion was positively euphoric about the Christmas dinner which he and his fellow Tommies achieved:

> You ought to have seen our table when it was laid out on Christmas Day. There are four of us in our dugout, and we each had a tinned ration of meat and vegetables, which was followed by a Christmas pudding, mince pies, almonds and raisins, and red and white wine. What a feed! And a glorious wood fire going all day. Cigarettes, tobacco, with cigars from the Germans galore. What strange warfare!

One of the most elaborate feasts eaten that day in or near the front line was that devised by some soldiers of the Honourable Artillery Company, who had a coke brazier burning at each end of their trench on which they heated and prepared their dishes one by one. Again featuring Maconochie's, the menu read:

HORS D'OEUVRES
sardines

SOUP
Turtle – Ivelcon – Oxo

FISH
Herrings

ENTREE
Meat and Vegetable Ration (consisting of Tinned Beef,
Potatoes, Carrots, Beans, Onions, and Gravy)

POULTRY
Turkey (Devilled or Roast)

SWEETS
Christmas Pudding (hot and alight with rum)
and Mince Pies

SAVOURY
Bread and Butter and Bloater Paste and
Pâté de Foie Gras

DESSERT
Dates, Figs, Apples, Almonds and Raisins,
Preserved Ginger,
Mixed Chocolates, Marrons Glacés
Black Coffee – Cocoa – Café au lait

LIQUEURS
Cognac Rum

Crackers and Cigars

Their officer was invited to join them at the pudding stage, and it was he who supplied the cigars. Their toasts were:

The King

The Other Sections

The People at Home

The Wounded in Hospital

The Boys in the Firing Trenches

and

A Silent Toast for those who have gone under

They were so well supplied that when they left the trenches on 27 December they were able to offer their successors a substantial seasonal bonus, as one of their number recorded:

> We made up a brazier well and left it for those who relieved us. Gee! they were glad and grateful for it, together with the half-bottle of rum we left them in a stone jar, a fowl we 'found' and plucked but not cooked, half a pig that somehow had got itself in the way of a few bullets from my automatic pistol, cheese, jam, and half a bottle of sauce sent me by a friend.

Not a few fowls, pigs and other livestock found their way into some unsuspected stockpot that Christmas Day. While the officers of the 3/Indian Cavalry were well cared for in a château near Béthune, the transport drivers attached to them were left to forage for themselves.

> On Xmas Day 1914 having nothing else in the way of Xmas fare we scrounged a goose belonging to the gentleman of the Château and having no other means of cooking it we trimmed him up and boiled him one end at a time in a small iron

bucket. A very welcome Xmas dinner followed by a couple of native cooked chapatis. But the hullaballoo when the maid of the house found their pet goose was missing was nobody's business and after the usual questioning we all fell for a dose of pay stoppage. A dear Xmas dinner but a long way in front of Bully and Biscuits.

Considerably more privileged than such deprived if resourceful Tommies, Captain Billy Congreve recorded in his diary the details of his own excellent lunch at 3rd Division Headquarters:

We have had a great Xmas dinner – oxtail (from a tin), fillet of beef with macaroni, *oie rôti*, plum pudding (on fire), caviare, champagne and port to drink. The chef quite rose to the occasion. It's not a bad Xmas Day, I hope the next I shall spend at home.

Hulse, too, did well, as he told his mother:

We had steak, mashed potatoes, plum-pudding, ginger biscuits, chocolate (hot), whisky and water, and finished up by drinking your health and all at home in best Russian Kümmel!

At British Headquarters in the rue St Bertin, St Omer, Field Marshal Sir John French entertained Generals Haig and Smith-Dorrien to lunch. On the previous night Haig had been very late to bed having spent much of the evening wrapping presents – sent to him from England by his wife Doris – for the thirty-six members of his staff, including servants. 'What an amount of pleasure it gave me', he confided in his diary, 'to distribute Doris's Xmas gifts in the midst of all my anxiety.' French had been distributing presents too, having motored over to see General Foch that morning and given him a small cigarette case and some cigars; it is noteworthy that here as at the front tobacco was the standard token of fraternization. The menu at GHQ is not recorded: what mattered was the announcement which French made over the luncheon table. The Commander-in-Chief had decided, he informed his guests, that the BEF should be formed into two Armies forthwith: Haig to command First Army, Smith-Dorrien to command Second Army, the change to be effected by the following day.

☆

At about 12.45 a lone biplane appeared over Sheerness heading in the direction of London. It was German. It got as far as Erith, some fourteen miles from the City, but was then accosted by three British aeroplanes which pursued it back down the Thames. It was finally lost in the fog over Essex and made its way home across the Channel. Subsequently *The Graphic*, in a feature about the event called 'A Santa Claus Surprise that Failed', wrote:

> If the much-vaunted air raiding of England is to be no more formidable than the Christmas Day attempt on London, there is not much occasion for alarm.

This was not the only air strike to be mounted on Christmas Day. The Germans bombed Warsaw, and the British carried out an ambitious attack by seven seaplanes on the north German seaport of Cuxhaven. The raid was hampered by fog and caused little damage but was reported with much pride in the British press.

The belligerent countries celebrated Christmas in their various ways. In Berlin the mood was, on the whole, serious and restrained. Reports spoke of shops and warehouses closing early 'owing to the war shadows in Berlin this Christmas' and suggested an almost deserted city, with no sound on Christmas night except the tolling of church bells, snow falling on Christmas Day itself, and the Christmas trees in almost every home hung with mourning. Other observers, however, described the streets in the centre as being crowded during the Christmas holidays, and pointed to a general attempt to prevent the war from impinging too much on the appearance and mood of the imperial capital, with the wounded (much evident in the early weeks) scrupulously kept from the public eye, the wearing of mourning discouraged, the restaurants busy, and Shakespeare still playing at one Berlin theatre in spite of the hatred of all things English. Yet most people seem to have commemorated Christmas quietly that year, with the obligatory tree, a gramophone, a carol or two. Similarly Miss Ethel Cooper in Leipzig had a series of 'very quiet evenings' over Christmas: 'There is', she wrote, 'absolutely no sort of festivity anywhere this year.'

Paris was observing an uncharacteristically religious calm, though people's spirits were lifted by the exceptional weather – precisely the same as that at the front, which was barely fifty miles away at its nearest point. 'It was kind of Nature', wrote an English resident, 'to look so beautiful on this particular Christmas Day; for even the saddest faces showed a gleam of pleasure in the glory of the morning.' Such celebrations as there were tended to be of a charitable kind. In the hospitals and refugee camps, there was a determined cheerfulness, with Christmas trees, presents, entertainments and good fare. But the city's mood was remarkably sombre. A British correspondent wrote: 'At a time when the rivers of France are almost literally running with blood, Christmas in Paris has never been more Christian.'

There were sufficient reminders of the war in London for some observers to claim that it was having a 'martial Christmas'. As well as the familiar khaki figures in the streets and on the posters, there were several thousand Canadians currently training on Salisbury Plain who had come to enjoy Christmas in the

Empire's capital. Christmas Day music in the main hotels was military and national, quite excluding the season's ragtime, and there were toasts at every table to relatives or friends in the army and navy. Many hotels had Belgian children as special guests at their Christmas trees. Meanwhile at the Earls Court Exhibition building three thousand Belgians were given Christmas dinner and presented with a huge Christmas tree; at Alexandra Palace another two thousand five hundred Belgians were similarly entertained. But the popular mood in London was buoyant, the principal thoroughfares were as thronged as usual, the hotels were packed for the traditional Christmas dinner and, though after dark searchlights played over a darkened sky, the general feeling was that London's Christmas Day was more nearly normal than that of the other belligerent capitals.

The British Royal Family was at Sandringham; after attending morning service in the church in Sandringham Park they settled down to their Christmas dinner. Then as now the popular press was fascinated by the activities of royalty, with the result that the readers of some Fleet Street newspapers knew in advance precisely what fare would be gracing the royal table. It was a stoutly traditional menu with scant concession to any defeatist spirit:

Turkey, goose, a baron of beef – as the tenants will have – venison from Sandringham Park, cygnet from the Thames, boar's head, mince pies, and a flaming plum pudding, which will be served by the King.

In contrast, the King's royal cousin, Wilhelm II, was at Military Headquarters at Douai, where he took part in a festive gathering of a thousand officers and soldiers. On long rows of tables stood Christmas trees shimmering with lights. Green fir-branches decorated walls and ceilings. Spiced cake, apples and nuts were given to all officers and men, and the men also received tobacco pouches and cigars. Carols were sung. But when the Kaiser came to speak his message was stern and unyielding, with no concession to the spirit of the season:

> We stand on hostile soil, the point of our sword turned to the enemy, our hearts turned to God. We say, as once the Great Elector said, 'To the dust with the enemies of Germany'. Amen.

Meanwhile, deep in Germany, in the prisoner-of-war camp at Sennelager in Westphalia, a special gift from the Kaiser was the one redeeming feature of the day, as remembered by Rifleman Plumridge of the 1/Rifle Brigade:

> On Christmas Day 1914 for dinner we had a few pieces of swede in hot water. A German Sgt Major came in and shouted 'Achtung, Englanders. His Imperial Majesty the Emperor has today given you all a Christmas present', and he dished out five cigars to each man. I smoked them in my pipe.

Royal gifts were much in evidence at the British front on Christmas Day. For every serving soldier from the Commander-in-Chief to the humblest private there was a Christmas card from the King and Queen, plus the special present from Princess Mary's Fund which had been trundling up by the trainload in the previous week. It was a tremendous task of distribution to get them to all the units in Flanders. Most battalions would have to wait until they were out on rest, but some did receive them in the trenches on Christmas Day itself – such as the 2/Scots Guards who were given theirs along with Lady Rawlinson's pudding (and a card from Lady Rawlinson as well) on Christmas morning. The card from the King and Queen carried their photographs and the touching message: 'With our best wishes for Christmas 1914. May God protect you and bring you home safe.' For the wounded there was a variation: 'May you soon be restored to health.' All this was fine and good for morale, but better still was Princess Mary's gift, now revealed in its not inconsiderable splendour: a beautifully designed, embossed brass box, containing cigarettes, tobacco, a Christmas card and a photograph of the Princess herself, together with a pipe. For non-smokers there was an alternative box containing acid drops and a khaki pencil case, while for the Indians the contents included sugar candy and a tin box of spices.

The box had been specifically devised as a permanent souvenir of Christmas spent in the field or on the seas and, indeed, many men carefully sent it to their families, often with the contents untouched to ensure its safe survival. This present was particularly appreciated by some of the very young soldiers, such as Rifleman Leslie Walkinton, who 'was rather pleased about the tobacco because my family at home thought I was too young to smoke and it made me feel rather older and bigger'. Princess Mary's photograph was also an immediate success; in the course of the day, according to Henry Williamson, the future novelist, then serving as a private soldier in the London Rifle Brigade, one found its way into the hands of a delighted German, who was heard going around saying, '*Ah, schöne, schöne Prinzessin*' ('Oh, beautiful, beautiful Princess').

The Germans had their royal gifts too, as has been indicated: from the Kaiser a cigar-case bearing the inscription '*Weihnacht im Felde 1914*' ('Christmas in the Field 1914'), and from Crown Prince Wilhelm a pipe with his own portrait on it for every member of his army – a Christmas memento, he explained, following the precedent set by his grandfather, then Crown Prince, in 1870, when German armies also spent Christmas in France.

☆

Have just finished dinner. Pork chop. Plum pudding. Mince pies. Ginger, and bottle of Wine and a cigar, and have drunk to all at home and especially to you, my darling one. Must go outside now to supervise the meetings of the men and the Germans.

So wrote Captain Armes, hurrying to finish his letter so that he could despatch it immediately to his wife and pass on as speedily as possible the news of the extraordinary events at the front. He was well aware that he was reporting an episode of some historic importance:

Keep the letter carefully and send copies to all. I think they will be interested. It did feel funny walking alone towards the enemy's trenches to meet someone halfway and to arrange a Xmas peace. It will be a thing to remember all one's life.

The task completed, he climbed over the parapet to rejoin the fraternizing crowds in No Man's Land.

In some areas the truce did not really begin until the afternoon. Near Houplines on the river Lys, where the 2/Royal Welch Fusiliers were in trenches that ran down to the water's edge, the mist lingered throughout the morning and the men were already at dinner when it finally dispersed. Captain C. I. Stockwell, one of the battalion company commanders, having seen that his men were being well fed, had just retired to his shelter to get his own meal, when the sergeant on duty suddenly ran in and said that half a dozen Saxons were to be seen standing unarmed on their parapet.

I ran out into the trench and found that all the men were holding their rifles at the ready on the parapet, and that the Saxons were shouting, 'Don't shoot. We don't want to fight today. We will send you some beer.' A cask was hoisted on to the parapet and three men started to roll it into the middle of No Man's Land. A lot more Saxons then appeared without arms. Things were getting a bit thick. My men were getting a bit excited, and the Saxons kept shouting to them to come out. We did not like to fire as they were all unarmed, but we had strict orders and someone might have fired, so I climbed over the parapet and shouted, in my best German, for the opposing Captain to appear. Our men were all chattering and saying, 'The Captain's going to speak to them.' We met and formally saluted. He introduced himself as Count Something-or-other, and seemed a very decent fellow. He could not talk a word of English. He then called out his subalterns and formally introduced them with much clicking of heels and saluting. They were all very well turned out, while I was in a goatskin coat. One of the subalterns could talk a few words of English, but not enough to carry on a conversation.

I said to the German Captain, 'My orders are to keep my men in the trench and allow no armistice. Don't you think it is dangerous, all your men running about in the open like this? Someone may open fire.' He called out an order, and all his men went back to their parapet, leaving me and the five German officers and a barrel of beer in the middle of No Man's Land. He then said, 'My orders are the same as yours, but could we not have a truce from shooting today? We don't want to shoot, do you?' I said, 'No, we certainly don't want to shoot, but I have my orders to obey' – to which he agreed. I then suggested that we should return to our trenches and that no one should come out of the trench. We agreed not to shoot until the following morning, when I was to signal that we were going to begin. He said, 'You had better take the beer; we have lots.' So I called up two men to bring the barrel to our side. I did not like to take their beer without giving something in exchange, and I suddenly had a brainwave. We had lots of plum puddings, so I sent for one and formally presented it to him in exchange for the beer. He then called out 'Waiter', and a German private whipped out six glasses and two bottles of beer, and with much bowing and saluting we solemnly drank it, amid cheers from both sides. We then all formally saluted and returned to our lines.

Frank Richards, author of the Tommy's classic *Old Soldiers Never Die*, was present as a member of the Welsh battalion; a rugged professional, he had joined the regiment in 1901, had served nearly seven years in India and Burma and, in a phrase not unfamiliar in the ranks, had 'risen to the rank of Private'. His version suggests that there was much more actual fraternizing than Stockwell's account allows, in spite of attempts to prevent it, and that there were some lively exchanges between Saxon and Welshman:

One of their men, speaking in English, mentioned that he had worked in Brighton for some years and that he was fed up to the neck with this damned war and would be glad when it was all over. We told him that he wasn't the only one that was fed up with it.

But his story of the parley in the middle is much the same as Stockwell's and he is one with his officer, as indeed are all the accounts, in portraying the rolling out into No Man's Land of a barrel or so of beer as the central feature of the fraternization on this sector. The beer had been purloined from the Frelinghien Brewery which stood virtually in the Saxon lines. Richards provides the scarcely necessary detail that 'the two barrels of beer were drunk', but not, apparently, with any very great enjoyment since he and his comrades thought that 'French beer was rotten stuff'. As if to vent their disapproval the British destroyed the brewery by shell-fire in February 1915.

Opposite 15th Brigade, between Ploegsteert and Wulverghem, the mist also lingered throughout the morning, inhibiting any friendly relations between opposing trenches. At about 2 p.m., however, an unarmed German officer was seen walking towards the trenches of the 1/Norfolks, with other Germans following him. Some of the Norfolks shouted to them telling them to come no nearer but they took no notice; so, to prevent them seeing the state of the British defences, the Norfolk men climbed out and advanced to meet them. It was the signal for a mass meeting in No Man's Land in which eventually between 200 and 400 British and Germans, including officers, took part and which continued for about one and a half hours, with much conversation and communal hymn-singing. Reporting the episode, the War Diary of the 15th Brigade noted that the Germans had said that they were not going to fire for three days. 'Little mention of war was made,' it added. 'They expected it to finish within 2 months at least.' The report also stated that more Germans had come out of the trenches than it was thought the trenches held.

At Port Arthur near Neuve Chapelle, Lieutenant-Colonel Lothian Nicholson, commanding officer of the 2/East Lancs, was more concerned with the state of his trenches than with striking up temporary friendships with the enemy. There had been, it was true, a little flurry of activity soon after daylight, when the Germans put up a few Christmas trees on their parapets and shouted 'Merry Christmas East Lancs' – 'pretty smart,' Nicholson noted in his diary, 'considering that it was our first tour in this line.' But the afternoon found him in urgent discussion with his Brigadier, Carter, and the Commander Royal Engineers, Rotherham, as to how to solve the 'water situation' of a stretch of line particularly vulnerable to flooding – 'they didn't get much beyond making futile suggestions & fixing a pump which was drained out 24 hours later'. As he was talking with the

Brigadier, however, he became suddenly aware of 'a lot of our men hobnobbing with the Hun in No Man's Land'. He decided to investigate:

> I went out . . . and found Fryer, one of our attached subalterns, talking fluent German to a German NCO. I gathered that they wanted leave to bury the dead of which there were a good many lying in No Man's Land. After vain endeavours to get hold of a German officer I sent the German NCO with a message to the Bn Commander that he could have an hour and a half & that we would bury all the dead lying close to our line & they could do the same with theirs. This was accepted and subsequently extended for another hour, in the course of which we buried all the dead & Sanders went out from the Adv. Post in the 3rd Sector & recovered the body of Dilworth, a Sher[wood] For[ester] who had been killed about a month before.

☆

It was not until the afternoon that fraternization got under way on the sector to the south of Neuve Chapelle held by the Indians of the Royal Garhwal Rifles.

At dawn on the other side of No Man's Land the officer on duty had reported to Captain Walther Stennes, 'Everything all right, but strange: not a shot fired'. Stennes went round and talked to the sentries, who all insisted that they had not heard or seen anything. Off duty, Stennes settled into his dugout and started reading; but his soldiers were still eager to continue the celebrations begun the previous night. Within earshot in the Indian trenches was the adjutant of the 2/39 Garhwal Rifles, Captain E. R. P. Berryman, who wrote in a letter to his mother:

> We heard them singing and shouting in their trenches, and about midday they began lifting up hats on sticks and showing

16. London Rifle Brigade church parade early Christmas morning for companies
not in front-line trenches. There is still a thick mist, and the field is white with frost

*'We found we were to bury our comrades that fell in the charge on the 18th of Dec.
So we all started digging and burying them side by side and made them a Cross out of the wood
of a biscuit box & laid them to rest'* (anon diary, Border Regt)

17. Preparations for the joint burial near Rue Petillon and the Sailly-Fromelles road.
The soldier with a shovel, left, is Sergeant Cyril Luckin, 55 Field Company,
Royal Engineers

18. Preparations for burial

19. Fraternization and photography in No Man's Land

20. British and German officers and men

21. British and German officers. The British (far right) are Second Lieutenant
The Hon. Harold B. Robson and a fellow officer of the Northumberland Hussars,
7th Division

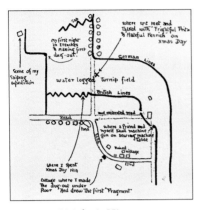

22 (*above*). His map
23 (*right*). '*Swapping Buttons*'
24 (*below*). Himself

TAKEN AT ST. YVON, XMAS DAY, 1914
OFFICERS, 2ND LIEUTENANT   1
BAIRNSFATHERS, BRUCE   1
HOLES, SHELL   1

☆

THE LONDON RIFLE BRIGADE (LRB)

These photographs were taken on Christmas Day on Rifleman Turner's 'pocket camera', and sent by Rifleman J. Selby Grigg to London newspaper for publication

25. Riflemen Andrew and Grigg posing with Saxons of the 106th and 104th Regiments

26. 'A crowd of some one hundred Tommies of each nationality holding a regular mothers' meeting between the trenches'

27. Rifleman Turner, (centre wearing goatskin coat) with two German officers

28 (*above*). A group of cheerful riflemen in Ploegsteert Wood, after their Christmas dinner

CAPT. SIR EDWARD HULSE AND CAPT. E. WARNER
(In the Trenches Christmas Day, 1914)

29 (*left*). Captain Sir Edward Hulse, author of the most famous account of the Christmas truce, photographed on Chistmas Day with a fellow officer

30. Hulse's battalion, the 2/Scots Guards, with Westphalians and Jägers, photographed on Christmas Day by Lieutenant Alan Swinton

'They were very nice fellows to look at . . . & one of them said, "We don't want to kill you and you don't want to kill us. So why shoot?" . . . I lined them up and took a photograph'

31. British and Germans photographed in No Man's Land on Boxing Day by Second Lieutenant Cyril Drummond, RFA

List of Casualties for 27th/12/14. 10

Reg't no	Rank & name	Nature of Casualty.	Date	How disposed of etc.
2270	Rfn	Brand a	Died of Wounds	25/12.	
2133	"	Byng x H.C	Missing		Known to be
1401	"	Souch x H.S	— Do —	25/12	Safe & not wounded
2788	"	Pearce x H.S	— Do —		With Germans.
1885	"	Hubbard a.S	Septic Heel	26/12	17th F.a
1684	"	Simmons H.S	— Do —	—"—	— Do —
1656	"	Johnson 2/	Rheumatism	—"—	— Do —.

x. These men foolishly walked
into the German trenches on Xmas
day when there was a sort of
an arrangement that "no shooting to
be done between daylight & dusk."
Please don't publish this

Can you send us an army
list — A Happy New Year to all

Yours

27/12/14   A.M.D a   S

32. Page from the Casualty Book of the Queen's Westminster Rifles.
The three men described as missing were held as prisoners of war after
fraternization on Christmas Eve (see page 82)

them above the trench, then they showed their heads, and then their bodies and finally they climbed out of their trenches into the open! Of course we could not shoot them in cold blood like that, tho' one or two shots were fired.

Also observing these developments was Private W. Weir of the 18th Hussars, attached to an Indian Cavalry Regiment, who was manning a Maxim gun in the 'gap' between the 1/39 and 2/39 Garhwal Rifles.

We were saluted by the Germans, whose trenches are only about sixty yards away, by them calling out to us in good English, 'A Happy Christmas to you all'. We took no notice of it at first, but about 1.30 p.m. we heard them calling again.

We looked out of our loopholes, and there they were all standing on top of their trench. We could hardly believe our eyes; we were just about to open fire when one of our officers gave us the order to unload our rifles. Seeing the Germans standing there without any rifles, we stood up and answered them. Then they started to cheer. One of their men shouted out, 'Here's some cigars for you. Come and fetch them.' We were not having any at first, as we thought it might be a trap for us. The German then told us to come over for them. They shouted, 'Come on, we will not fire on you.' The fellow who threw the cigars then came down off the top of his trench and picked up the box again and started to walk over towards our trenches. Seeing this I climbed over the parapet of our trench to meet him. When we met in the middle he handed me the cigars and said, 'A happy Christmas to you.' I hardly knew what to do at first, but I shook hands with him and wished him the compliments of the season also.

As soon as the Germans saw us shake hands they cheered like mad. They then started to come towards our trench. Our boys, all Indians by the way, started out to meet them as well.

The scene that followed can hardly be described. To see our

greatest enemy shaking hands with our Indian troops and giving them cigars and cigarettes was a sight I shall never forget.

As the fraternization began, a German sergeant reported to Stennes in his dugout: 'Captain, come out, the British have started waving in their trenches, but there is no shooting, and our men are doing the same.'

I did not even take time to don my tunic, but rushed out and saw a strange unforgettable picture. The soldiers who were not on duty were standing upright on top of their trenches without their weapons, waving and shouting 'Merry Christmas'. I ordered half of the company back into the trenches, told them to arm and reinforce the sentries, and to be on the alert; but there must be no shooting and they were to avoid any menacing movement. Meanwhile some soldiers had advanced into No Man's Land. Intensely we watched the strange sight as the soldiers met in the middle of No Man's Land, shook hands, talked and strolled about. Then a man of my company came running back and reported that a British officer wanted to talk to me.

The British officer was Lieutenant-Colonel D. H. Drake-Brockman, commanding the 2/39 Garhwal Rifles. Back at the Battalion HQ, he had that morning been making arrangements for artillery fire to knock out the German pump which he suspected was responsible for the water flowing into the British lines. After some difficulty in aligning the correct range, and a first effort narrowly missing their own parapet, shells had been dropped on the pump's vicinity, though Drake-Brockman did not think it had been hit, as the flooding was as bad as ever.

He had also been showing around some officers of the Worcesters, who were to relieve them, and was returning to his dugout at Battalion HQ in the orchard of a ruined farm when he was suddenly approached by his somewhat breathless adjutant:

> Captain Berryman came running up with the news that 'the Germans were out of their trenches'. 'The devil they are!' I replied, and went up with him. Sure enough I found a number sitting on the parapet of No. 2 Company's trench, and also out in front of No. 1 Company. They were trying to converse with our men and giving them cigarettes, biscuits and boxes of cigars. As I could speak German I conversed with them. They all belonged to the 16th Regiment . . . They seemed very jolly, as if they had had a good dinner. One of them said to me that there must be *'Friede auf der Erde'* ['Peace on Earth'] on this day, being Christmas Day. They seemed convinced that they were winning, and one of them said, with a wave of his hand, that the Russians were quite out of it. He gave me a bundle of his newspapers to corroborate his statement.

Captain Walther Stennes also marched off to the middle of No Man's Land:

> Here I met two English, one Indian and one German officer of the neighbouring Company; we shook hands, wished each other a merry Xmas, agreed that both sides would abstain from any hostile activity until next day at noon, then we exchanged some small presents like plum pudding, cakes, whisky, brandy, and so did our men.

It was all very strange, as Captain Berryman explained in the letter he wrote about the event to his mother:

> For an hour both sides walked about in the space between the two lines of trenches, talking and laughing, swapping baccy and cigarettes, biscuits, etc. . . . you would never believe that we had been fighting for weeks.

On this front too there were dead to be buried, as Private Weir reported:

> One of the Germans came up and asked me if I would like to bury a few dead Indians that were lying about their trenches. My chum and I set to work and buried about a dozen of them, for which the Germans thanked us.
>
> All the Germans looked very fit. They were also very well clothed and looked well fed. One thing I did notice was that there were Iron Crosses galore amongst them; about one man out of every six had one on [see page 298]. One of their officers, a captain, clasped his hands together and looked towards heaven and said, 'My God, why cannot we have peace and let us all go home!'

Approved by officers on both sides, the fraternization between the 2/39 Garhwal Rifles and the Westphalians was conducted throughout in a friendly spirit and led to no unfortunate consequences. In the case of the 1/39th battalion on their right, however, the reaction of one of their senior officers produced a somewhat different result. Major Kenneth Henderson, the officer in question, took a far less sympathetic view of the Christmas truce than Lieutenant-Colonel Drake-Brockman:

> Hearing of the fraternization I hastened to the scene to investigate, and found the whole of No Man's Land crowded with our men and the Germans amicably intermixed. I could distinguish German officers and confabbing with them [Captain] Kenny and [Lieutenant] Welchman . . . For a moment I gazed at the curious sight, and then realized how absolutely wrong and dangerous it was, and decided to stop it. I therefore stood up on the parapet and blew my whistle and signalled and shouted for all to come back. It was amusing to notice that the first to clear off were the Germans. They all bolted like rabbits at the sound of my whistle evidently expecting a ruse,

or having a guilty conscience, while our men continued to stand irresolutely for a second or two, uncertain of where the whistle came from and what its meaning was. Within a few minutes however normal conditions were restored and after scolding Kenny and Welchman a bit I decided to go off myself to Battalion HQ and report the matter.

That same evening Captain W. G. S. Kenny had 'the honour' to submit a report on the meeting with the Germans and on the German trenches to the Acting Adjutant of the 1/39 Garhwal Rifles, Captain J. Lumb (see Appendix A). He hoped to show that much useful information had been obtained about the enemy's dispositions during his parleys in No Man's Land, but his reports failed to lessen the displeasure he had incurred through Henderson's precipitate action. The latter's account concludes:

> Needless to say the news caused the greatest perturbation when it reached higher quarters and for dear old Kenny the results were tragically serious. I heard the Commander-in-Charge had stopped leave for all officers who participated in the 'Xmas truce': a truly unnecessarily terrible penalty. It was a pure error of judgement which infected a very large stretch of the whole British front and an expression of the Commander-in-Chief's displeasure would have been a safe and complete deterrent from any repetition. But it is too often forgotten that the object of all punishment is not to penalize the offenders for what is past and done, but to deter others for the future. In Kenny's case and possibly in many others a terrible cruelty was done by this order because he was killed before he ever got leave, and his mother and relations had not seen him for years . . .

It appears in fact that the decision to withhold Captain Kenny's leave was a local one, taken at no higher level than that of the battalion commander. Both Captain Kenny and Lieutenant Welchman were killed at the Battle of Neuve Chapelle on 10 March 1915: Lieutenant Welchman as he reached the German trenches, and Captain Kenny (who was the only British officer of the 1/39th to reach the enemy trenches alive) while returning, wounded, with some German prisoners.

Among the prisoners taken by the Garhwal Rifles at the Battle of Neuve Chapelle were some of the men who had come out on Christmas Day during the informal armistice.

☆

Elsewhere in many areas fraternization begun earlier in the day continued all Christmas afternoon. Rifleman Bernard Brookes had been to church in the morning and had then been on duty from 12 noon to 2 p.m. at battalion headquarters, so it was not until relatively late that he was able to go out to join his fellow Queen's Westminsters and meet what he called 'our friends the enemy'. By this time fraternization was beginning to take some rather bizarre forms:

> Many of the Germs had costumes on which had been taken from the houses nearby, and one facetious fellow had a Blouse, Skirt, Top Hat and umbrella, which grotesque figure caused much merriment.

Fritz had no monopoly in such entertainments, as a Royal Artilleryman observed:

> A couple of bright sparks from the Staffords (1/N. Staffs) who had been prowling around some ruined houses, appeared – one clad in a tail-coat, black trousers, and an old battered silk hat that had seen better days, the other decked out in blouse and skirt, an old bonnet and a broken umbrella. They paraded up and down the line of the trenches and were joined by another

joker who had found a broken bicycle with almost square wheels, which he trundled up and down.

The 2/Wiltshire Regiment and the friendly Germans opposite had earlier been presented with a similar diversion, as a former subaltern of the Wiltshires, E. L. Francis, remembered:

> My own platoon Sergeant was a very cheerful reservist in his mid-thirties and well earned his nickname of Chirpy. He added a good deal to the informal Christmas party by going out to meet the Germans wearing a large skirt which he had found in a deserted farmhouse; this led to some earthy Teutonic byplay and caused plenty of laughs.

There were those, however, on both sides, who saw the opportunity to make some military gain while these cheerful distractions were taking place. While the sergeant of the 2/Wiltshires was performing his drag act to general acclaim, Second Lieutenant Francis was struck by the curious behaviour of one of the enemy:

> Both sides seemed to be imbued with the Christmas Spirit until I noticed a German officer who was walking up and down between the trenches and gradually getting nearer to ours. I pointed this out to my friend and fellow subaltern, Frank Strawson, and we started to walk parallel with the German officer. We rode him off in true polo style and he returned disgruntled to his own trenches.

A more successful reconnaissance was carried out by Major Arbuthnot, officer commanding 24 Battery, 38th Brigade, Royal Field Artillery, at La Chapelle d'Armentières, in the area held by the Queen's Westminster Rifles, as one of his Gunners described:

> My OC put on a German uniform and had a good look around the German lines. He spotted what he wanted to find – a

German machine-gun post which had given our infantry a deal
of trouble; he also saw the German billets in a village called
Wez-Macquart.

Attempts were often made to keep the wandering soldiery
of one nation from approaching too near the trenches and
emplacements of the other. In some areas a more or less notional
halfway line was agreed; but, as more and more men crowded
into No Man's Land and as the mood of good humour and
camaraderie held, the situation became increasingly difficult to
control. People were, according to one report, 'strolling about
as if in Hyde Park'. 'We were like a crowd of kids with a day's
holiday,' wrote Rifleman G. Eade of the 3/Rifle Brigade, and
added:

> Of course, we were not allowed to go into their trenches or
> they into ours, but we met halfway and in some places even
> got as far as their wire entanglements.

In such circumstances it was impossible to prevent at least
some of the enemy from peering into forbidden zones or picking
up the kind of random intelligence only accessible in normal
times to a trench raid. However, there were those who attempted,
if vainly, to sweep back the advancing tide, as Rifleman P. H.
Jones of the Queen's Westminster Rifles noted in his diary:

> One little officer, who looked about sixteen, amused us very
> much by clearing some North Staffords away from his machine-
> gun emplacement. 'No, no,' he said. 'It shall not so be. You
> shall not so near come.' We gravely saluted him and turned
> about, but he followed us and finally had his photo taken arm
> in arm with one of our officers.

Henry Williamson, of the London Rifle Brigade, met with
a similar rebuff.

I wanted to get right behind their lines but a German officer came up to me and asked, 'What do you do?' 'Admiring your beautiful field fortifications,' I told him. And he smiled and saluted and I went back and told my second lieutenant, who ordered me not to do it again.

☆

'In most cases', wrote an officer of a Glasgow regiment, 'the only reservation was that men were not to go into the other side's trenches, but in some instances the order was not obeyed and groups were entertained in the hostile dugouts.' Stories of such episodes soon circulated. Two Germans, it was believed, took Christmas dinner with two officers of the Scots Guards, while six men of the Worcestershire Regiment had lunch with the Germans. 'Some of our people', wrote an officer of the RAMC (reporting at second-hand but with considerable confidence), 'actually went into their trenches and stayed there for some time, being entertained by the enemy! All joined together in a sing-song, each taking it in turn to sing a song, and finally they ended up with "God Save the King", in which the Saxon sang most heartily!! This is absolutely true. One of our men was given a bottle of wine in which to drink the King's health.' A less florid – and perhaps more reliable – reference occurs in the War Diary of the 11th Infantry Brigade:

> Several officers visited German trenches – most of which well made but partly full of water, and a lot of enemy wore gum boots. Trenches v. thickly manned. 1 man per yard or 2 yards in places. Much valuable information gained regarding enemy's wire entanglements.

But sometimes men were invited into enemy trenches for a more serious purpose. Quite early on Christmas Day Second

Lieutenant R. D. Gillespie of 2/Gordon Highlanders was taken into German lines to be shown a grave with the inscription: 'To a Brave British Officer'.

Yet visits to the other side's trenches did not always end happily. Some men who got too close for the enemy's comfort found themselves, as in the case of the riflemen of the Queen's Westminster Rifles the previous night, taken prisoners of war. One such was a German who, according to the account by former Lance-Corporal George Ashurst, proposed an armistice to the 2/Lancashire Fusiliers:

> Coming across from the German trenches was a solitary German, carrying a white flag high above his head. Having come about halfway to our lines he suddenly stopped and waited. Then one of our men was seen to go out and meet him, to bring him in to our lines . . . Unfortunately [he] had not been blindfolded . . . and consequently he had to be made a prisoner of war. He protested and was awfully upset about it, but he had seen the position behind our lines and that must be kept from the enemy at all costs.

Lieutenant William Tyrrell, the medical officer of Ashurst's battalion, commented angrily in his diary:

> Germans send in party and white flag. Our B. F--1 of a sentry brings one in without blindfolding him and of course he had to be made prisoner.

Elsewhere two Germans of a *Landsturm* Regiment (a unit of reservists over forty brought to the front because of heavy losses in the regular regiments) who came across to British lines in friendly mood were arrested by an 'extra-officious soldier' and held in the dampest corner of the trench. For them, however, there was a more fortunate outcome.

Presently an officer came along. 'What in the world have you got there?' said he to the brave British soldier who was guarding his shivering treasures. 'Beggin' your pardon, Sir, a couple of land-streamers, by the look of them. Said they'd come to wish us many happy returns; so I nabbed them, Sir.'

Realizing that this was hardly playing the game, the officer read the sentry a little homily on the amenities of the festive season and asked the plump 'landstreamers' to depart, with the compliments of the season, to their own lines.

While all this byplay was going on, many men seized the opportunity presented by the armistice to better their living conditions. 'I have been taking advantage of the truce to improve my "dugout",' wrote Second Lieutenant Dougan Chater to his mother on Christmas Day. 'We put on a proper roof this morning and now we have got a tiled fireplace and brushwood and straw on the floor.' Sometimes implements were shared with the enemy: Harold Startin of the 1/Leicesters remembered that the Germans 'willingly lent us some of their tools to carry out our improvements'. The ruined buildings nearby were raided for coal, firewood, furniture and whatever other comforts might be found. Lieutenant J. D. Wyatt, of 2/Yorks, commenting some days later on the fact that his dugout was more or less rainproof at last, added as a final flourish: 'We have also 2 easy chairs – loot.' In addition, working on trenches in full view of enemy lines, previously unthinkable, became almost common practice before Christmas Day was out. In some areas, indeed, this was to become almost second nature and to go on for a considerable time, and to become the major reason – or the major pretext – for continuing the truce well into the New Year.

☆

There was much taking of photographs on Christmas Day 1914, enemy photographing enemy, enemy standing cheerfully side by side with enemy as the cameras clicked. At this stage of the war there were still many private cameras at the front, British and German, officers and men having tucked their Kodaks into their baggage as they marched away much as if they were going on a prolonged and exciting holiday. Nor was there anything particularly underhand about this. There was indeed a general regulation against the taking of photographs by soldiers on active service, and a crackdown on cameras began soon after Christmas 1914; yet the fact remains that newspapers such as the *Daily Mail* were offering substantial payments for war photographs throughout much of 1915. However, with the arrival of official war photographers the heyday of the amateur passed.

But that moment had not yet arrived. Thus Captain Armes, referring in his letter to his wife to pictures taken on Christmas Day ('a group of German officers, a German officer and myself, and a group of British and German soldiers') could write: 'I hope the photos come out all right. Probably you will see them in some paper.' Indeed, a number of such photographs *did* find their way into the columns of the British press, some of them to be much reproduced elsewhere, with the result that they have become minor classics among the images of the Great War.

The Germans were aware of this possibility too, and were eager to offer their own contributions for editorial consideration by British publications. A British subaltern, in a letter written on New Year's Day and published in many newspapers, wrote:

> The [German] officers were amusing themselves by taking photographs of mixed groups. The Germans brought us copies to send to the English illustrated newspapers, as they received them regularly.

It should be added that perhaps the most widely distributed of all the photographs of the truce, which appeared in such newspapers as the *Daily Mirror* and the *Daily Mail*, may well have reached Fleet Street as a result of an approach of this kind, since the *Mail* described it as being probably taken by a German officer.

Far more photographs, however, were 'snapped' during the Christmas truce than have survived – or at any rate have appeared in the public domain. Many letters and accounts refer to photographs being taken; and there seems to have been little concern for rank or status as men photographed officers and officers photographed men – no doubt enthusiasm and the novelty of the occasion overbore normal considerations. Typical of many, a member of the London Rifle Brigade reported that 'a German officer took a photo of English and German soldiers arm in arm with exchanged caps and helmets'. Other accounts suggest that whole groups of friendly enemies were rounded up before the camera like guests at a wedding. 'My captain, with another officer and two German officers, surrounded by swarms of English and German "Tommies", had their photographs taken.' 'Some Uhlan officers, who had been transferred to the Infantry, came out and posed for their photograph in the centre of a group of British and German soldiery. They were magnificently polished and clean, which unfortunately the British officers were not.'

British and Germans stood together – and, on the front occupied by the Garhwal Rifles, Indians and Germans stood together, as Private Weir described:

> We then had our photographs taken by a German who was the proud possessor of a small camera. There were Indians and Germans shaking hands when he pulled the shutter of his

camera. He also took a photograph of three of our officers and three of their officers; our officers were placed between theirs.

Second Lieutenant Bruce Bairnsfather also found himself being photographed out in No Man's Land surrounded by British and Germans; he later described the event in characteristic style:

> Suddenly one of the Boches ran back to his trench and presently appeared with a large camera. I posed in a mixed group for several photographs, and have ever since wished I had fixed up some arrangement for getting a copy. No doubt framed editions of this photograph are reposing on some Hun mantelpiece, showing clearly and unmistakably to admiring strafers how a group of perfidious English surrendered unconditionally on Christmas Day to the brave Deutschers.

In other instances, arrangements were made on the spot so that the participants might have the opportunity to study the results, as Second Lieutenant Dougan Chater reported following more photography on Boxing Day:

> Some of our officers were taking groups of English and German soldiers . . . We are at any rate having another truce on New Year's Day, as the Germans want to see how the photos come out.

☆

To many people it has come to be accepted that the central feature of the Christmas truce of 1914 was a game, or possibly games, of football in which British and Germans took part. Indeed, to some the whole event is not so much 'the truce' as 'the football match'. It is, of course, an attractive idea, carrying as it does not only the heart-warming thought of enemies at friendly play, but also the appealing if politically naïve implication that nations would be far better employed in settling their differences on the fields of sport rather than on the field of war. Yet there are those, including some veterans of 1914, who doubt if any football match took place at all.

There is no question that if the fraternizing soldiers had found occasion to play each other at any game it would have been football – or 'footer' as it was frequently called. It was an immensely popular sport at the time and the natural recreation of thousands of men when out on rest. Matches between platoons, companies, battalions were constantly taking place. There are even stories of games being played 'while in billets a few yards from the enemy, shells whistling over'. Another contemporary report refers to 'footballs which so many privates carry tied to their knapsacks' (though it should be added that many old soldiers pooh-pooh the idea that footballs would be carried into the trenches). Nor was football enjoyed only by the ordinary Tommy. For example, on 22 December, Major John Charteris, staff officer to General Sir Douglas Haig, having nothing much to do, 'turned out to play football for the Staff against a team of Cavalry. The Prince of Wales was playing . . .'

The Germans were enthusiasts too. When Lieutenant Stewart of 2/Argyll and Sutherland Highlanders was given the photograph of the 133rd Saxon Regiment's pre-war football team, this was plainly intended as a signal honour. On Christmas Day itself an officer of a Highland Regiment found himself deep in conversation with a keen German sportsman – a 'great big sergeant' – whose main regret seemed to be that the war had spoilt his football:

> He toured Britain last year with the Leipzig team and beat Glasgow Celtic 1–0. All day we walked to and fro with

newspapers and our little photographs, and parted regretting that it was our duty to go for each other.

But he continued:

We arranged . . . to have a 2-hour interval on Boxing Day from 2–4 p.m. for a football match. This, however, was prevented by our superiors at HQ.

This letter points to one definite fact: there is no question that football was discussed between British and Germans and the idea of playing a game was seriously canvassed – and not only at one point of the line. Most frequently, as in the letter already quoted, the proposal was to play on Boxing Day. Private Tapp wrote: 'We are trying to arrange a football match with them for tomorrow, Boxing Day'; this plan failed owing to the resumption of artillery fire the next morning. Lieutenant-Colonel Fisher-Rowe of 1/Grenadier Guards wrote on 27 December: 'They [the Germans] wanted to play the Kiddies [the 2/Scots Guards] at football yesterday but the Kiddies couldn't supply the ball.'

Perhaps the most determined initiative in this context came from the Commanding Officer of an Infantry Battalion (unfortunately no details as to his identity were supplied) whose letter was quoted in the *South Wales Echo* on 2 January 1915:

I said if they would have an armistice on New Year's Day we would play them at football between our lines.

In the afternoon at 3 p.m. our doctor thought he would go and see the Germans so boldly walked down the road to the trenches and talked to them. They were very full of the football idea of mine on New Year's Day. I said if they would like another armistice then I would turn out a team and play them among the shell-holes, and they were quite keen. Happily, there won't be any obstacles like dead Germans lying about unless they try on another attack before then. I wonder if it will come off?

There is no hint that this match happened either; indeed, apart from any other considerations, the break in the weather on the 27th would have made it virtually impossible.

Yet there are a sufficient number of references to games which allegedly took place for it to be difficult to believe that this is all smoke without fire; and, interestingly enough, most of the likely contenders happened on Christmas Day itself. Lieutenant Charles Brewer of 2/Bedfordshires wrote in a contemporary letter: 'Higher up in the line – you would scarcely believe it – they are playing a football match.' In a brief contemporary diary, Gunner C. L. B. Burrows, of 104 Battery, 22nd Brigade, noted: 'Our infantry played a football match with them [the Saxons opposite] and exchanged cigarettes etc. in No Man's land.' It might well be argued that these two were hearsay reports, but in his account, the German Hugo Klemm wrote: 'Everywhere you looked the occupants from the trenches stood around talking to each other and even playing football.' Similarly Lieutenant Johannes Niemann, in the same regiment, implies first-hand experience in his account:

> Suddenly a Tommy came with a football, kicking already and making fun, and then began a football match. We marked the goals with our caps. Teams were quickly established for a match on the frozen mud, and the Fritzes beat the Tommies 3–2.

As it happens this score coincides precisely with that to be found in one of the first references to a football game in contemporary newspapers – in a Christmas Day letter by an anonymous major of the RAMC quoted in *The Times* on New Year's Day:

> The . . . Regiment actually had a football match with the
> Saxons, who beat them 3–2!!! [see page 299]

It must be admitted that this reference would be more
satisfactory if *The Times*'s sub-editors had been less coy with the
name of the major and the regiment.

To accept this evidence, however, is to fly in the face of
vigorous statements from impressive witnesses to whom the
idea of any kind of football game in No Man's Land was always
incredible. In a postwar memoir Private Alexander Runcie,
6/Gordon Highlanders, stated:

> Some chroniclers of the truce incident have claimed that a
> football match was played in no man's land; this is not the
> case as the shell-holes, ditch, barbed wire, and churned-up
> condition of this part of the ground rendered it impossible to
> do so.

Stories of kick-abouts with made-up footballs have tended
to strain the credulity of old soldiers somewhat less. A New
Year's Day letter in the *Manchester Guardian* from a British
officer referred to a football match with a bully-beef tin; and
the History of the Lancashire Fusiliers records that '"A" Company
played a football match against the enemy with an old tin for
a ball: they won 3–2!' Lance-Corporal George Ashurst was with
the Lancashire Fusiliers in the line at Christmas; his account
mentions no game with the Germans, however, though he
records that 'some of our boys tied up a sandbag and used it as
a football, while a party of Germans enjoyed themselves sliding
on a little frozen pond just in rear of their trench'. A former
member of the Kensingtons, on the other hand, G. Gilbert,
wrote in 1963:

Soon there were dozens of us fraternizing even to the extent of kicking a made-up football about in No Man's Land.

A letter of 28 December by Lance-Corporal Jack Quayle, of the Queen's Westminster Rifles, offers both an interesting football reference and a variant of the practice of pressing unlikely objects into service for sporting purposes. He stated that on Christmas morning sentries were re-posted as a precautionary measure because of the early morning fog: however, 'nothing happened and as the fog lifted they reported that the Germans were playing footer. We then climbed out at the back area armed with an entrenching tool haft and a jam tin and played rounders.'

Yet stories of actual footballs in the line *do* occur in convincing contemporary accounts and there seems no reason to doubt their evidence more than that in the other letters from the front which were rushed into print over the weeks following Christmas. Another member of the Queen's Westminster Rifles wrote, in a letter printed both in London and New York before the end of the year (in fact the earliest letter on the truce to be published):

> On Christmas Day we had a football out in front of the trenches and asked the Germans to send a team to play us but either they considered the ground too hard, as it had been freezing all night and was a ploughed field or their officers put the bar up.

The latter explanation seems the more likely as it is clear from Quayle's evidence quoted above that the Germans had been playing that very morning. Either way this account coincides well with Rifleman Leslie Walkinton's Boxing Day letter, in which he wrote:

> Some of them were trying to arrange a football match, but it didn't come off.

Given all the circumstances – the uneven, shell-pocked ground (which had at least been hardened by the recent frost), the crowds of men milling about, the difficulties of language – if, given all this, a football *had* suddenly appeared in No Man's Land, arguably the most likely outcome would not be a formal game with eleven men neatly attacking opposing goals, but a disorganized, untidy affair with everybody joining in as much or as little as they wanted to – one diversion among the others rather than a major event. An account along these lines emerged in 1983, when a former Territorial of 6/Cheshires, Ernie Williams, told his story of Christmas 1914 in a television interview. Williams was at Wulverghem, where, as he recalls it, No Man's Land was not as broken up by shell-fire as it was elsewhere:

> The ball appeared from somewhere, I don't know where, but it came from their side – it wasn't from our side that the ball came. They made up some goals and one fellow went in goal and then it was just a general kickabout. I should think there were about a couple of hundred taking part. I had a go at the ball. I was pretty good then, at nineteen. Everybody seemed to be enjoying themselves. There was no sort of ill-will between us . . . There was no referee, and no score, no tally at all. It was simply a mêlée – nothing like the soccer you see on television. The boots we wore were a menace – those great big boots we had on – and in those days the balls were made of leather and they soon got very soggy . . .

There is a contemporary letter which precisely confirms Williams's account – published in a local Cheshire newspaper and written by Sergeant-Major Naden of the same battalion, it states:

> We had a rare old jollification, which included football, in which the Germans took part.

A memoir by a Brigadier C. E. M. Richards, who in 1914 was serving as a Lieutenant in the 1/East Lancashires at Ploegsteert, provides an illuminating postscript to this discussion. He had watched askance as members of his battalion, including the CO, fraternized with the enemy, so he had been immensely relieved when everybody was back in trenches and, as he put it, 'the good old sniping started again – just to make sure that the war was still on'. The day's surprises, however, were not yet over:

> That evening I received a signal from Battalion Headquarters, telling me to make a football pitch in No Mans Land, by filling up shell-holes etc., and to challenge the enemy to a Football Match on the 1st January.
>
> I was furious and took no action at all. I wish I had kept that signal. Stupidly I destroyed it – I was so angry. It would now have been a good souvenir.
>
> The proposed match did not take place.

His story is significant in that it supports the argument that the ground between the lines was hardly fit for a serious game of football; it also shows that at one point at least there was a definite intention to mount a proper match on a genuinely level playing-field, while at the same time underlining the general rule that such ambitious ideas tended to be bright hopes that ultimately came to nothing.

☆

As the daylight began to fade there was a general exodus from No Man's Land. In the area occupied by the Queen's Westminsters an officer fired a Very light – a prearranged signal that men should return to their posts. 'Altogether we had a great day with our enemies,' wrote Rifleman P. H. Jones of the Queen's

Westminster Rifles in his diary, 'and parted with much hand-shaking and mutual goodwill.'

Sergeant Lovell of 3/Rifle Brigade, back in his trenches at dusk, hastened to describe all that had happened in a letter to his parents. He concluded:

> Even as I write I can scarcely credit what I have seen and done. This has indeed been a wonderful day.

Rifleman Eade of the same battalion returned to his lines much struck with a conversation which he had just concluded with a German bombardier who had lived for a time in London and spoke good English. As they parted the German said:

> Today we have peace. Tomorrow you fight for your country; I fight for mine – good luck.

Captain Armes, 1/North Staffs, was thoughtful as he returned to his trenches:

> I left our friends on Xmas Day in a quiet mood. I stood upon the parapet & had a final look round and not a shot was fired.

At the end of the day there was a friendly gesture from the Germans who had collaborated with the Scots Guards and other battalions in the joint burial service in No Man's Land. Earlier, George Paynter, the 2/Scots Guards' CO, had presented one German officer with a scarf as a token of gratitude for his care of the wounded. 'That same evening', wrote Hulse, 'a German orderly came to the halfway line, and brought a pair of warm, woolly gloves as a present in return for George.' The donor was Major Thomas, who had just received them as a Christmas gift.

There was a burst of singing opposite 2/Border Regiment when the Germans struck up with 'God Save the King', in 'as good English as they could'. The Tommies gave three cheers in return:

> So we all had a good sing-song that night in our trenches.
> But we did not forget to have our lookout as I do not think
> we became friends.

In some areas there was a swift return to normality. The 2/Devons had had a very relaxed Christmas Day, they had been 'walking about on top of the trenches', as Sergeant William Williamson recorded, 'as if no War was on'. The Germans had 'played the game' and there had been no firing. But suddenly the mood changed:

> When darkness came on, we had the order, Strictest discipline
> to be carried out during the night, and each man stood at
> his post, in dead silence. We only fired 24 rounds during
> the night, and that was at a German who got as far as our
> barbed wire, I fancy he must have been under the influence
> of drink.

Rifleman Bernard Brookes, of the Queen's Westminster Rifles, concluded his account of Christmas Day on an even more sombre note:

> The Germs wanted to continue a partial truce until New Year,
> for as some of them said, they were heartily sick of the war,
> and did not want to fight; but as we were to leave the trenches
> next morning, and naturally did not want them to know, we
> insisted on the truce ending at Midnight, at which time our
> artillery sent over to them four shells of small calibre to let
> them know that the truce, at which the whole World would
> wonder, was ended, and in its place, Death and Bloodshed
> would once more reign supreme.

Fortunately, over much of the line the truce had a long way

yet to run, but this was not the only sector to hear that night the all too familiar booming of the guns.

☆

One German account of a fraternization which merits inclusion but which is difficult to accommodate with the known disposition of British forces is that included in the Official History of the 143rd Infantry Regiment. They were in trenches at Hill 59, just to the south of the more famous Hill 60, but approximately two miles to the north of the most northerly units of the British 3rd Division, in what was at this time essentially a French-held sector. Nevertheless the writer, named as Reserve Lieutenant Meinicke, clearly had no doubt that the enemy with whom he and his comrades fraternized were British – or, as he described them, English. Unfortunately he offered no more precise identification. Any question mark there might be, however, over who precisely fraternized with whom does not affect the nature and quality of the experience. His brief but moving description reads as follows:

On the second day of Christmas [i.e. Christmas Day] 1914 there was a little armistice between us and the enemy. A comrade of our company held a sign over the parapet with the inscription '*Fröhliche Weihnachten*' (Merry Christmas). The English immediately responded in like manner. An English soldier shouted to us in perfect German, asking if we wanted to remove the dead between the lines. (There were about fifty to sixty in front of our position at that time.) After a short deliberation we came to an agreement and some of our men climbed over the parapet, as also did some of the English. Afterwards the Englishmen asked us to sing some Christmas songs. Things soon became very animated on both front lines. As a precaution some of our troops held their machine-guns at the ready. An English soldier came towards us and exchanged cigarettes and chocolate. The sight of opposing troops chatting to each other along a stretch of several hundred metres was a very strange one. As darkness fell both sides went back to their trenches and recommenced hostilities.

Such attempts at fraternization can hardly have been approved of by the High Command; they remain, however, a wonderful testament to the human spirit [see page 299].

☆

Rifleman A. E. Watts, of the Queen's Westminster Rifles, in the same letter in which he enthusiastically described his Christmas lunch in the trenches, concluded on a more reflective note:

> It sounds hardly feasible that one day you go and shake hands with the enemy, and the next, if he shows his head above the trench, you try and pierce him with a bullet.
>
> Perhaps it was just as well our battalion came out the next morning. Somehow it seemed to alter the feelings of one towards the Germans. We have no bitter feelings like the French and Belgians. I very much doubt if they would have done such a thing as we did.

A similar thought was expressed by Private George Martin, 4/Seaforth Highlanders:

> You would not find French and Germans exchanging cigar-ettes, I think, even if it were the morning of Judgment Day. You have only to mention '*allemands*' [French for Germans] to a Frenchman to learn that all the hatred is not confined to Germany.

Yet, as has already been shown, there were a number of incidents of seasonal friendliness involving the French and

Belgians on Christmas Eve, and the same was true of Christmas Day itself. Likewise there were also outbreaks of bitter and unseasonal violence.

For the Belgian soldier who had attended midnight mass to the sound of gunfire, there was an astonishing change by the following morning:

> Now I am going to tell you something which you will think incredible, but I give you my word that it is true. At dawn the Germans displayed a placard over the trenches on which was written 'Happy Christmas' and then, leaving their trenches, unarmed, they advanced towards us singing and shouting 'Comrades!' No one fired. We also had left our trenches and, separated from each other only by the half-frozen Yser, we exchanged presents. They gave us cigars, and we threw them some chocolate. Thus almost fraternizing we passed all the morning.
>
> Unlikely, indeed, but true. I saw it, but thought I was dreaming. They asked us to spend Christmas without firing, and the whole day passed without any fighting. At 8 o'clock in the evening we were relieved by other soldiers and returned to the rear without being disturbed.
>
> Was it not splendid? Think you that we were wrong? We have been criticized here; it is said that we ought to have fired. But would it not have been dastardly? And then, why kill one another on such a festival day?

Robert de Wilde, Captain Commandant of Belgian Artillery, who had attended midnight mass in a barn at Pervyse, within sight of the flares fired by the Germans from their trenches, witnessed nothing unusual on Christmas Day on his front but recorded a memorable fraternization at nearby Dixmude, where the Germans and the Belgians were dug in on opposite banks of the river Yser. Sixty unarmed Germans emerged from their lines and sang carols, asked for a one-day's truce, and threw across the river one of the treasures from the collegiate church of Dixmude – which they had previously purloined – as a pledge of good faith. 'They have also thrown chocolate to us,' wrote de Wilde. 'We have responded with cigars, and the festival of Christmas has momentarily united in the same emotion enemies of yesterday and tomorrow.'

As for the French front, that the Bavarians of I Corps in the vicinity of Arras were 'much inclined to fraternize with the French' found its way into the journal of the British Commander-in-Chief, while the War Diary of the French 139th Infantry Brigade then stationed near Ablain, St Nazaire in Artois, recorded another example of Bavarians and *poilus* striking up friendly relations. Its Christmas Day entry read:

> No activity at all on the part of the enemy.
>
> During the night and in the course of today, the 25th, communications, strictly frowned upon by the authorities, have been established between the French and the Bavarians and from trench to trench (with conversations, the sending by the enemy of friendly messages, cigarettes, etc. . . . There have even been visits to the German trenches).

For the 56th Infantry Brigade, however, near Foucaucourt in Picardy, the day began in peace, but ended with a particularly harsh return to the normality of trench warfare:

> A calm day; a completely spontaneous truce is established along the whole front in this sector, notably at the two extremities, where French and German soldiers come out here and there from the trenches to exchange newspapers and cigarettes.
>
> However the General Commanding our Division decides to ward off an expected underground attack so our sappers

proceed to place a charge of 800 kilos of powder under the German advanced trench.

At 23.00 hours everything is ready for the explosion, the order to light the fuse is given, but there being a misfire, the operation is recommenced and the explosion takes place at 23.45.

Immediately a detachment rushes forward to take possession of the crater and exploit the incident, but the enemy being on the alert, greets them with rocket flares, hand grenades and above all rifle fire. Finally they execute a counter-attack and our detachment withdraws with some difficulty, using the bayonet.

Another account tells of a joint burial in which the French 29th Regiment was involved, but which was characterized by a much less cordial atmosphere than that which prevailed in similar episodes on the British front:

The meeting was an awkward one, as the French came out with shovels while the Germans brought cigars. After a French corporal had shaken hands with a German, salutes and cigars were exchanged, the bodies collected and buried, the men returned in silence, and in the evening firing began again.

Instances of Germans emerging from their trenches to propose a Christmas cease-fire only to be met by a hail of bullets, as took place at certain points in the British sector, occurred on the French front too. *La Gazette de France* of 10 January reported an event in the Rheims–Verdun area:

On Christmas Day the Germans left their trenches shouting 'Two days' truce!' Their ruse did not succeed. Almost all of them were shot down by an immediate fusillade.

Yet there were also friendlier episodes. The German 1/Garde-Grenadier Regiment was stationed near Puisieux, in the region which would become famous a year and a half later as the battlefield of the Somme – at this stage of the war a relatively untroubled sector. Grenadier Thimian of No. 2 Company wrote in his diary:

> Up to the afternoon of Christmas Day it was remarkably quiet and then something happened which I shall never forget. I was on guard duty when I saw a Frenchman climbing out of his trench. I had just taken aim when I suddenly noticed that someone had climbed out from our side too. The two of them walked slowly and stealthily towards each other and shook hands. They were followed by several others from their side and ours. The French looked ill-fed and poorly clothed and almost all of them were old. They begged for tobacco. We chatted for about 45 minutes and then everybody went quietly back to their trenches.

One other incident of Franco-German fraternization had an unusual twist to it. A Mannheim newspaper published a postcard from a German soldier in Flanders which was subsequently printed in the *New York Herald* under the headline: FRENCH AND GERMANS AGREE TO TRUCE IN TRENCHES: BAR BRITONS. Following a suggestion from the French that some German dead lying between the trenches should be buried, some twenty men of both sides, including a French and a German officer, gathered in No Man's Land:

> There was general handshaking; the dead were buried; cigars, cigarettes and newspapers were exchanged and a general celebration ensued. Then the Frenchmen suggested that we shoot no longer, promised that they themselves would not resume hostilities in that event. But they added: 'Beat those Britishers.

We have no use for them.' Well, we gladly agreed to this. Again there was handshaking, arms were resumed, and everybody crawled back to his trench. It was peace in the midst of war.

It should be added that this story was not published in Britain.

Chapter Seven

Boxing Day

At the front men woke with the memories of their unusual Christmas Day still fresh in their minds. 'I wouldn't have missed the experience of yesterday', wrote one soldier on Boxing Day, 'for the most gorgeous Christmas dinner in England.' It was an attitude shared by many.

But the story was by no means over. Boxing Day also was to have its range of curious incidents as the armies began the process – brief in some sectors, remarkably long-lasting in others – of going back to war. Private Tapp was up late, at 7.40: *'had to be called too'*, he noted in his diary, 'as the officer was waiting for his breakfast.' A glance towards No Man's Land showed that things were much as they had been:

> I am surprised to see the Germans and our fellows still walking on top. It's too ridiculous for words, we are all mixing up again.

Soon, however, there was the first hint of a return to routine warfare:

> 8.40 a.m. one of our Officers tells them to get back in their trenches as our artillery are going to shell them at 9 a.m. Some of them say 'we will get in your trenches we shall be safer'. This will stop the football match. Shells are exchanged for a

few hours but we all stand up at intervals, no fear of being shot with a bullet. Of course our artillery are a long way from us, same as theirs is from them, so they know nothing about our little holiday.

By the river Lys, the senior officers of the 2/Royal Welch Fusiliers had also decided that the time had come to recommence hostilities. There was, however, no hasty recourse to machine-gun or rifle fire. Everything was done with studied decorum. At 8.30 a.m. Captain Stockwell fired three shots in the air, had a 'flag', as he called it, put up with 'Merry Christmas' on it, and climbed on to the parapet. The Germans responded with a sheet with 'Thank you' on it, after which the German captain also emerged into full view. The two officers bowed, saluted, then got down into their respective trenches; the German captain fired two shots in the air and the war was on again.

In fact, hostilities were only notionally resumed. As Private Frank Richards described it:

During the whole of Boxing Day we never fired a shot, and they the same, each side seemed to be waiting for the other to set the ball a-rolling. One of their men shouted across in English and inquired how we had enjoyed the beer. We shouted back and told him it was very weak but that we were very grateful for it. We were conversing off and on during the whole of the day.

There was much uncertainty in both camps on Boxing Day as to the other side's intentions. It was plain that there was a widespread if only half-admitted reluctance to begin fighting again. It was also clear that many had no desire to harm the men with whom they had been on such good terms. In the case of the 1/North Staffs, when the 107th Saxon Regiment opposite gave formal notice of their intention to discontinue the truce, they accompanied it with a friendly warning so that nobody should actually get hurt. As the British Regiment's Official History recorded:

> Shortly after 'Stand down' next morning 'C' Company Commander was informed that a German officer wished to speak to him in No Man's Land. On going out he found a very polite and spotless individual awaiting him, who, after an exchange of compliments, informed him that his Colonel had given orders for a renewal of hostilities at mid-day and might the men be warned to keep down, please? 'C' Company Commander thanked the German officer for his courtesy, whereupon, saluting and bowing from the waist, he replied, 'We are Saxons; you are Anglo Saxons; word of a gentleman is for us as for you.' The troops were duly warned to keep down, but just before hostilities were due to re-open a tin was thrown into 'A' Company's lines with a piece of paper in it bearing the inscription, 'We shoot to the air' and sure enough at the appointed hour a few vague shots were fired high over the trenches. Then all was quiet again and the unofficial truce continued.

The 107th was in XIX Saxon Corps, in one of whose regiments there was almost a mutiny when the order was given to resume hostilities. Vize-Feldwebel Lange told the story to the Australian Ethel Cooper when on leave in Leipzig and she recorded it in a letter to her sister:

> The difficulty began on the 26th, when the order to fire was given, for the men *struck*. Herr Lange says that in the accumulated years he had never heard such language as the officers indulged in, while they stormed up and down, and got, as the only result, the answer, 'We can't – they are good fellows, and we can't.' Finally, the officers turned on the men with, 'Fire,

or we do – and not at the *enemy*!' Not a shot had come from
the other side, but at last they fired, and an answering fire
came back, but not a man fell. 'We spent that day and the
next', said Herr Lange, 'wasting ammunition in trying to shoot
the stars down from the sky.'

As agreed, the 1/Royal Irish Rifles near Laventie had ended
their truce with the Germans at midnight on Christmas Day
with the firing of a single revolver shot. A party of Germans
who had come across towards 'B' Company's trench just before
midnight had been peremptorily ordered back. But Boxing Day
found the atmosphere on the front very relaxed. As their battalion
War Diary noted: 'The Germans throughout the morning
appeared to have *no intention* of opening fire on us.'

One of the numerous battalions which had collaborated with
the Germans on Christmas Day in a joint burial was 2/Queens.
They had buried their own fallen on 20 December (see page
55), but their main task on Christmas Day was to bury the dead
of their sister battalion, the 2/Royal Warwicks, which was now
out of the line in billets; the Queens' War Diary notes that, '71
bodies were collected chiefly Warwicks'. However, the task had
been abandoned unfinished at 4 p.m. and it had been agreed
that the work should resume next morning. The battalion's
diary entry for Boxing Day is particularly interesting because
it offers clear evidence that this action was fully supported on
the German side in that members of the Staff came to observe.
Indeed, they came also to make their own special gesture of
goodwill. Several had appeared on Christmas Day but now there
were many more:

> 26 Dec. Armistice re-commenced as arranged at 9.0 a.m. A
> large number of Staff Officers appeared during the day – all
> were immaculately dressed without a speck of mud on them,

mostly in fur-lined coats. They furnished us with a list of officers lately taken prisoner and asked that their relatives might be informed. They also promised to try and obtain the release of 2nd Lieut Rought and Walmisley, who had been taken prisoners during the armistice on the 19th inst. Owing to frost the ground was very hard and the graves were not completed till 1.0 p.m. when the chaplain read the burial service, in the presence of the digging party, some officers of the Queens and 8 or 10 German officers. The body of 2nd Lieut Bernard, Royal Warwicks, was found and buried. In addition to the 55th Regt men of 7th, 15th and 22nd Regts were noticed. Armistice concluded at 3.30 p.m.

Some had their first experience of the Christmas truce on Boxing Day. Second Lieutenant Cyril Drummond, Royal Field Artillery, had been out on rest until late on Christmas evening. Shortly after breakfast, he and his telephonist set off from their artillery lines to take up their duties in an observation post which they had established in a ruined house at St Yvon, just to the north of Ploegsteert Wood. As they walked down the road towards the front they were confronted by an amazing sight:

> Looking down towards the trenches it was just like Earls Court Exhibition. There were the two sets of front trenches only a few yards apart, and yet there were soldiers, both British and German, standing on top of them, digging or repairing the trench in some way, without ever shooting at each other. It was an extraordinary situation. And so my telephonist and I walked down the sunken road in full view of everybody in Germany, with no one taking any notice of us.

Within minutes Drummond was out in No Man's Land conversing and exchanging souvenirs. After a while, having brought his camera with him, he rounded up a group of friendly enemies and took a photograph (see illustration 31).

Another newcomer to the truce on Boxing Day was Second Lieutenant John Wedderburn-Maxwell, also of the Royal Field Artillery, who had come up to the front near Fauquissart from the artillery lines the previous evening when the day's proceedings were over. His fellow officers' account of what had taken place left him, as he said in a letter to his father, 'terribly jealous of having missed such an experience', and determined to make up for it at the earliest opportunity. A first foray beyond the wire ended when a heavy battery of British artillery, after shooting into some building some way behind the German lines, suddenly reduced the range and dropped a round into a German trench not far away:

> I thought this would stir them all up and made a dash for our trench and into it like a rabbit, but the 'Allemands' didn't seem to mind tho' they went to ground for a few minutes and appeared again later.

About midday he walked across open ground to the battalion headquarters of the Royal Irish Rifles, to have lunch with the Colonel, noting as he did so that 'our people and theirs still seemed quite friendly'. So in the afternoon he made up his mind if at all possible 'to hold a conversation with a Boche'.

> Taking a tin of cigarettes I set out along our trenches with a corporal from the Battery (who happened to be up here and wanted to come badly). I made my way through the barbed wire in front of our trenches and when about halfway across waved to some of them in front to come over, upon which two came to meet us and four more rolled up later. One was a German–American who could talk fair English. I gave them cigarettes and was given a box of tobacco which I will send

home as a souvenir of what is probably the most extraordinary event of the whole war – a soldier's truce without any higher sanction by officers and generals, with firing going on to the right and rather further away to the left. We strolled up and down for about ½ hour, shook hands, said goodbye, saluted and returned to our lines.

Second Lieutenant Dougan Chater was also out in No Man's Land on Boxing Day. There was another parley in the middle, and more exchanging of autographs and cigarettes. Photographs were taken; and it was on this occasion that the Gordons and the Germans made provisional arrangements for another truce on New Year's Day, 'as the Germans wanted to see how the photographs came out'. Chater also took advantage of the truce and the beautiful weather to take several walks along the line. 'It is difficult to realize what this means,' he wrote, 'but of course in the ordinary way there is not a sign of life above ground.'

Private Tapp too was out walking:

I take a stroll to a cottage near their trenches where neither side dare go at ordinary times. I am out after coal, meet a few Germans on the way, they have come to buy one of our army knives. I don't want to sell mine so we exchange coins, I have got 3, also five rounds of ammunition, I give one pkt of cigarettes get cigars in return, then I go for the coal, a German comes in with a bag to get some too, he helps me fill my bag so it was only polite to help him fill his, it didn't take long to clear all the coal out of that cottage . . . we could not have done that last time we were here, one fire would have caused vollies [sic] to be sent over.

Even in areas where there had been hard fighting up to Christmas Boxing Day was relatively peaceful. When to the north of Givenchy, two platoons of the Cameron Highlanders came under sniper fire while digging support trenches well out of sight of the Germans, the cause was traced to the fact that the Berkshires to their front were amusing themselves holding up caps as targets for German marksmen to fire at. Here and there, however, more hostile gunfire claimed its victims. The 2/Seaforths had one man wounded on Boxing Day – the same Corporal Ferguson, 'Fergie', who had been a ringleader in the fraternization of Christmas Eve. Boxing Day, in fact, was to be his last day as a fighting soldier. He described what happened:

> 26 December – They have not fired yet, but the artillery have been busy, and they have the range of our trench; they have started shelling on the right; word is passed along for our section to retire to reserve trenches. I had just left my mud hut to carry out the order; the last shell I noticed had smashed our telephone wires, and the next shell I didn't know was going to strike me – but it did!
>
> Result: arm amputated at elbow and shrapnel wound in thigh. In all I had six pieces of shrapnel and two bullets removed from me; but I know it was not our new-made friends the Bavarians who shot me, but the artillery of the Prussians – 'The dogs.'

Ferguson's story should not be left at this point, however; his account was dictated in hospital in Nottingham soon after his return home. 'I am at present in DRI (Derbyshire Royal Infirmary),' he wrote, in the final paragraph of his remarkable story, 'and words fail me in trying to express my appreciation of the attentions and kindness of our Sister and nurses.' He later married the nurse to whom he dictated his story.

☆

On the evening of Boxing Day, General Smith-Dorrien went down to the trenches. He had already issued, on Christmas Day itself, a stern document signed by his Chief of Staff pointing out that his instruction of 5 December on the subject of the maintenance of the offensive spirit and the avoidance of military lethargy had 'not received sufficient attention' (see page 43). So it must be presumed that he was not expecting to be overly impressed when only the next day he made his random checks at two points in the line. The subsequent 'confidential memorandum' to all the commanders of II Corps was signed by Smith-Dorrien himself and pulled no punches. He was, he wrote, 'considerably disappointed with the state of affairs I found' and, 'generally speaking, was struck by the apathy of everything I saw'; only the Field Companies of the Royal Engineers – 'for whom I have nothing but praise' – escaped castigation. It was perhaps fortunate for the units he visited that they were not engaged in fraternizing; but when he got back to his headquarters he was further incensed to hear that such strictly forbidden activities had indeed been taking place. His memorandum ended:

> I would add that, on my return, I was shown a report from one section of how, on Christmas Day, a friendly gathering had taken place of Germans and British on the neutral ground between the two lines, recounting that many officers had taken part in it. This is only illustrative of the apathetic state we are gradually sinking into, apart also from illustrating that any orders I issue on the subject are useless, for I have issued the strictest orders that on no account is intercourse to be allowed between the opposing troops. To finish this war quickly, we must keep up the fighting spirit and do all we can to discourage friendly intercourse.
>
> I am calling for particulars as to names of officers and units

who took part in this Christmas gathering, with a view to disciplinary action.

News of the truce had spread in other directions as well. The 2/Royal Welch Fusiliers, after fraternizing with the enemy and, as we have seen, drinking looted French beer, were relieved on the evening of Boxing Day by the 2/Durham Light Infantry. According to Frank Richards they told the Welshmen that the French 'had heard how we had spent Christmas day and were saying all manner of nasty things about the British Army':

> Going through Armentières that night some of the French women were standing in the doors spitting and shouting at us: 'You no bon, you English soldiers, you boko kamerade Allemenge.' We cursed them back until we were blue in the nose . . .

There was one more flurry of excitement at the front before Boxing Day ended. A German deserter crossed to the trenches of the Kensingtons with the news that there was to be an attack that night at 12.15 a.m. The Kensingtons were in process of pulling out to their billets at Laventie, but had to return immediately to the front where, as their War Diary put it, 'we lay in a field most of the night, but nothing happened'. The artillery in the whole area opened up on the enemy's trenches and the area beyond at 11.15 p.m. and many units found themselves on full alert, but there was no response or movement of any kind on the part of the Germans. The anger which this episode aroused among the British was reflected strongly in the accounts of some of those who found their Boxing Day peace thus brusquely disturbed. Second Lieutenant J. D. Wyatt, of 2/Yorks, had been attempting to cut a ditch with a working party all day:

Saturday Dec. 26th

. . . Back after a long day at this pursuit, and turned out soon after got into bed. 'Stand to!' Ready at a moment's notice. No end of guns firing. Perhaps Germans attack.

Sunday Dec. 27th

After messing about 3 hours were told to stay in billets ready dressed, so lay down as I was. Had a very uncomfortable night & hear the whole thing was 'wind up' pure & simple. Sickening! Last night in billets spoilt.

Lieutenant-Colonel Lothian Nicholson, commanding officer of the 2/East Lancs, reacted with similar asperity, having lain down in a wet ploughed field for an hour and only got his men under cover at 3 a.m. Commenting later on what he called 'this fuss', he wrote:

It was never ascertained whether there was ever any real intention of attack. Possibly the man was sent over purposely so that the Hun Command, by means of their spies behind the lines, could find out what steps we took to reinforce the line.

It was perhaps fortunate for the German who had sparked off all this activity that he was picked up by the Kensingtons and not by the more volatile soldiers of 1/Royal Irish Rifles next to them. They too had been on their way out to billets and had taken most unkindly to a dismal night in the open waiting for an attack that never came. Their War Diary commented caustically:

The deserter who caused the alarm on the night 26th–27th *unfortunately* did not fall into the Battn's hands.

In fact, the anticipated onslaught on the British lines appears to have been a figment of the German deserter's imagination.

The next morning Hulse, seeing some of his men laughing with a group of Germans, went out to find what was amusing them and found that they were discussing the false alarm of the previous night. The enemy too, he discovered, had spent many long, dark hours on full alert, not because they were preparing to attack but because of the furious cannonade from the British artillery, which convinced them that the *British* were about to advance against the *German* lines. 'They assured me', wrote Hulse, 'that they had heard nothing of an attack and I fully believe them, as it is inconceivable that they would have allowed us to put up the formidable obstacles which we had [on the two previous nights] if they had contemplated an offensive movement.'

Chapter Eight

'The Long Truce is Broken'

The bracing weather which had provided so appropriate a setting for the events of Christmas now began to change. A sprinkling of snow had fallen on Boxing Day itself but after dark it turned to sleet and by the morning of the 27th the front was back in the grip of the usual, soaking Flanders rain. After their dreary night alert the 1/Royal Irish Rifles, in billets in Laventie, spent their first day out of the line making up for lost sleep and scraping mud from their boots, uniforms and guns.

Major Buchanan-Dunlop, still in the line, wrote that day to his wife:

> Last night turned very wet and unpleasant . . . The mud was *awful*, 'knee-deep' doesn't look formidable when written down, but in reality it's pretty bad. My subaltern, six feet high, stuck so fast that he had to be pulled out by his men.

Once the rain returned, it continued. A violent storm with thunder, hail and very high winds fell on the Western Front on the night of 28–29 December. The trenches were never to be in worse condition. Early in the New Year Hulse would be informing his mother, not without some glee:

In one of our communication trenches which is deeper than
most, 11 ft 6 in, the water has now attained the astounding
and almost comic depth of nine feet!

But flooding, as ever, produced mud and mud was never a
laughing matter. The ghastly conditions of the Third Battle of
Ypres, when drowning in mud became a common occurrence,
were almost three years ahead, but even in this first winter of
the war it claimed its victims. In mid-January 1915 General
Smith-Dorrien noted in his diary:

Two unfortunate Cameron Highlanders disappeared in a
morass, one was never found and the other died on being
recovered. I am afraid that a young officer of the RFA has also
been lost in the same way.

So the weather was back to 'business as usual' and so too in
many areas was the war. There would not be a great deal of
activity on the British front for some time, and no large-scale
fighting until the Battle of Neuve Chapelle in March 1915, but
for many units the truce was now behind them, beginning its
process of slipping back into history. Yet in certain sectors the
mood inspired by the events of Christmas lingered on with
incredible stubbornness. Some German regiments continued to
show themselves remarkably eager to maintain their friendly
relations with the British, while the British for their part were
prepared to go along with them, either arguing military
advantage (as in the matter of improving trenches) or openly
admitting that they were happy to have the threat of snipers'
bullets and random artillery fire temporarily withdrawn.

There were two main areas where the truce took root. To the
north of the British line, Ploegsteert Wood was already beginning to confirm its reputation as a relatively 'cushy' sector. It

was during this period that much work was carried out on constructing a line of breastworks in the wood, which was dubbed the 'Tourist Line' because it was a safe show-piece for visitors. To the south of Armentières, the region of Rue du Bois, Fleurbaix and Laventie – also to have a benign reputation throughout the war – continued extremely quiet. There were friendly episodes in other areas, and occasional casualties in these areas but, by and large, in spite of some stern attempts to tell the enemy the truce could not continue, there was to be peace and goodwill here for some considerable time – in some cases well into January, in certain other cases into February and even March.

☆

That it was possible for the truce to continue openly in this way inevitably raises an important question not yet discussed: what was the attitude of the High Command (in particular the British High Command) to the Christmas truce?

It was a common assumption of the men at the front that the 'top brass' would be automatically against any gesture of friendship towards the enemy – or, indeed, any accommodation with him of any kind. 'It is one of the fundamental rules of soldiering that you don't fraternize,' commented Leslie Walkinton over sixty years later, adding, in relation to Christmas 1914, that 'it made us all roar with laughter to think of the generals going purple in the face' at the thought of Tommy and Fritz meeting together between their trenches. Writing on Christmas Day itself Private Tapp confided to his diary: 'I don't know what our General would say if he knew about this.' Bruce Bairnsfather wrote of his parleys with the Germans: 'A sort of feeling that the authorities on both sides were not very enthusiastic about this fraternizing seemed to creep across the gathering.' And certainly this was the attitude of General Sir Horace Smith-Dorrien, who condemned the whole affair in precisely the terms that most ordinary soldiers would have expected. Nor would the average Tommy have quarrelled with Smith-Dorrien's statement in his personal diary where, after expressing his great annoyance at the truce, he wrote: 'War to the knife is the only way to carry on a campaign of this sort.'

Field Marshal Sir John French reacted with similar exasperation but, ruminating on the event later, called to question his own initial response. He wrote in his book *1914*:

> When this [i.e. the fraternization] was reported to me I issued immediate orders to prevent any recurrence of such conduct, and called the local commanders to strict account, which resulted in a good deal of trouble.
>
> I have since often thought deeply over the principle involved in the manifestation of such sentiments between hostile armies in the field. I am not sure that, had the question of the agreement upon an armistice for the day been submitted to me, I should have dissented from it.
>
> I have always attached the utmost importance to the maintenance of that chivalry in war which has almost invariably characterized every campaign of modern times in which this country has been engaged.

And he went on to describe his own experience at Christmas in the Boer War:

> I was in charge of the operations against General Beyers in the Western Transvaal during the latter part of December 1900. On the afternoon of Christmas Eve a flag of truce – that symbol of civilization and chivalry in war which has been practically unknown during this war with Germany – appeared at our outposts, and a young Dutch officer was brought to my Headquarters carrying a request from Beyers regarding the burial of his dead.

Some important movements were then in progress, and I told him we must of necessity detain him there till the next day, but I hoped we would be able to make him as comfortable as possible. When he started back to his General on Christmas morning I gave him a small box of cigars and a bottle of whisky, asking him to present them to Beyers as a Christmas offering from me.

I had forgotten the incident when a few days later, two cavalry soldiers who had been taken prisoners by the enemy marched back into camp with horses, arms and equipment complete. They brought me a note from Beyers, thanking me for my gift on Christmas Day and telling me that, although he had no whisky or cigars to offer in return, he hoped I would regard his liberation of these men in the light of a Christmas gift . . .

In the swift and kaleidoscopic changes which occur in world politics, the friend of today may be the enemy of tomorrow. Soldiers should have no politics, but should cultivate a freemasonry of their own and, emulating the knights of old, should honour a brave enemy only second to a comrade, and like them rejoice to split a friendly lance today and ride boot to boot in the charge tomorrow.

One senior commander who had very strong ideas indeed on the subject of relations with the enemy and who was determined that there should be no concessions in his sector was Major-General J. A. L. Haldane, GOC of 3rd Division. He had been in Manchuria during the Russo-Japanese War of 1904–5 and had noted the risks of a slackening of endeavour during periods of military stalemate. As far back as September 1914, at the time of the first entrenchment on the Aisne, he had insisted (as he would later put it in his autobiography) on 'an aggressive policy – that is to say, no opportunity should be lost for inflicting casualties on our opponent and not yielding to the temptation to adopt a pacific attitude or . . . to fraternise with him'. Three months later he had taken similar action:

> As Christmas approached, aware that the Germans paid more attention to that season than ever we do, I issued orders with the object of discouraging any approach to friendly overtures in the front-line between our men and theirs. I had procured the report of Lord Bryce's committee on the atrocities committed in Belgium towards the inhabitants of that State and had issued several copies to the troops so that they might not forget the brutal kind of enemy to whom they were opposed. I had no fear of weakness as regards the behaviour of the Scottish and Irish soldiers, but their more tender-hearted and forgetful comrades of the southern kingdom could not be trusted to exhibit the proper attitude. On my front, therefore, no fraternisation took place.

If any comment was made by General Sir Douglas Haig it appears not to have survived – though it is important to add that there was very little fraternization at Christmas on the front held by his I Corps. (He would be much more concerned with such fraternizations as occurred at Christmas 1915, by which time he would be Commander-in-Chief.) However, Lieutenant-General Sir Henry Rawlinson in command of IV Corps made a number of references to the truce, both officially and privately, which are far less condemnatory than might have been anticipated. In a report on operations in his Corps area between 22 and 31 December he stated:

> On the occasion of Christmas overtures were made on the German side for an informal armistice. These were not entertained on the section held by the 8th Division. An informal armistice on the 26th and 27th was, however, agreed to by the GOC, 7th Division, both in order to bury the large numbers

of dead still lying between the lines as a consequence of the attacks of the 18th December, and also to make better progress with the urgent task of clearing the rivière des Layes and the drainage ditches.

It is true that in this official document his comments were only about the military aspects of the armistice, but he also noted the events of Christmas Day in his personal diary without anything approaching Smith-Dorrien's exasperation.

Merville Dec. 27th

There has been a certain friendliness between our men and the Germans in the trenches – Xmas day was looked on mutually as a peace day and both sides went out freely in front of their trenches and buried the dead which were still lying out in the fire-swept zone – Germans looked very clean and smart – Put on their best clean clothes for the occasion I fancy – They conversed freely and exchanged cigarettes – I am rather suspicious of them – But many of them expressed themselves as heartily sick of the war and anxious to get home to their wives and families.

The only action he took, in fact, was to send one of his staff officers to collect the details of what had happened on the front occupied by 7th Division. More, it is noteworthy that Rawlinson was still writing in his diary about the continuance of friendly relations between the Germans and some of the units of 7th Division as late as 10 January 1915 and doing so without any hint of disapproval. (It should be noted, however, that he was wrong in his claim that fraternization had not occurred in front of 8th Division. Of twelve battalions in the line in this division six actively fraternized, and five observed some sort of truce.)

Major-General Thompson Capper, commanding 7th Division, was plainly at one with Rawlinson in taking a pragmatic attitude. In his report on operations in IV Corps during the period 22–29 December, he commented:

> Recently, I have purposely kept things rather quiet, as so much work has had to be done at close range from the enemy, that I could only carry it out by exercising a certain amount of forbearance.

At the lower level of brigadier-general, a similar view prevailed in some sectors: no conniving at fraternization, but a realistic use of the lull to improve what all commanders knew were very inadequate lines of defence. On 28 December 11th Brigade signalled to the 1/Somerset Light Infantry, the 1/East Lancs and the 1/Rifle Brigade at Ploegsteert:

> It appears that there is still cessation of hostilities in some parts of our line. The GOC [General Officer Commanding] trusts that you are availing yourself of any opportunity to strengthen our defences. He wishes me again to remind you not to allow the enemy near our defences.

There were German commanders who took the same view. In the Rue du Bois sector where at one point the lines were barely thirty yards apart any necessary labour would obviously be far better carried out with the enemy in tolerant rather than aggressive mood. It was here that the 107th Saxon Regiment had declared its intention to return to war only to resume the unofficial peace after a flurry of token fire. Honour satisfied, they then proceeded to get on with the task of trench improvements. This action was openly justified in the Official History of one of the other regiments in this corps:

> Because of heavy rain the conditions were intolerable and the position untenable. Army High Command were keen not to allow the position to deteriorate, and therefore allowed an

informal truce in this sector, so work could be carried on without hindrance.

That the generals grasped the practical advantages to be gained by the Christmas truce is the conclusion drawn by John Buchan in his *History of the Great War*:

> Possibly it was connived at by the commanders on both sides, for some of our trenches were nearly flooded, and the Germans had much timbering to do.

This view was endorsed by Graham Williams, who was there at the time and had thought much about the event since:

> Contrary to reports I have read regarding this truce, which state that it was only maintained by the rank and file of both sides, and that the officers were dead against it, the reverse was the case in our sector, where it was encouraged, by Brigade at least, if not by Division, and even higher. It enabled necessary work on our defences to be carried out in daylight, uninterrupted by machine-gun fire.

The ambivalent attitude of the generals to the truce inevitably led to some hesitation and lack of clarity in the manner in which it was dealt with. The Germans were more forthright than the British, and the sooner to react. By an army order of 29 December, all fraternization was forbidden, as were all approaches to the enemy in the trenches; all acts contrary to the order were to be punished as high treason. This strongly worded edict was publicized both in the German and the Allied press. By contrast, no parallel order on the British side was given such publicity and, indeed, no written order emanating from GHQ appears to have been preserved. The nearest surviving equivalent from a British source is an order of 1 January 1915 stating: 'Commander Second Army directs that informal understandings with enemy are to cease. Officers and NCOs allowing them are to be brought before a court martial.' This was, however, once again the inevitable Smith-Dorrien, now striding the wider stage of an army as opposed to a corps. The instruction was passed on as a routine order with little urgency on 2 January (see page 300).

In the event, despite Smith-Dorrien's instruction, it appears no one was penalized and no one court-martialled. The disciplinary action which he proposed to take subsequent to the reports of fraternizing which he heard on Boxing Day was not brought into effect. French's reference to calling the local commanders to 'strict account' as a result of which there was a 'good deal of trouble' seems to have been an exaggeration, in that no stories have survived of COs reprimanded, demoted or sent home. Only the unfortunate Kenny and Welchman of the 1/39 Garhwal Rifles seem to have suffered stoppage of leave; while by contrast the Commanding Officer of the 2/39th, Lieutenant-Colonel Drake-Brockman, and the Adjutant, Captain Berryman, were soon to be enjoying the sight of 'Blighty' so dear to all the British members of the Indian Corps after their long separation from home. On the whole, in fact, the fraternization left remarkably few victims of official displeasure at any level.

There remains the tradition, widely believed, that certain units were punished in some way for their participation by, for example, being taken out of the line as untrustworthy. There appears to be no evidence of this. The tradition is perhaps stronger still on the German side; but a specific story to the effect that certain Saxon regiments were sent to the Russian front for fraternizing has proved to be without foundation. Weeks later, according to their Regimental Histories, they were still in the same area of the Western Front; and at certain times during the next months they would find themselves opposite their 'friends' from Christmas Day.

But this is to anticipate.

☆

The rain which lashed down on 27 December, restoring the front to its usual dismal colours and its usual air of soaking desolation, failed to keep the Saxons who had been fraternizing with the 1/Leicesters in their own lines, as Major Buchanan-Dunlop told his wife:

> Such a curious situation has arisen on our left. The Saxons all today have been out of their trenches and had tea with our men halfway between the trenches. They only fire four shots a day. Our men were rather non-plussed, as owing to the friendly relations between the two parties they couldn't very well take them prisoner, when two of their officers and 70 men came into our trenches and have refused to return. They insist on staying.

Opposite the Scottish regiments of the 20th Brigade the Germans showed a similar enthusiasm for the truce to continue on the 27th:

> The Germans tried to come over and enjoy another day's so-called 'armistice' but were informed that they must keep in their trenches. They seemed to be quite indignant and said they wouldn't fire if we didn't, but if we had orders to fire to signal to them with three volleys first fired in the air.

But there was no firing and the quiescent mood lingered on. Lieutenant-Colonel Fisher-Rowe, whose 1/Grenadier Guards had been out of the line over Christmas and had now returned to his sector, relieving the 2/Scots Guards, wrote to his wife on the 27th:

> We are all very peaceful . . . [The Germans] say they want
> the truce to go on till after New Year and I am sure I have
> no objection. A rest from bullets will be distinctly a change.

On the 28th Hulse, in the comfort of his farm billet behind
the line, and prompted by the continuance of the cease-fire to
analyse what was happening, set down his explanation in a long
letter to his mother. The Germans were, he thought, 'pretty sick
of fighting and found the truce a welcome respite'; their keen-
ness to keep it going was shown by the fact that 'they made us
prolong it by continually coming to talk'. It was also significant
that 'they were the troops we had attacked, and some of them
expressed admiration for us, etc. and they had also suffered a
good deal by it and, one way and another, they were quite ready
to have a respite and to improve their own comforts and trenches
like us'. In addition, he detected what he called 'a deeper and
also fairly obvious reason', in that he saw the present lull as part
of an overall German strategy to hold the present situation in
France and Belgium, while deciding the main issue of the war
in the east. Such attacks as the Germans had made on the Western
Front lately 'have only been bluff, in order to make us believe
that they are still trying to advance here'. In support of this he
cited a falling-off of artillery fire in the past two months, and
an absence of shrapnel fire over the previous three weeks.
'However', he concluded, 'it is all very curious.'

Private Tapp of the 1/Royal Warwicks at Ploegsteert was
also puzzled by what was taking place and sought for explana-
tions:

> I can't understand the friendship between our fellows and the
> Germans. It may be they are short of ammunition, if so, it is
> a clever trick of theirs.

Others saw simpler and less subtle causes. Lance-Corporal Bell of the London Rifle Brigade spent part of the 28th in what was left of the roof of a bombarded house on sniper duty, 'but owing to the truce there is nothing to do. We can all see the fraternization going on.' On the 30th he commented in his diary:

> Truce continues; most amazing. Starting with the 'peace and goodwill' idea on Christmas Day, it was found so mutually pleasant and convenient that neither side, though keeping close watch, fires a shot.

It was also, some thought, practical common sense. Captain Maurice Mascall, of the Royal Garrison Artillery, wrote on 28 December:

> There is no sniping, and the men of both sides stand up and repair their parapets, and wave to each other, and sometimes make each other tea, and it is all most gentlemanly! Also it is very sensible, as this useless and annoying sniping can have no real effect on the progress of the campaign.

Lieutenant-Colonel Fisher-Rowe shared the same attitude:

> I don't think that they want to start more than we do as it only means a few of each side being hit and does not affect the end of the war.

The war had become so friendly at Ploegsteert that all warlike spirit seemed to have evaporated. On 29 December Captain Mascall came down from the artillery lines to do some drawing:

> Having said in my last letter that there were no birds in the wood, I saw *five* sitting in the same tree this morning. I was sketching in front of our line, when suddenly a German appeared at the window of a ruined house opposite me, waving a cigar box in his hand. He was followed by several others,

and then several of our men left their trenches, and the two parties advanced and met halfway. There was great saluting and bowing, and then an interchange of cigarettes, and then they separated with every mark of admiration.

Isn't this an extraordinary state of affairs! They seem to get more friendly every day, and Heaven knows how they will ever start fighting again.

On occasions the truce had to be temporarily broken when the appearance of some high-ranking commander on the German side required a token display of firing. True to the friendly spirit which prevailed the Germans informed the British in advance. Lance-Corporal Bell wrote in his diary on 30 December:

The other day the German CO opposite expected a visit from a general, and said he would be opening fire between 11 and 12, and we had better keep our heads down.

There was a similar event on the 30th itself, as Second Lieutenant J. D. Wyatt of the 2/Yorks commented:

Dec. 30th. Still no war! At about lunchtime however a message came down the line to say that the Germans had sent across to say that their General was coming along in the afternoon, so we had better keep down, as they might have to do a little shooting to make things look right!!! And this is war!! A few shots came over at about 3.30 p.m.

News of this reached the Corps Commander Sir Henry Rawlinson who noted in his diary: 'A German shouted out to our men the other day, "Look out – we have a General coming down to the trenches so we must fire for an hour."' No doubt he found some pleasure in reporting the deception played on one of his opposites in the German military hierarchy.

In these days following Christmas, indeed, in the main

trucing areas, it became a commonplace to walk and work freely in the open, unworried by the prospect of sniper fire. There was an incredible sense of relief, after weeks of crouching below ground level, at being able to stand upright and see beyond the horizon of sandbagged parapet. As Lieutenant-Colonel Fisher-Rowe put it: 'It makes such a lot of difference having your eyes 5 feet instead of a few inches above the level of the ground.'

Fisher-Rowe also wrote: 'Walking about on top brings the Germans curiously near to us.' And indeed Germans as well as British were fascinated by what was going on just a few yards away on the other side of No Man's Land. The following extract from a Saxon regimental history refers to the part of the line near Rue du Bois where both sides were working simultaneously on their defences:

> During the following days we saw among our neighbours strange sights. Every morning on the other side brown figures and on our side grey figures crept up from their holes in the ground scarcely 60 metres away from each other, and began to build and work with wood and wire on trench fortification.
>
> It was fascinating to watch how when the bell rang the English soldiers would lay down their pickaxes, spades and tools and take their breakfast in protection of their trenches, and half an hour later on the Sergeant's whistle, stream again over the tops of their parapets . . .
>
> This relaxation in Rue du Bois sector naturally spread to neighbouring company sectors of our regiment, where there were the same intolerable conditions – only the lines were further apart. Firing didn't cease altogether in these particular sectors.

There were, however, further examples at this time of the risks of fraternization. In some areas 'visiting' the enemy's lines was getting rather out of hand, and measures were taken to curtail it. The War Diary of 20th Brigade reported on 27 December that four Scots Guardsmen were 'enticed' into the German trenches, among them the scout, Murker, who had gone out into No Man's Land to arrange the truce on Christmas Eve – 'needless to say they have not returned'. There was immediate retaliation; forty Germans who paid a visit to the trenches of 2/Border were kept as prisoners!

In one instance (unfortunately unplaced and undated, being based on a hearsay report) there seems to have been a flurry of action due to the refusal of a group of enemy soldiers to quit the freedom of No Man's Land when expected to do so. The episode was described in a letter written some weeks later by Lieutenant H. Wyllie of the 9/Hampshires:

> Heard a most amusing story about the Christmas truce from one of the staff officials here who was in the trenches at the time.
>
> A party of unarmed Saxons continued to wander about between the lines after the prescribed time was up. They were duly warned by our men but took no notice whereupon one of our officers ordered some men to fire over them. This had no effect so a German officer sang out, 'Fire at them. I can't get the beggars in.' The English officer would not do this as they were unarmed but he rang up a battery to put a few shells over the German trench which they did, but the Saxons quite unperturbed sat down just outside our wire line and watched their pals getting shelled.

Such occurrences were rare, however. Indeed, it was more common for dealings between the two sides to be conducted with the utmost politeness, as in the case of 11th Brigade on the edge of Ploegsteert Wood, who received a series of signals from the Saxons opposite in the week following Christmas. On the 27th, the 1/Hampshires had taken a message from them announcing:

> Gentlemen, our automatic fire has been ordered from the Colonel to begin the fire again at midnight, we take it honour to award you of this fact.

Later that day the Adjutant of the Hampshires sent a signal quoting this message to 11th Brigade Headquarters, where it came to the notice of the Brigade commander. The signal prompted the following comment written along the margin in pencil:

> The GOC presumes you have sent a courteous answer to this.

There were further contacts next day. At 10.50 a.m. the following signal was despatched from Brigade headquarters to the Hampshires:

> The GOC would like you to pass over one or two papers and I send you three suitable ones for that purpose.

But such friendly gestures were not meant to imply any weakening of resolve or lowering of guard. The signal continued:

> The GOC hopes we are taking every advantage of the lull to strengthen our defences. You do not of course allow any Saxons to overlook your forward trench.

Similar messages were sent to the other battalions of the brigade. There was a flurry of shots later that day which wounded three men but this was immediately followed by an apology from the Germans and on the whole this stretch of front remained extremely quiet.

On the 29th, however, there came the anti-fraternization order from German Headquarters which presumably led to the following signal at 4 p.m. on the 30th:

Dear Camarades, I beg to inform you that is forbidden us to go out to you, but we will remain your comrades. If we shall be forced to fire we will fire too high. Please tell us if you are English or Irishmen. Offering you some cigars, I remain, yours truly . . .

As a token of his appreciation a company commander of the Hampshires presented the Germans with a box of chocolates.

In fact, some sniping did take place on the 31st. Two men of the 1/Somerset Light Infantry were killed, while the 1/Rifle Brigade next to them lost one man killed and one wounded. But this was on New Year's Eve and, once again, as at Christmas there was the urge to celebrate. The German Karl Aldag described events on his sector:

On New Year's Eve we called across to tell each other the time and agreed to fire a salvo at 12. It was a cold night. We sang songs, and they clapped (we were only 60–70 yards apart); we played the mouth-organ and they sang and we clapped. Then I asked if they hadn't got any musical instruments, and they produced some bagpipes (they are the Scots Guards, with the short petticoats and bare legs) and they played some of their beautiful elegies on them, and sang, too. Then at 12 we all fired salvos *into the air*! Then there were a few shots from our guns (I don't know what they were firing at) and the usually so dangerous Very lights crackled like fireworks, and we waved torches and cheered.

We had brewed some grog and drank the toast of the Kaiser and the New Year. It was a real good 'Sylvester', just like peace-time!

It should be said that Aldag was no doubt confusing the Scots Guards with the Gordon Highlanders in the matter of the 'short petticoats and bare legs'. The Scots Guards have never been a kilted regiment.

For the Germans it was the feast of St Sylvester, a traditional day for family festivities, and for the Scots opposite the celebration was Hogmanay, with Hulse, as usual, at the centre of events:

> We had another comic episode on New Year's Eve. Punctually at 11 p.m. (German war time is an hour ahead of ours), the whole of the German trenches were illuminated at intervals of 15 to 20 yards. They all shouted, and then began singing their New Year and Patriotic Songs. We watched them quietly, and they lit a few bonfires as well. Just as they were settling down for the night again, our own midnight hour approached, and I had warned my company as to how I intended to receive the New Year. At midnight I fired a star-shell, which was the signal, and the whole line fired a volley and then another star-shell and three hearty cheers, yet another star-shell, and the whole of us, led by myself and the Platoon Sergeant nearest to me, broke into 'Auld Lang Syne'. We sang it three times, and were materially assisted by the enemy, who also joined in. At the end, three more hearty cheers and then silence. It was extraordinary hearing 'Auld Lang Syne' gradually dying away right down the line into the 8th Division. I fired three more star-shells in different directions, to see that none of the enemy were crawling about near our wire and, finding all clear, I retired to my leaking bug-hutch.

But the night was not yet over: there was another curious episode to come:

> I had warned all sentries as usual, and had succeeded in getting about ¾ of an hour's sleep, when the Platoon Sergeant of No. 12 (my Platoon number from 9–12) burst in and informed me, most laconically, 'German to see you, Sir!'

I struck a light, tumbled out, and heard a voice outside saying, '*Offizier? Hauptmann?*' and found a little fellow, fairly clean and fairly superior to the average German private, being well hustled and pushed between two fixed bayonets. The minute he saw me he came up, saluted, covered in smiles, and awfully pleased with himself, said, '*Nach London, Nach London?*' I replied, 'No, my lad, *Nach* the Isle of Man' [the Isle of Man was well known as a detention centre for enemy aliens] on which the escort burst in loud guffaws! He could not talk a word of English except 'Happy New Year', which he kept on wishing us. He was a genuine deserter, and had come in absolutely unarmed. I went rapidly through his pockets, which were bulging on every side, and found no papers or anything of any value, but an incredible amount of every kind of food and comestibles. He had come in fully provided for the journey, and was annoyingly pleased with himself.

I ordered him to be marched up to Battalion Headquarters under escort, and telephoned up to George and had him woken to tell him that I was sending him a New Year's present. I enclose receipt for prisoner, which is rather interesting as it is the first bit of work, or writing, which 1915 brought me, and was considered by the ultra-superstitious private soldier, of which there are many, as a good augury.

It may have been the result of my telling them on the 25th that any of them who wished to report themselves at my barbed wire after dark would be fed and given a free passage to England! From what I could make out about a lot of talk from him, about 'three camaraden', I gathered that three of his pals were going to come in and give themselves up at 3 a.m. but they disappointed us and did not show up. He told me that he had a wife and two children, and never wished to see a rifle again – at least, that is what I gathered from a few words which I could understand.

The London Rifle Brigade had a similar unexpected visitor on New Year's Eve, an extremely inebriated German clutching a bottle of beer in each hand and determined to see in the New Year with his English friends. There was much debate as to whether he should be taken prisoner, as in theory he had seen the British dispositions and should therefore be able to report on them. But since it was quite clear that in practice he was incapable of apprehending anything it was decided to despatch him back to his lines. Two riflemen, one of whom was Graham Williams – summoned to interpret – were detailed to see him off:

> We managed to heave him up on to the parapet, then we each took hold of one of his arms and led him back across No Man's Land. And there he was between us, staggering along singing a very bawdy song at the top of his voice until we reached the German wire where there was a gap which he had obviously come through. I said to the other chap: 'I don't think we'll go any further; if we get into their trench they might want to keep us there.' So we headed the German in the right direction, wished him a Happy New Year and left him to it.

A machine-gun crew of the 2/Bedfordshires at La Boutillerie had an unexpectedly alarming transition to the new year. The Germans had been active in improving their trenches since Christmas and the crew feared they would almost certainly have marked their gun-position and would shell them out of it the moment hostilities recommenced. It was therefore decided to take evasive action by repositioning the gun a hundred yards or so along the trench. Having prepared the gun-pit the previous night, the crew made ready for the moving. One of their number, Private W. A. Quinton, described what happened:

> Still being on friendly terms with the enemy, and our trenches being knee-deep in mud and water, we took the easiest course

and travelled along the top behind our own trench. We started off, well loaded with our kit, the gun, tripod and boxes of belt ammunition, and our rifles slung across our backs by the slings. We made very slow progress as the ground was heavy with mud (the snow having thawed) and in addition to this we had to negotiate the communication trenches that ran at right angles to the firing-line. These were about 4 ft wide and we crossed by taking a sort of staggering leap, and throwing the heavy stuff across to the outstretched arms of those already over.

An hour had passed and we had covered about three parts of the total distance when without a word of warning something happened that caused us to fall as one man, flat on our stomachs in the mud. The Germans had opened fire! Rifles and machine-guns cracked. They had done the dirty on us! We crouched there in the mud, and the names we called those Germans must have turned the air blue. Yet – strange, we could not feel the 'pinging' of any bullets around us. The explanation came in the next few moments, when a voice from our front-line yelled, 'Hi, you fellows, what's up? They ain't firing across 'ere. They warned us what they were going to do. *They're firing in the air to celebrate the coming-in of the New Year.*' I looked at my watch. It was exactly two minutes past midnight. Having made sure that the voice from the trench had spoken the truth, we staggered to our feet and continued our journey.

How easily mistakes can be made. Being out of the trench we did not know of this midnight arrangement, and it was lucky for the Germans that we had not misunderstood their intentions and opened fire with our machine-gun. This certainly would have broken up the temporary armistice.

'And so', Quinton's account continues, 'this unofficial armistice with the enemy still held good. Not a shot from either side.'

☆

But where there had been no truce at Christmas, New Year was characterized by a similarly bellicose mood. 3rd Division, at the northern end of the line, reported on New Year's Day:

> Enemy exposed himself above parapet singing & cheering night of 31st Dec./1st Jan. & was fired on by Lincolns with rapid fire. Artillery made very good shooting against the enemy's trenches this day.

In the southern sector the 2/Grenadier Guards were back in the same trenches in which they had spent so wretched a Christmas Eve. The CO of the battalion, Lieutenant-Colonel Wilfrid Smith, wrote home:

> I saw the New Year in last night in the most depressing way, wet, cold, slush and bullets and rockets. The Germans sung carols, so our men shot at them to keep them quiet . . . Never was warfare made more difficult.

Where the Indians had fraternized with the Westphalians, the 2/Worcesters now held the line. There was a thunder of defiant gunfire from both sides to greet the New Year. As a gesture of hostility to the enemy, the Worcesters added to the general salvo with the firing of a newly devised trench mortar made from an iron drain pipe and named 'Archibald'. The Tickler's jam-tin bombs it launched towards the Germans were now to be filled with nails instead of plum and apple.

☆

The end of the year saw the publication in many newspapers of letters from soldiers telling of 'the Wonderful Day'. This was the start of a steady stream which was to continue in the daily and weekly press until late January. The *New York Times*, sharing the same source as the London *Daily News*, broke the story across

the Atlantic on New Year's Eve under the breezy headline FOES
IN TRENCHES SWAP PIES FOR WINE. The news took
longer to reach Australia, appearing as late as 9 February.

Shortly photographs began to appear. One in particular, of a
crowd of some twenty-five British and Germans in No Man's
Land, was given wide currency in the popular press, appearing as
TOMMY'S TRUCE BETWEEN THE TRENCHES in the
Daily Sketch and AN HISTORIC GROUP in the *Daily Mirror*.

That all this ran counter to the prevailing mood of anti-
Germanism caused few qualms. Now editors who had found
such rich column inches in berating the Hun and his frightful-
ness coined phrases like 'Amiable Germans', 'Good-hearted
Bavarians', 'Chat and Chaff with the Germans', 'How the Enemy
Joked' or, more grandly, 'The Power of Peace in the Time of
War'. Moreover, the same edition might carry cheerful yarns
of fraternizing on one page while publishing the latest horror
stories on another. On 9 January, for example, when the *Daily
Graphic* published the photograph of British and Germans
described above, they also ran a story headed: TORTURING
PRIESTS – GERMAN CRUELTY TO DESOLATED
BELGIUM – REVOLTING DEEDS.

What principally kept the story going were the letters and
their accompanying headlines: there were relatively few edito-
rials. Such comments as there were, however, were remarkably
benign. When the news broke the first reaction was not to
condemn but to be amazed that the truce had happened at all.
On 1 January, in one of the very first editorial references, the
South Wales Echo wrote:

> When the history of the war is written one of the episodes
> which chroniclers will seize upon as one of its most surprising
> features will undoubtedly be the manner in which the foes

celebrated Christmas. How they fraternized in each other's trenches, played football, rode races, held sing-songs, and scrupulously adhered to their unofficial truce will certainly go down as one of the greatest surprises of a surprising war.

The *Daily Mirror* gave the truce a column-length leader on the 2nd. The burden of its thoughtful, indeed challenging, message was that it was hard for human nature 'to keep up the gospel of hate when chance throws men into a companionship of toil and danger':

> The soldier's heart has rarely any hatred in it. He goes out to fight because that is his job. What came before – the causes for the war and the why and wherefore – bother him little. He fights for his country and against his country's enemies. Collectively, they are to be condemned and blown to pieces. Individually, he knows they're not bad sorts.

Hatred, the writer added, was to be found 'mainly at home':

> The diplomats and counts and Kaisers and Crown Princes, the journalists and statesmen and loafers in cafés, the people growing apoplectic-red in Berlin streets – these mobilize in hatred. The soldier has other things to think about. He has to work and win. Consequently he has not time for rage, and blind furies only overwhelm him when the blood is up over fierce tussles in the heat of the thing. At other times the insane childishness is apparent to him. He sees the absurdity . . .

Warming to his theme, the writer cited a story from the Eastern Front, of Austrians and Russians playing leapfrog together:

> Not bad sorts again! How unpatriotic! An Austrian liking a Russian!

His final thoughts were, however, gloomy and fatalistic. The war would, and must, go on.

> But now an end to the truce. The news, bad and good, begins again. 1915 darkens over. Again we who watch have to mourn many of our finest men. The lull is finished. The absurdity and the tragedy renew themselves.

Five days later, with the story supported by a positive explosion of letters from the front, the *Daily Telegraph* featured a long article by E. Ashmead Bartlett, a seasoned war correspondent in earlier campaigns, which began:

> probably no news since the war began has made a greater sensation, and certainly none has made better reading than the accounts which have come through from the trenches of the unofficial armistice established between certain sections of the German line and our own on Christmas Eve and Christmas Day . . . All this seems incredible in view of the ferocity of the combatants during months past and of the authenticated tales of German atrocities and trickery. It seems to prove the assertion of many that the German soldier is a good-hearted peace-loving individual once he is outside the influence of the Prussian military machine.

Reserving his particular animus for the Prussians and Prussian militarism, he seized on the stories which identified the Saxons and Bavarians as the principal fraternizers, seeing in them possible evidence of a desire on the part of the non-Prussian states of the German Empire to make a separate peace with the Allies. He also reminded his readers that these incidents 'which have caused profound interest and have given rise to much divergent comment' were 'no new feature of warfare':

In fact, it seems to be a common phenomenon of war, however bitter the struggle and however much the two nations may hate one another, that after a time a feeling of friendship will spring up between the troops in the front ranks if they are kept for any length of time opposite one another. This arises from a growing feeling of respect for your adversary and, sharing common hardships and common dangers as they do, the national feeling gives way before the fellow-feeling for the man opposite, who, after all, is not responsible for the war and is only obeying orders . . .

Whatever happens in the future let it not be forgotten that the brave Bavarians and Saxons exchanged greetings and gifts and the dead whilst the author of all Europe's miseries was publicly announcing 'that to the enemy I send bullets and bayonets'.

The Scotsman echoed the same sentiments the following day, when the *Manchester Guardian* printed an even more emotional article. Harking back to the long-outdated mediaeval concept of the 'truce of God' – a pause in fighting to observe the sacred feasts of the Church – the writer commented:

[Now] there comes the proof that this oldest and most wonderful sort of truce is not dead . . . From its occasion, of course, it can be claimed as a truce of God, but it was not a truce of God in the sense that it was authorized and enjoined by the Church. It was a thing more hopeful than even such a truce as that would have been. It was the simple and unex-amined impulse of human souls, drawn together in the face of a common and desperate plight . . . Those of us who are left at home may well think of that Christmas truce . . . with wonder and thankfulness. For the men who kept it proved, as men will always prove when the challenge is given with suffi-cient directness for the little catchwords and calculations to slip away for a moment, that the human soul stands out a quite simple thing and of infinite goodwill.

The Times made a small but significant reference to it *en passant* in a leader of 4 January:

> We cherish no anger against the masses of our enemies. We pity them for the ease with which they have suffered themselves to be blinded and misled; but, as the wonderful scenes in the trenches showed, there is no malice on our side, and none in many of those who have been marshalled against us.

A further item in *The Times* – the letter from a German lieutenant quoted on page 130 – plainly provoked a more critical reaction in at least one distinguished household. On 28 January Mrs Thomas Hardy wrote to Alda, Lady Hoare, who had written disapprovingly of the truce to the Hardys: 'My husband (& I too) agree with what you say about the hobnobbing of the Germans and the English at Christmas. In today's *Times* there is a letter from a German lieutenant to an English battalion refusing the Christmas truce. Although the arguments he uses against England are quite futile & founded on lies, yet the spirit is the right one.'

The German press, if it commented on the truce at all, generally took a far harder line, though at least one newspaper, the *Berliner Tageblatt*, under the headline DEUTSCH–ENGLISCHE WEIHNACHTSFEIERN IM FELDE (German–English Christmas Celebrations in the Field) reprinted in translation a letter by an officer of a Highland regiment which had been published in *The Times*. The *Tägliche Rundschau* of Berlin printed a long article pointing out the dangers of fraternization with this as its central message:

> War is no sport and we are sorry to say that those who made

these overtures or took part in them did not clearly understand the gravity of their situation.

The magazine *Reclams Universum* of Leipzig printed two letters from German soldiers who had fraternized and also reprinted drawings from British illustrated magazines depicting various aspects of the truce. Its comments were sarcastic and scathing: these pictures of 'English gentlemen' celebrating their friendship with the 'German barbarians' were a great exaggeration of what had taken place and though it was admitted that, 'impressed by the spirit of peace at Christmas', both sides *did* meet between the trenches, there were none of the 'orgies of brotherly love' of the sort publicized by the British press. Leipzig being one of the principal cities of Saxony, it must be deduced that whatever pro-Anglo-Saxon attitudes were held by the Saxon soldiers at the front, they were not necessarily shared by the guardians of public opinion back home.

The Times History of the War – published at the time, not written with postwar hindsight – was as reproachful of the German press, and of German official attitudes generally, as *Reclams Universum* was of the British:

> This wonderful Christmas outburst [i.e. the truce] is a text from which many morals might be preached, and the reader will doubtless draw his own. Among the first which will occur to him is that, from the German side, this exhibition of goodwill consorted badly with the enemy's avowed policy of 'frightfulness'. It received, therefore, as may easily be imagined, no support from the German Higher Command . . . German newspaper writers, composing their lucubrations in the reposeful atmosphere of their offices, drew from it, doubtless by order, many lugubrious deductions. In their safe places it was evident that making or countenancing these Christmas

overtures showed that the soldiers responsible for them mistook the seriousness of the situation, and these backsliders in the policy of 'frightfulness' were reminded that 'the Highest authority of the Army' shared the opinion. But as both the 'Higher authority' and the writers had taken particular care never to expose themselves to any personal danger, the value of their views as to the desirability of a little relaxation from the nerve-trying stress of a continued residence in the trenches, may be disregarded, perhaps with feelings not unmixed with a little contempt.

☆

One of the earliest pictures to appear in the press in connection with the truce was printed in the *Daily Sketch* on 5 January. Under the headline MAJOR WHO SANG CAROLS BETWEEN THE TRENCHES was a photograph of Major Buchanan-Dunlop. He was described as 'one of the moving spirits of the Christmas truce' and 'the leading chorister' in the Christmas festivities in his sector (see illustration 40).

The story had, in fact, broken on the previous day when the *The Scotsman* published a letter by Buchanan-Dunlop to a member of the staff of Loretto School, and had given his account added authority by reporting a sermon preached at St Paul's Episcopal Church, Edinburgh, by the Revd G. N. Price, Head-master of Loretto Preparatory School, and Buchanan-Dunlop's personal friend. Price had become very emotional in describing the events of Christmas on the Western Front:

> During the past few days you may have read in your papers, or in letters that have actually come from the trenches, as I have done, of the marvel of the Christmas Day just past – how in many parts of the firing line there was, by mutual consent, a truce of God; how friend and foe met to exchange some small

luxury; how they sang one to another the old Christmas carols and hymns . . . Is it merely fanciful to say that, on that anniversary of the birth of God's Son, there must have been some gracious influence of the spirit of Christ brooding over the combatants and suggesting, though but for a brief moment, the brotherhood of man in the great family of the Father?

Also on the 4th, the *Daily Mail* – without giving Buchanan-Dunlop's name – had printed a paragraph about him which included a list of the carols, taken from the Loretto Christmas concert programme, in which he had led the singing on Christmas Eve.

It was, however, the publicity following the photograph and headline in the *Daily Sketch* that caused the furore which followed. On 6 January Buchanan-Dunlop wrote to his wife:

> The General is on leave in England, but comes back Friday. I'm rather apprehensive of what he'll say when he does come. He is upset at the informal truce on Christmas Day, and now – my photo is in the *Daily Sketch* as 'one of the leaders in arranging the Christmas Truce'. It isn't true of course, but there it is, it was another Regiment that arranged it, but he won't think so.

On 7 January he had a memo from his commanding officer requesting a full explanation – 'apparently Army Headquarters are moving in the matter. It's rather a nuisance altogether, however I shall doubtless survive it.' On the 8th he received in the post 'letters from any number of folk . . . and *four* copies of the *Daily Sketch*, underlined and blue-pencilled. Sir H. Smith-Dorrien is awfully angry about it . . . The Brigadier-General came hurrying to our Headquarters to investigate directly he heard about it. However, I have no military career to blast, for certainly I shouldn't dream of staying in the service if Sconnie

wants me back and I can get to Loretto again. Also I don't mind
generals, and am not at all afraid of them.' (Sconnie was A. R.
Smith, Headmaster of Loretto Senior School; Buchanan-Dunlop
was a Territorial serving with a Regular battalion – hence his
reference to his military career not being at risk.)

The matter was to grumble on with some acrimony for most
of January. The General – Brigadier-General Ingouville-Williams
– vented his anger and frustration by accusing Buchanan-Dunlop
of having disobeyed orders, not in relation to the singing which
had started the whole story, but because he had left his trenches
to fraternize on Christmas Day in spite of explicit instructions
from the General himself requiring that 'the sentries were to
be extra-vigilant'. Buchanan-Dunlop argued that he had *not*
disobeyed orders, in that he had made sure the trenches were
securely guarded before he left them. He also felt greatly
aggrieved in that he had told the General on Christmas Day
precisely what he had done and the General had said nothing
– a fact which now he 'rather conveniently forgot'.

> He ought *then* and *there*, if he considered I had done anything
> wrong, to have written at once to the Colonel, and said so.
> It's not as if he had heard of it just now for the first time. No,
> it's just that he is annoyed at seeing his beloved Brigade prac-
> tically ridiculed in the cheap press, and he's determined to
> 'take it out' of somebody.

There was no talk of reprimands or courts martial, but the
unhappy major was left with the stain of disobedience against
his name:

> So when I met [the General] alone one morning in the trenches,
> I began to talk to him about it – he said the incident was
> closed and he didn't want to hear anything more about it; but
> I stuck to my guns and said I regretted extremely that I had

given him occasion to think that I had disobeyed his orders, but that I had been genuinely astonished when I heard he considered I had done so; but that I saw *his* point of view as well as my own. He said that I had now to 'redeem my character'.

I quite like the man really, but he is odd, altho' a good soldier.

There was to be a curious little postscript to the affair a day or so later:

A general staff officer from Army Headquarters came down with the General to see our trenches. I was showing the latter a barricade I had made, and the former said to our Colonel 'Who is that officer?' When the Colonel told him, he said 'Oh, the notorious Major B-D' and with that he screwed an eyeglass into his eye and had a good look at me. This the CO told me. (He was an Indian Cavalry officer, so what *could* he know about trenches?)

It is believed in his family that Buchanan-Dunlop failed to receive a DSO that he should have been awarded because of his involvement in the Christmas truce. However, he recovered from the event sufficiently to become, in due course, commanding officer of his battalion with the rank of Lieutenant-Colonel. He survived this war and the next one (winning the OBE for his work in the Home Guard and as Army Welfare Officer in the Lothians) and died in 1947 aged seventy-three. Ingouville-Williams commanded 34th Division with the rank of Major-General during the Battle of the Somme. He comes out less than gloriously in this present story but his reputation was that of a popular general who shared the dangers of his men. He was killed by shell-fire on 22 July 1916.

☆

Meanwhile, one by one, the trucing areas were going back to war.

On 3 January the 6/Gordon Highlanders had been approached by a German officer, accompanied by an orderly acting as interpreter. They asked to speak to a British officer. Captain Dawson, of 'D' Company, left the British trench and advanced into the open to meet them. The two officers gravely saluted, then the German officer informed Dawson that instructions had been received that the ordinary conditions of warfare must be resumed. The Gordons' Regimental History described the moment of the resumption of hostilities:

> A '*feu de joie*' passed from the 2nd Gordons through the 6th to the Guards, rifles being in the proper position, muzzles well in the air. Immediately after, a message passed right along the front, 'Pass it along – the Kaiser's dead.' The truce was over.

As late as 5 January Hulse was still writing to the effect that the Westphalian Regiment opposite them, the 158th, had not fired a shot since Christmas. In fact, he had been amusing himself over several days by climbing up a tree with his glasses to study the German lines, having found to his pleasure that he was opposite 'the fat, heavy-jowled brute' of a German officer to whom he had talked on Christmas Day. 'Every morning he has had four men scooping the water out just round his dugout and, judging by the amount of pumping which they do, I should say they are worse off than we are.' But he was writing this in billets and when Lieutenant-Colonel Fisher-Rowe's 1/Grenadier Guards returned to the line on this sector that same day they found that it was 'business as usual'. 'There is a German Maxim having a good go,' he wrote to his wife, 'and our guns also are busy.' And the next day: 'Our guns are now firing hard and making a beast of a row and the enemy are also shelling over us feeling for our guns.' However, things still remained relatively quiet, and Sir Henry Rawlinson was writing of the continuance of friendly relations on this front as late as 10 January.

It was on the 10th that the 2/Leinsters received orders to open fire on the enemy to prevent them from carrying on their work on their trenches in daylight. This also stopped the Leinsters from working on theirs: 'This will mean considerable delay in completion of new breastwork,' commented their War Diary. The enemy did not fire back. Indeed, there was very little firing during the rest of the month. On the 19th, the Diary noted 'Some enemy were seen today in front of our line apparently wearing kilts!!!'

At Ploegsteert on 11 January the Somerset Light Infantry recorded their return to war:

> The truce came to an abrupt end today and sniping started again in earnest.

The 1/Royal Warwicks were entrenched not far to the north, where Corporal Samuel Judd had written 'War declared' in his diary the previous day, following some busy sniper fire in which a comrade of his had been hit. However, on the 12th Private Tapp was noting a 'quiet time in trenches this time, very little sniping', adding that 'we can fetch water now without being sniped at'. Yet a fellow Warwicks who stepped outside a ruined house which they had been using as sleeping quarters with his cigarette alight had a dozen shots fired at him. 'He won't smoke a cigarette there again,' Tapp commented wryly.

But the war was claiming its victims, as it always did, even in relatively peaceful times and 'cushy' sectors. Karl Aldag wrote home on 10 January describing the death of a comrade:

> There was a fellow with whom I was on sentry duty yesterday morning; he sang a chorale and then one of those old, slow,

rather melancholy army songs; in spite of all he had gone through he was still a cheerful country lad. One hour later he was dead, with his face in the mud.

This was Aldag's last letter: five days later he was himself killed. The circumstances of his death are not known.

On 23 January the 1/Royal Warwicks went back to the front after a few days in billets. There was a different atmosphere now. The Royal Dublin Fusiliers had been 'shelled pretty heavy', noted Tapp, and over the next few days the German artillery viciously probed their line. The infantry opposite were also in aggressive mood: 'We catch them at our barbed wire again . . . they have left 3 dead behind, I do not know how long they will stay there as it is dangerous to fetch them in, the shells shake the whole trench and the jar nearly puts the candle out.' On the 26th the shelling was very severe:

I thought my time had come as one dropped a few yards away . . . making a hole as big as a cellar . . . My Of came along to see if I was alright.

Later the shelling stopped for about five minutes, with unfortunate consequences for some of Tapp's comrades:

Our fellows thought they had sent their limit over so they started getting out, stood talking in a bunch, a shell came and killed a corporal and wounded 2 sergeants and one colour sergeant, this happened six yards away they went down like logs without a murmur, no time to get out of the way of these shells, they are no sooner fired than they are at their destination, they are still sending the rifle grenades over but we can get out of the way of them as the shot goes

Thus William Tapp's diary came to its abrupt end in the middle of a sentence. He is officially described as having died of wounds. He left a widow and one child, a son. It is not known where he was buried, but in four years of war many graves lost their identification or were destroyed by shell-fire. He is one of the 54,896 men whose names are commemorated on the Menin Gate at Ypres.

☆

The 1/Leicesters, having lost two men killed on Christmas Day, had only one fatal casualty in the whole of January. But the new month brought an abrupt change of mood. On 3 February Major Buchanan-Dunlop wrote to his wife:

> Just a little note before I go off to the trenches. The long truce between the Saxons and ourselves is broken, and there is brisk fighting there now.

Yet this was not quite the end of the story. Three days later Sergeant E. W. Castle, a member of the Army Service Corps working on the staff of General Smith-Dorrien as a shorthand writer and confidential clerk, noted in his diary:

> It appears our men and the Germans (Saxons) near Armentières have been chumming up again, and do not fire on each other. This has come to the notice of Sir John French, and they are all wild that this goes on notwithstanding all the orders we give on the subject – for any kind of fraternizing with the enemy is forbidden. *We are to be at War.*

Even this did not pull down the curtain on the Christmas truce. Astonishingly, post-Christmas goodwill lingered on in one area at least for several weeks more. Returning to the front in mid-March after being wounded, Captain F. E. Packe, now assigned to the 1/Welch Regiment, found himself in a very different kind of war from the one he had left during the First

Battle of Ypres several months earlier. On the 19th he wrote to
his mother:

> On Sunday [14 March] we moved up to the trenches; the
> regiment we relieved had been there for months and it was an
> absurdly quiet spot, it was one of those places where they
> fraternized with the Germans at Xmas and a certain amount
> of the truce has gone on apparently, anyhow there was very
> little firing by day and never really heavy by night and I only
> had one man hit in two nights – not badly – and he was the
> only casualty in the regiment! We never had a single shell the
> whole time I was there.

The 'absurdly quiet spot' was Ploegsteert, where Packe's
1/Welch, still in the process of being acclimatized to the Western Front, briefly found themselves in the area of 10th Brigade,
in which Bairnsfather's Warwickshires had celebrated Christmas
with 'Frightful Fritz and Hateful Heinrich' and where on Boxing
Day Second Lieutenant Drummond had found the Germans
'very nice fellows' and taken his fine photograph.

Having lasted so long, the peaceable mood was scarcely likely
to change greatly before Easter, which came early that year, on
4 April, and so it proved. Indeed the approach of another sacred
season prompted a further surge of the fraternizing spirit on the
part of the enemy in several sections of the line – though by
now those who hoped to initiate, in however modest a way, a
rerun of Christmas would find that, at last, for the British this
was a gesture too far.

The day before Good Friday, 1 April, was exceptionally quiet
in some sectors. The London Rifle Brigade were still at Ploegsteert Wood – a stone's throw south of where Packe's battalion
had been under two weeks earlier – their first real blooding in
the Second Battle of Ypres, yet to come. After dark some lights

Christmas Day.

Dearest Mother,

I am writing this in the trenches in my "dug out" – with a wood fire going and plenty of straw it is rather cosy although it is freezing hard and real Christmas weather –

I think I have seen one of the most extraordinary sights today that anyone has ever seen – About 10 oclock this morning I was peeping over the parapet when I saw a German, waving his arms, and presently two of them got out of their trenches and came towards ours – We were just going to fire on them when we saw they had no rifles so one of our men went out to meet them and in about two minutes the ground between the two lines of trenches was swarming with men and officers of both sides, shaking hands and wishing each other a happy Christmas – This continued for about half an hour when most of the men were ordered back to the trenches.

33. From a letter written by Second Lieutenant Dougan Chater,
2/Gordon Highlanders

34. Photograph of the 133rd Saxon Regiment's pre-war football team, given to Lieutenant Ian Stewart on Christmas Eve in exchange for a tin of bully beef (see page 79)

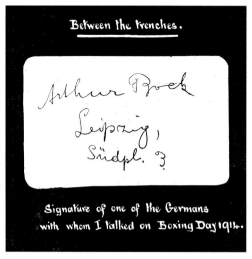

35. From the album of Rifleman David Smith,
London Rifle Brigade

36. A German soldier showed this photograph to some Tommies on Christmas Day. One of the British, a sergeant, looked at it a long time and said: 'When the war is over, I would like to marry your eldest daughter, she is beautiful.' The German was delighted as the said 'eldest daughter' was his wife and the mother of the other two. He told the story on his return, and the whole family was much taken by the incident, which was recounted many times over the years

37. British non-commissioned officers with their souvenirs of the truce – a German song book, a bayonet and several pickelhaubes

'Bon Jour Fritz . . . Salaam Salaam'

38 (*above*). A cartoon impression of the truce by Captain E. R. P. Berryman, 2/39 Garhwal Rifles, from a letter to his brother, 1 January 1915

'I have just been through one of the most extraordinary scenes imaginable'
(see page 84)

39 (*left*). Captain R. J. Armes, 1/North Staffordshire Regiment, experienced Regular soldier and enthusiastic participant in the Christmas truce. He survived the war, retiring in 1919 with the rank of Brevet Colonel

DAILY SKETCH.

Cardigan jackets are comforting things at the front. You can send them through the "Daily Sketch."

Telephones: Editorial and Publishing: 9570 Holborn. Advertisement: 2376 Holborn. BRITAIN'S BEST PICTURE PAPER. LONDON: Shoe Lane, E.C. MANCHESTER: Withy Grove.

MAJOR WHO SANG CAROLS BETWEEN THE TRENCHES.

Major Buchanan-Dunlop, the leading "chorister"   *The Germans' melodeon-player accompanied the singers*

40. The newspaper story which caused Major Buchanan-Dunlop so much trouble (see page 224). 'I shall now be known as "the leading chorister" – luckily I've grown a beard so no one will recognize me'

The Daily Mirror

Friday, January 8, 1915

CERTIFIED CIRCULATION LARGER THAN ANY OTHER DAILY NEWSPAPER IN THE WORLD

WHY DELAY? THE DAILY MIRROR OVERSEAS WEEKLY EDITION contains all the Latest and Best War Pictures and News, and is therefore the Best Weekly Newspaper for your friends abroad. You can obtain it from your Newsagent for 3d. per copy.
Subscription rates (prepaid), post free, to Canada 12s 6d; elsewhere 10s 10d per year. Address—Manager, "Overseas Daily Mirror," 23-29, Bouverie Street, London, E.C.

AN HISTORIC GROUP: BRITISH AND GERMAN SOLDIERS PHOTOGRAPHED TOGETHER.

41. The photograph which appeared in several British newspapers on 8 January 1915

Aus der Londoner „Sphere": „Wie Engländer und Deutſche ſich am
Chriſtfeſt verbrüderten."

Aus dem Londoner „Graphic": „Der Weihnachts-Waffenſtillſtand in den
Schützengräben: Freund und Feind auf der Haſenjagd."

Aus „Illuſtrated London News": „Engliſche und deutſche Soldaten Arm in Arm. Verbrüderung zwiſchen Sachſen und Angelſachſen auf dem
Schlachtfeld zur Weihnachtszeit."

42. Reproduction of drawings from the British *Sphere, Graphic* and
Illustrated London News, by *Reclams Universum* of Leipzig, 21 January 1915.
The accompanying caption poured scorn on 'the great English magazines which
since the outbreak of war have made an unbelievable performance of disparaging and
decrying the "German Huns", and 'have in their Christmas editions run a series of
"imaginative illustrations" in stark contrast to their previous attitude' (see page 223)

43. *'Talkers and Fighters'*: an American comment on the Christmas truce,
New York Evening Sun, 22 January 1915

'There was a certain amount of friendly backchat with the Saxons opposite, mostly about being made to work so hard by our bosses' (Lieutenant Ian Stewart, 2/Argyll & Sutherland Highlanders)

44. 2/Argyll & Sutherland Highlanders constructing a breastwork of mud and hurdles, Rue du Bois trenches near Grande Flamengrie Farm, January 1915. The German trench line is in front of the trees on the left

45. The Scots Guards' front-line trench at Laventie, December 1915 – the sector where the 1st and 2nd Battalions of the Scots Guards fraternized with the Germans on Christmas Day 1915

were put up on the German trenches opposite. The Germans had a band in their lines, which played '*Deutschland über Alles*' followed by 'God Save the King', and both sides sent up several flares amid cheers. But, as Rifleman J. C. Abery wrote in his diary, 'after a bit they sent over two grenades and laid out a number of our fellows so we promptly replied and that put the lid on: the night was a series of explosions.'

On Easter Day, the Germans made a more substantial bid for a truce, at Kemmel, apparently taking their cue from what they assumed to be encouragement on the part of the British. The 8/Sherwood Foresters, like the 1/Welch, were new to the front – indeed the process of introducing them to trench life had begun only the previous week – and they were clearly uncertain as to how to react when their innocent celebration of Easter produced a surprising result. They were soon to find out. The story is well told in the battalion Diary:

> 9.0 a.m. 'C' Coy sing Hymns and the Enemy make overtures for a truce – by showing the white flag – and about 40/50 of their men appear. GOC asked for instructions – and we [were] told that no truce can be allowed – that the enemy are to be warned that we shall fire on them if they don't withdraw. They do this, before the message reaches O. C. Coy. The interlude has given Capt Martyn a good chance to inspect the German line and our own.
>
> 11.0 p.m. Sniping breaks out very badly in the evening . . .

Reporting this event in his diary, Sergeant Castle wrote of the Germans: 'They evidently wanted another Xmas gathering.'

There was a similar incident opposite Captain Packe's 1/Welch Regiment, now in trenches between Ploegsteert and Kemmel, to the east of Dranoutre; in a letter of 8 April he wrote:

On Easter Day the Germans tried to fraternize showing white flags etc – they threw potatoes into one trench – but orders are very strict on the subject so we ignored them.

The 1/Welch's Diary was dismissively curt:

Easter Day – Germans showed white flag in several places, but advances were not met. Orders were issued by Bde [Brigade] to avoid fraternising.

In fact all such 'advances' were met with a distinctly frigid response. If there had been ambiguity as to how the British should react back in December, there was no such ambiguity now. It can reasonably be claimed that the Christmas truce lasted in places *almost* to Easter, but there is also little doubt that *by* Easter it was over and done with, consigned to history, a thing of the past. The long truce was finally broken, after a little over a hundred days.

☆

There was another very important reason why it should have ended. If certain sectors had remained more or less peaceful till Easter, elsewhere by this time a great deal had happened. On 10 March the British had launched their first offensive since the advent of trench warfare, at Neuve Chapelle. It had been a hard-fought battle spread over three days, beginning with a successful attack which caught the Germans seriously off guard, but ending in disappointment as the enemy rallied, fought back and regained virtually all the ground they had lost.

It claimed many lives. Among them was Wilbert Spencer of the 2/Wiltshires. His attitude to the Germans, which had been so benign six months earlier, had undergone a significant change by the time he went 'over the top' at Neuve Chapelle.

As early as 3 January, after one of his men had died with his head on his, Spencer's, knee, he had written to his family:

> In many ways I am sorry to be fighting the Germans but when one sees how they ruined such thousands of innocent folk and when you see a Tommy lying with his brains blown out by a German bullet it is hard to have sympathy with them.

He was now eager for action, his early encounters with the Germans having scarcely advanced the British cause; but in the event his fighting war lasted less than one day. He was killed by shell-fire on the evening of 10 March – just two weeks short of his eighteenth birthday.

That same day in March also saw the deaths, already described (see page 158) of Captain Kenny and Lieutenant Welchman of the 1/39 Garhwal Rifles, and on the 12th there was another notable casualty, when Sir Edward Hulse, now a Captain, joined the battle with his 2/Scots Guards.

As they were advancing across open ploughed land his Commanding Officer, George Paynter, fell wounded. Hulse, who had gained cover, unhesitatingly went to see if he could give Paynter any assistance. In so doing he was shot and killed. He was buried in the Rue David Military Cemetery nearby. His mother published his remarkable correspondence and later his account of Christmas Day was included by Lord Birkenhead in his famous anthology *Five Hundred Best English Letters*. There is a tablet to his memory in Salisbury Cathedral. He was twenty-five.

Yet another participant in this story died on the day after Hulse, having taken part in the same attack. This was Lieutenant-Colonel Laurence Fisher-Rowe, Commanding Officer of the 1/Grenadier Guards. Towards evening on 12 March, Lieutenant J. D. Wyatt of 2/Yorks, after being wounded, was attempting to make his way back to a dressing station when he came upon '4 huge Grenadiers carrying a stretcher. I was told to follow them to the Doctor. They were carrying Col. Fisher-Rowe, I gathered.' Fisher-Rowe died of wounds on 13 March. He was buried in the military enclave of the communal cemetery of the little township of Estaires. He was forty-eight. Also in the same cemetery lies another participant in the truce, Second Lieutenant Arthur Pelham-Burn of the 6/Gordon Highlanders, who had been so moved by the joint burial service in No Man's Land on Christmas Day. He was killed in action on 2 May 1915, aged nineteen.

☆

One question remains to be asked: was the Christmas truce a significant event, or was it simply an agreeable irrelevance, a sentimental aside in the dialogue of war?

For some men, undoubtedly, it meant little. Taking part in it was a boyish prank, a bit of fun, a dormitory feast when the masters weren't looking. Others, by contrast, took it very seriously. However, the idea that it might somehow stop the fighting – bring the warring nations to their senses, as it were – was never more than a pipedream. There was no chance that this could have happened. But the possibility did occur to people at the time. An editorial paragraph in the *Herald* on 2 January 1915 stated:

> The picture is gladdening in one respect, saddening in others. It is especially saddening to think that such soldiers are not in charge of the affairs of Europe instead of the diplomats and potentates. If they were we would have a natural and human Europe.

At the front Captain Jack, whose battalion, the 1/Cameronians, had not been involved in the truce, speculated in his diary on 13 January (having only just realized that the truce had taken place):

> It is interesting to visualize the close of a campaign owing to the opposing armies – neither of them defeated – having become too friendly to continue the fight.

Putting it at its simplest, the German captain with whom Private Weir conversed 'clapped his hand together and looked towards heaven and said, "My God, why cannot we have peace and let us all go home?"'

Such an idea remained ever afterwards with some men who took part. Speaking in 1981, Albert Moren said:

> If the truce had gone on and on, there's no telling what could have happened. It could have meant the end of the war. After all they didn't want war, and we didn't want war and it could have ended up by finishing the war altogether.

The not dissimilar thought that if the soldiers had had their way the awfulness that was to come might have been avoided underlay the highly emotional comment of Josef Sewald in 1964:

> It is wonderful to think that the thought of Bethlehem brought these men together. They heard the voice of 2000 years back, but the rulers did not hear, and so the war went on for four years and millions of young men had to die.

Perhaps the most eloquent statement of this view was made in the House of Commons in 1930 by the Liberal MP for Banff, Major Murdoch McKenzie Wood, who had been at the front in 1914 with the Gordon Highlanders. In a debate on the rights of conscientious objectors, he rebutted the claim of another member that men only entered the army in order to kill, stating that he joined up early in order to *prevent* killing; indeed, during the whole of the war he had never had the slightest animosity against anyone, 'even against those who were opposed to us':

> In the early stages of the War, at Christmas 1914, I was in the front trenches, and took part in what was well known at the time as truce. We went over in front of the trenches, and shook hands with many of our German enemies. A great number of people think we did something that was degrading. I will not discuss that at the moment. The fact is that we did it, and I then came to the conclusion that I have held very firmly ever since, that if we had been left to ourselves there would never have been another shot fired. For a fortnight that truce went on. We were on the most friendly terms, and it was only the fact that we were being controlled by others that made it necessary for us to start trying to shoot one another again.

The notion that such an abrupt end to hostilities might conceivably have taken place even lodged in the minds of some participants of the Second World War. Describing the truce as 'the most significant moment in history', an RAF flying officer wrote:

> There remains for all time an enormous 'if' from that date. If only all the soldiers along the whole of the Western Front had . . . come out and refused to go back to the slaughter. If only this precious peace had spread, the whole of history would be different. There would never have risen to power a mad Dictator and [other] dictators in Europe, no more millions of lives lost, no concentration camps and most important of all men and women would have exerted the power on their politicians which so-called democracy is supposed to give them . . . Politicians do not listen to those whom they claim to represent and the failure to take notice of the fragile peace declared for

that brief precious period led to the anti-government revolution throughout Europe.

Yet it has to be said that such thoughts were veritable will-o'-the-wisps in the political climate of Europe in 1914. It was the determination not only of governments but also of peoples that the war should be fought, and most soldiers, even while shaking hands with the enemy and exchanging souvenirs, accepted without question that the killing would resume sooner or later. When Bruce Bairnsfather wrote of Christmas that there was 'not an atom of hate on either side that day,' he added:

> And yet, on our side, not for a moment was the will to war and the will to beat them relaxed. It was just like the interval between the rounds of a friendly boxing match.

There were, of course, many for whom even that brief interlude was a lapse, an unprofessional aberration, to be viewed with anger and contempt. The following is from a letter by Captain Tom Ingram, a medical officer attached to 1/King's Shropshire Light Infantry, written on 6 January 1915; a letter which is not only outspokenly critical of the whole fraternization, but which also, while naming no names, makes it clear that Brigadier-General Ingouville-Williams was not alone in his disapproval of the activities of Major Buchanan-Dunlop and the 1/Leicesters:

> All this friendly peace business at Christmas is rotten; we aren't here to pal up with the enemy and sing carols with him. One regiment especially distinguished themselves by their friendliness to the enemy at Xmas, and their second in command went and sang in the German trenches. This particular regiment is in our brigade and has not been so distinguished when fighting had to be done; in fact quite the contrary.

Indeed, as Ingram's letter went on to make evident, matters had gone beyond mere criticism; trucers and non-trucers had actually come to blows:

> Our men are awfully sick with them over the whole thing, and last night there was a bit of a scrap in the town between some of ours and the carol singing lot. Two or three other regiments who were too pally at Xmas have also had to fight their friends since: good thing too.

Ingram believed that far too many were adopting a casual attitude to the war: 'They don't take things seriously enough,' he commented in the same letter. Yet for the great mass of those who had sung carols or fraternized there was never the slightest doubt that the war would go on and that they would continue to carry out their duties, as though the events of Christmas had never taken place.

Most survivors took this view. Asked almost seventy years after, whether, if the soldiers had had their way, they would have stopped fighting and gone home, Graham Williams replied:

> I'm quite sure that wouldn't have been the case – I'm quite definite about that. We all wanted to win the war and to see the Germans beaten. It was all right just having the truce and meeting the Germans, but as for ending the war, no, that was quite out of the question. In any case, we all expected the war would end next spring – we were quite certain that would finish the war off.

Leslie Walkinton expressed a similar attitude:

> If it had been left to the soldiers? But of course it couldn't have been left to the soldiers, because if it were they would have started arguing amongst themselves, wouldn't they, before very long. It's just a happy dream. I suppose like a lot

of schoolboys one often thought at school if only the masters would let us get on with this that or the other, everything would be perfect . . . No, it didn't affect my attitude to the war in the least.

Even the *Manchester Guardian*'s commentator in January 1915 – after rhapsodizing over the restoration of the ancient concept of the 'truce of God' – went on to admit that the soldiers who had fraternized were quite right to return to their lines and get on with the war; there was, after all, much unfinished business:

> 'But they went back into their trenches', a perfectly enlightened and quite inhuman observer from another planet would perhaps say, 'and are now hard at it again, slaying and being slain. Evidently their glimpses of the wiser and better way was interesting but of no very great practical importance.' To which, of course, we might reply with great reason that there was very much to be done yet – that Belgium must be freed from the hideous yoke that has been thrust upon her, that Germany must be taught that Culture cannot be carried by the sword . . .

Nevertheless, the truce of Christmas 1914 cannot be dismissed as an event of no importance. It halted however briefly the juggernaut of war, gave some men an insight they were never to forget, made some men think twice about the nationally inspired animosities to which they were expected to subscribe. Second Lieutenant A. P. Sinkinson wrote of Christmas Day:

> As I walked slowly back to our own trenches I thought of Mr Asquith's sentence about not sheathing the sword until the enemy be finally crushed. It is all very well for Englishmen living comfortably at home to talk in flowing periods, but when you are out here you begin to realize that sustained hatred is impossible.

It should be added, however, that such insights could lead to unfortunate consequences. Henry Williamson, the novelist, was profoundly moved by his participation in the truce and thereafter – in reaction to the conditioning of hatred to which he, like all his generation, had been subjected – came to hold an uncritical admiration for all things German. This led him to conceive a profound fellow-feeling for Hitler (like himself, an ordinary soldier at the time of the truce) and even to toy with the fantasy that he had actually met Hitler in No Man's Land in 1914. In fact the future Chancellor of Germany was not far off, but his 16th Bavarian Reserve Infantry Regiment was out of the line over the Christmas period. From such Damascus-Road discoveries Williamson went on to support Hitler's political creed and to try to implant it in Britain – for which fascist tendencies he was never quite forgiven. Happily, he will be remembered more for such classics as *Tarka the Otter* than for his well-intentioned but misguided philandering with totalitarian politics.

But if the insights inspired by the Christmas truce could drive some men to excess, it could also make even dedicated professional soldiers see, if only briefly, the whole idea of war in a new light – or at any rate glimpse the thought that war might not be as natural to an intelligent species as had always been assumed. Captain Jack of the 1/Cameronians wrote on 13 January 1915:

> These incidents seem to suggest that, except in the temper of battle or some great grievance, educated men have no desire to kill one another; and that, were it not for aggressive National Policies, or the fear of them by others, war between civilized peoples would seldom take place.

Events, indeed, are more than just the sum of what happened at a particular time and place; they are also what people subsequently make of them. So this transient episode of peace in a long and brutal war has become far more than a temporary unofficial celebration in No Man's Land. It can now be seen as a small but significant gesture against the tide of international and nationalist rivalry and hatred which was flowing strongly in 1914 and flows strongly – and no less dangerously – a century later. No doubt the claim of an Old Contemptible who took part in the truce that 'perhaps never before and probably never again will the world see such a demonstration of the Brotherhood of Man between opposing warring forces' could be considered overstated and over-sentimental. The same might be said of a historian of the time, G. H. Perris, who, in a weighty volume on the 1914 campaigns published just one year later, wrote: 'The vision of these hours of reconciliation will last when many a day of dear-bought but necessary victory has sunk into oblivion.' But it is these interpretations of the truce which attract people today and will doubtless continue to do so.

Perhaps a final comment, which sums up the pressures and insights of Christmas 1914, might be left to Private William Tapp, who chronicled the truce day by day in his diary and at times almost hour by hour. On Christmas Day itself he wrote:

> They say they are not going to fire again if we don't but of course we must and shall do, but it doesn't seem right to be killing each other at Xmas time.

Chapter Nine

Christmas 1915

The year that followed was one of few achievements and much disappointment. Nineteen fifteen did not provide the decisive breakthrough which the soldiers in France expected. By the end of it the trench lines were virtually where they had been at the beginning; the principal difference was that they were greater in depth, more sophisticated, more difficult to attack. Also more extensive, behind the lines, were the military cemeteries. A. J. P. Taylor has called 1915 a year of 'battles which have no meaning except as names on a war memorial'. They were small in scale compared with the great set-pieces of later years, and from the Allied point of view they were almost totally disastrous. They created the track record of brave but melancholy failure which has become the brand-image of the Western Front. They killed and wounded thousands of men.

Nineteen fifteen also has the distinction of being the year which saw the first use of poison gas, the start of the Zeppelin bombing raids on Britain and the launching of submarine warfare. In May a U-boat sank the *Lusitania*, with the loss of nearly two thousand passengers and crew, including over a hundred Americans, and the world gasped at a stunning example of German frightfulness. It was not a good year for the further-ance of friendly relations between opposing forces.

There were, however, some attempts at breaking the prevailing hostile mood.

In August a Frenchman took to singing at night in the trenches near Evricourt in Picardy. Herbert Sulzbach, a gunner with the 63rd (Frankfurt) Field Artillery Regiment, was at the artillery observation post in the German front line one night when the Frenchman suddenly struck up on the other side of No Man's Land:

> We stepped out of the dugout into the trench and, quite incredibly, there was a marvellous tenor voice ringing out through the night with an aria from *Rigoletto*. The whole company were standing in the trench listening to the 'enemy' and, when he had finished, applauding so loud that the good Frenchman must certainly have heard it and is sure to have been moved by it in some way or other as much as we were by his wonderful singing. What an extraordinary contrast! You fire on each other, you kill each other, and then all of a sudden a Frenchman starts to sing, and the music makes us forget the whole war: music seems to overcome every kind of difference. Anyway, that was an experience much more splendid than anything you can express in words.

In November there was a prolonged if small-scale fraternization at St Eloi, a point to the south of Ypres not occupied at Christmas 1914, where British and Germans were about two hundred yards apart on opposite sides of a huge mine crater – 'big enough to drop a house into,' as one Tommy described it. The 1/10 Liverpool Scottish relieved a Northumberland battalion in the line on 22 November. When Private Edmund Herd and four others were detailed to take over a listening-post in advance of the main British trenches, the Northumberlands who had been occupying it told them that the Saxons opposite were

distinctly friendly and that if they heard a low whistle that
would mean that the Saxons were coming out and that the
Liverpools should respond if they intended to meet them halfway.
Herd described what then took place:

> Our post discussed the matter which appealed to us as an
> adventure, although a risky one, and it was agreed that I should
> go. Sometime later in the night we heard the whistle and
> responded. A German appeared over his parapet and out I got
> over our low parapet. When we were both about 8 or 9 yards
> away from our respective posts, another German followed the
> first and his appearance brought Jack out of our post imme-
> diately. The situation was very exciting. I could see that the
> Germans had no rifles. Neither had we, but I had my bayonet
> and I had taken the precaution of placing a Mills bomb in my
> pocket. I think Jack was similarly armed. Anyway, we met
> our opposites about halfway across and talked in English for
> perhaps five or ten minutes, then returned to our posts.

Herd went out several times during the week in which his
battalion was in the line. Bully beef and jam were exchanged
for cigars and cigarettes on one occasion, on another the Saxons
brought out wine, and on a third Private Herd returned with
a cap badge, a trench knife and the photograph of one of the
Saxons, who turned out to have been a waiter at the Hotel Cecil
in London. One night the ex-waiter gave a colleague of Herd's
a letter to be posted to a girl in London, but the Tommies'
response to this was less generous than it might have been the
previous year. They destroyed it.

And so Christmas came around again, with a much larger
British army manning a considerably longer stretch of line and
with Sir Douglas Haig as its newly appointed Commander-in-
Chief – Sir John French having followed the deposed Smith-

Dorrien into exile in England. There was no repetition of the Christmas card weather which had provided so appropriate a backcloth to the events of 1914; instead it was dull, wet and mild. And, if there was any urge to restage the Christmas celebrations of the previous December, there were now firm instructions on hand making it plain that such excesses were strictly prohibited. For instance, in a signal of 19 December, the GOC of the 47th (London) Division reminded the units under his command of the 'unauthorized truce' of Christmas Day 1914 and impressed upon them 'that nothing of the kind is to be allowed on the Divisional Front this year'. The 140th Infantry Brigade passed on the order to the brigade's battalions with the following rider:

> The Brigadier wishes you to give the strictest orders to all ranks on the subject, and any man attempting to communicate either by signal or word of mouth or by any other means is to be seriously punished. All snipers and machine-guns are to be in readiness to fire on any German showing above the parapet.

There are numerous accounts of such orders being passed on to British troops at Christmas 1915. Private H. E. Dickson of the Royal Scots was in billets at Bouzincourt on the Somme and remembered such an order being read to the battalion by its commanding officer, Colonel Gemmel – 'and that was it. No truce this time.' The battalion spent Christmas Eve digging trenches at Aveluy in the Ancre Valley being strafed by 'whizz-bangs'. Lieutenant Gordon Barber of the 1/Queen's Own Cameron Highlanders recorded in his diary 'an order from GHQ saying it was hoped that there would be no repetition of the regrettable occurrences of last Christmas Day, and that any German who ventured to show himself was to be shot at once'.

He regretted the prohibition because his trenches were at Loos and the ground in front of them, three hundred yards across, was littered with the dead – mostly British – of the disastrous battle fought there last September. 'That is one reason why I should, in a way, like to see a truce on Christmas Day, just to bury the poor fellows who are lying out in No Man's Land, a terrible tribute to the patriotism and self-sacrifice that this war has taught us to know. Another reason is that the sight of so many of our dead must, to a certain degree, tell on the morale of our men.' G. A. Leonard, then a sixteen-year-old Pioneer of 25th Division, recalled the shock of being warned, at a parade before going up the line at Ploegsteert, of the death penalty if the truce of the previous Christmas happened again, though it should be added that there were no official orders of such severity; possibly the idea that the ultimate sanction for fraternization might be the firing squad was the interpretation of some local commander.

Lieutenant Wyn Griffith of the 15/Royal Welch Fusiliers wrote of 'strict orders . . . that we must confine our goodwill not only to fellow Christians, but to Christians of allied nationality. We were to remain throughout possessed by the spirit of hate, answering any advances with lead.' However, at least in one area, there was a restriction in the amount of practical animosity to be directed at the enemy at Christmas. Billy Congreve, now Brigade Major of 76th Brigade, had worked out 'a gorgeous Boche strafe for Xmas Day – just to show how much we can really hate'. But in the event this did not come to pass. He wrote in his diary on 24 December:

> Awful rot; a wire came from the division this morning, saying: 'No action is to be taken by us on Xmas Day which is likely to provoke retaliation on the part of the Germans.' Was *ever*

such an order given before? I expect the corps commander is leaving off trousers and putting on skirts. I am especially annoyed, as I had taken some trouble in organizing our 'hate'.

As for the Germans, there was an unambiguous order forbidding friendly relations with the enemy and threatening the direst consequences:

> Any attempt at fraternization with the enemy (agreement not to fire, mutual visits, exchange of news, etc.) such as occurred last year at Christmas and New Year at several points on the Western Front, is strictly forbidden; this crime will be considered as verging on high treason.
>
> General HQ have issued instructions, dated the 12th inst [December], that fire will be opened on every man who leaves the trench and moves in the direction of the enemy without orders, as well as on every French soldier who does not make it clear that he is a deserter.

For many, perhaps most, there was no impulse to show a friendly Christmas face to the enemy. A young officer of the Queen's Westminster Rifles, Roland Bull, who had not been in France in 1914, wrote from 'front-line trenches' to his uncle:

> We had a pseudo-merry Christmas in the front line – there was no fraternizing like last year – people remembered the *Lusitania* a bit, I think, but the Huns shouted across and wished us a merry Xmas but all they got from us & the heavies was two hours of 9.2 howitzer in their front parapet.

The Canadians were now in the line and they reported that on Christmas Day the Germans showed a desire to fraternize, but a few rounds from their artillery batteries stopped this. There was also an attempt to erect a Christmas tree opposite

British trenches near Roulers, but the party involved was fired on and one man was hit.

From the German side an officer of the 73rd Hanoverian Regiment, Ernst Jünger, recorded a gesture by the British which produced a similarly violent response:

> We spent Christmas Eve in the line. The men stood in the mud and sang Christmas carols that were drowned by the enemy machine-guns. On Christmas Day we lost a man in No. 3 platoon by a flanking shot through the head. Immediately after, the English attempted a friendly overture and put up a Christmas tree on their parapet. But our fellows were so embittered that they fired and knocked it over. And this in turn was answered with rifle grenades. In this miserable fashion we celebrated Christmas Day.

Lieutenant Gordon Barber noted the peculiar behaviour of the French to the right of his Queen's Own Cameron Highlanders at Loos, who exchanged carols with the Germans for most of the night, subsequently went out to meet them 'for about three minutes' and then, the moment they got back to their trenches, 'put over covey after covey of rifle grenades. A true conception of the Christmas spirit!'

☆

Yet in places there was an echo of the mood and atmosphere of 1914.

Fritz Zeck was a nineteen-year-old *gefreiter* (lance-corporal) of the 235th Reserve Infantry Regiment. He and his brother had joined the colours on the outbreak of war and within weeks were in action at Langemarck, where so many of Germany's young volunteers marched singing into battle only to be slaughtered in their hundreds. Zeck's brother was killed and he himself was severely wounded so that he was not in the line at Christmas 1914 – indeed, he did not complete his convalescence until the summer of 1915. Shortly afterwards he received an extraordinary instruction from his Company Commander – to prepare a soldiers' choir to sing carols in the front line the following Christmas, the carols to be also heard by the English opposite. He had been chosen for this task because he had a modest knowledge of the violin and his ability to speak Dutch helped in the matter of obtaining music, carol books and, appropriately enough, a violin to help in leading the singing:

> About 50 men who could 'sing' were chosen from the battalion and the practice began . . . The result was perhaps not very pleasing, but at least the carols were heard, loud and clear.
>
> Shortly before Christmas we were ready. In the trench it was comparatively quiet with little artillery activity and isolated rifle and machine-gun fire . . . We assembled about two thirds of the rehearsed singers into the front trench as twilight fell. We were only about 60–80 metres away from the English positions.
>
> We climbed out of the trench and sang our first carol, 'Stille Nacht, Heilige Nacht'. When the sound had faded away, we could see in the light of some flares some English on the top of their trench breastworks listening to us. As the carols went on, more and more joined them, so that finally a large group stood listening in the open.
>
> After we had sung all our carols we could hear a few calls from opposite which we could not quite comprehend. We too called something across and both parties disappeared into their trenches.
>
> During this night no shot fell.

The event at Langemarck did not involve actual fraternization: singers and listeners stayed strictly on their own side of

No Man's Land. But near Laventie, on the old trucing ground of 1914, several battalions were involved in a memorable if brief meeting between the trenches which caused a small sensation at the time and resulted in two officers being court-martialled. The units concerned were from the newly formed Guards Division under Major-General Lord Cavan and included the 1 and 2/Scots Guards, the 1/Coldstream Guards and some men of the 4/Coldstreams; also the 14 and 15/Royal Welch Fusiliers, new to the line and attached to the Guards for instruction.

This was familiar territory to the men of 1914 and, indeed, only a little to the south of the point where Hulse's Scots Guards and the Gordon Highlanders had had their long peace with the Germans the previous winter. Though the lines had shifted somewhat, the same willow-lined ditch ran through the middle of No Man's Land, with the difference that, a year later, the willows were grotesquely twisted and bent by shell-fire. Now on the night of Christmas Eve it was beginning to happen all over again, as the sounds of merrymaking and singing came from the German trenches and shouts of 'Merry Christmas, Tommy' and 'Merry Christmas, Fritz' were exchanged between the lines. Former Private Felstead of the 15/Royal Welch Fusiliers recalled that the Germans, no doubt acknowledging the nationality of the new arrivals on the British side, sang 'All through the Night', to which the Welshmen replied with 'Good King Wenceslas' and other carols. Then at dawn 'both sides poked their heads up and started to climb out of their respective trenches and we met halfway'. Wyn Griffith, witnessing this scene, wrote of 'a rush of men from both sides, carrying tins of meat, biscuits and other commodities for barter', and added: 'This was the first time I had seen No Man's Land, and it was now Every Man's Land, or nearly so.' Wilfred Ewart of the

1/Scots Guards also described this remarkable and moving event which, as in the case of Christmas 1914, was not without its minor tragedies:

> A British sergeant is shot dead almost at the outset, as he stands on the parapet. But this makes no difference. It must be an accident. The supreme craving of humanity, the irresistible, spontaneous impulse born of a common faith and a common fear, fully triumph.
>
> And so the grey and khaki figures surge towards each other as one man. The movement has started on the right. It spreads like contagion. Only we officers, the sentries and a few non-commissioned officers remain in our trench. The men meet at the willow-lined stream; they even cross it and mingle together in a haphazard throng. They talk and gesticulate, and shake hands over and over again. They pat each other on the shoulder and laugh like schoolboys, and leap across the little stream for fun. And when an Englishman falls in and a Boche helps him out there is a shout of laughter that echoes back to the trenches.
>
> The Germans exchange cigars and pieces of sausage, and sauerkraut and concentrated coffee for cigarettes and bully beef and ration biscuits and tobacco. They express mutual admiration by pointing and signs. It is our leather waistcoats and trench coats that attract their attention; it is their trench overalls, made of coarse canvas, that attract ours. We shout 'Hullo, Fritz!' 'Good Morning, Fritz!' 'Merry Christmas!' 'Happy Christmas!' 'How's your father?' 'Come over and call!' 'Come and have breakfast', and the like, amid roars of laughter . . .
>
> Then from the trenches of the 95th Bavarian Reserve Infantry Regiment two officers in black accoutrements and shiny field boots come out, wishing to take photographs of our Tommies, and offering them cigars. Their request is refused,

and presently they say: 'You will have five minutes to get back to your trenches before our artillery will open fire.'

And it does. And two or three men are wounded almost at once. But for twenty-four hours not a shot [from the trenches] is fired on either side. A common brotherhood of suffering – or is it an act of God, or just human curiosity? – has united Englishmen and Bavarians this grey Christmas morning which no one on either side who has taken part in this quaint scene will ever forget.

It was the same story, and the same cause. As ex-Private Bertie Felstead put it nearly seventy years later:

The Germans were men of their FATHERLAND and we of our MOTHERLAND and Human nature being what it is the Feelings built up overnight and so both sides got up from their front-line trenches to meet halfway in No Man's Land.

This time, however, unlike the previous year it was all over very quickly. Ex-Private Harold Diffey of the 15/Royal Welch Fusiliers described what happened:

After about 20 to 30 minutes a Staff Officer with red tabs, a Major and a vociferous Sgt-Major appeared yelling, 'You came out to fight the Huns, not to make friends with them.' So our lads reluctantly returned followed by a salvo from our 18-pounders which ended this episode.

But in fact the episode was not quite over. There was a considerable *fracas* to follow, at the centre of which were two officers of the 1/Scots Guards, Captain Miles Barne, in temporary command, and Captain Sir Iain Colquhoun, a company commander, who had allowed the truce to take place on his front. Colquhoun's personal diary records the events of Christmas day as he saw them:

When having breakfast about 9 a.m. a sentry reported to me that the Germans were standing up on their parapets and walking towards our barbed wire. I ran out to our Firing Trenches and saw our men looking over the parapet and the Germans outside our barbed wire. A German officer came forward and asked me for a truce for Xmas. I replied that this was impossible. He then asked for ¾ hour to bury his dead. I agreed. The Germans then started burying their dead and we did the same. This was finished in ½ hr's time. Our men and the Germans then talked and exchanged cigars, cigarettes etc for ¼ of an hour and, when the time was up, I blew a whistle and both sides returned to their trenches. For the rest of the day the Germans walked about and sat on their parapets. Our men did much the same, but remained in their trenches. Not a shot was fired.

By the next morning the matter was beginning to blow up into a minor scandal. Colquhoun wrote:

Went at 10 a.m. to Winchester House to explain to a Court of Inquiry my conduct on Christmas Day. The Brigadier (who came round my trenches 10 mins after my truce was over) doesn't mind a bit, but the Major-General [Cavan] is furious about it. The Coldstream and our 2nd Batt. are also implicated.

Indeed, Lord Cavan was *very* furious about the affair, and had already, on Christmas Day itself, forwarded a report to his Corps Commander, in which he stated that he 'regretted the incident more than I can say' and that he had ordered a full and searching enquiry as to how 'my implicit orders came to be disobeyed'.

In the event, Barne and Colquhoun were placed under close arrest on 4 January and ordered not to leave their billets while awaiting court martial; the other officers involved were not to be proceeded against. However, the next day Colquhoun received a letter from his wife, Dinah – who was no other than the niece of Margot Asquith, wife of the Prime Minister – informing him that the baby she was expecting was starting and would he please come quickly home. He was promptly given five days' leave. He returned to find that the Prime Minister's distinguished and brilliant son by his first marriage, Raymond Asquith, then serving as an officer in the Grenadier Guards, had been appointed Prisoner's Friend. The two men had not met, but Asquith immediately took a liking to Colquhoun – 'arrogant, independent and brave. He is quite indifferent about his case and hardly interested enough to talk about it.' By contrast he found Barne 'terribly depressed' and 'pretty mopy', though Asquith was sure they could be got off with 'a lightish punishment'.

The court martial took place on 18 January. Asquith called his own part in it 'a pretty bloody and exhausting struggle', adding that he became 'much attached to Colquhoun in the course of the case . . . His deportment was quite faultless, both before and during the proceedings . . . and there is no doubt that he is a man of exceptional dash and courage.' In the outcome, it was Colquhoun's excellent military record that proved the best defence. Barne was acquitted, while Colquhoun was sentenced to be 'reprimanded'; but on the day that the sentence was announced the Commander-in-Chief, Haig, confirmed the proceedings but remitted the sentence 'because of Sir Iain's distinguished conduct in the field. He has been with me since "the retreat" and was wounded at the Battle of Ypres in end of October 1914.'

The later history of those involved in this story is worth recording. Barne was eventually promoted major but was killed in 1917 when a damaged British aeroplane accidentally released a bomb on the British lines. Sir Iain Colquhoun of Luss, to give him his full title, became a brigadier-general and survived the war. Raymond Asquith was killed in the Guards' attack on the Somme on 15 September 1916.

Postscript

The Christmas truce of 1914, like its small-scale counterpart of one year later, was soon left behind by the march of events. As the numbers drawn to the Western Front grew larger and humanity seemed lost in longer and greater battles and new and ever more formidable technology, so the idea of shaking hands, joking and exchanging souvenirs with the enemy in No Man's Land appeared increasingly remote and unreal, until even those who had taken part could find it difficult to accept that such events had actually occurred. As former Private W. A. Quinton wrote, looking back on the war from the perspective of the 1920s: 'Men who joined us later were inclined to disbelieve us when we spoke of the incident, and no wonder, for as the months rolled by, we who were actually there could hardly realize that it had happened, except for the fact that every little detail stood out so well in our memory!'

Yet echoes of that remarkable opt-out from hostility continued to reverberate, evoking in some at least a genuine sense of nostalgia. An officer of the Royal Field Artillery, Second Lieutenant Edward Beddington-Behrens, wrote this in a letter dated Boxing Day 1916:

> Everything was done to prevent any fraternizing between the two sides as the Boche would use the opportunity by getting useful information. Besides, things have got past the stage when one can fraternize with the enemy, there is too much hatred flying about, it would also induce bad discipline to our troops. However I must say going to talk to the Boche in No Man's Land like we did the first Xmas rather appeals to

one's sporting instincts, don't you think so? Instead, however, the artillery had a Christmas strafe at all hours of the day and night.

Yet even in the harsher climate of this third wartime Christmas the fraternizing instinct was not quite dead. Private Walter Hoskyn, serving with the 5/King's Liverpool Regiment in the Ypres sector, recorded the following episode in his diary:

> On Xmas Day weather was fine, no firing of any description. Fritz showed himself during the day and invited us into no man's land to meet half way.
>
> Major Gordon saw them and ordered two snipers to fire on them, which they did. The Batn called him a dirty dog and so he was. It was an unBritish act, as the 9th KLR were doing work in our trenches and encouraged Fritz by shouting and waving.

Hoskyn recorded that after the lull on the 25th hostilities were resumed with particular vigour. 'I suppose with no firing on Xmas Day,' he commented, 'both sides had a surplus amount of ammunition so let it go at one another. Very lively indeed towards evening.'

Other evidence suggests that certain unofficial accommodations with the enemy were in operation at this period, more as a consequence of the conditions than of the season. The sheer awfulness of the terrain in some sectors during the winter of 1916–17 – considered at the time to be the worst in European memory – was a powerful factor in enforcing a hands-off mentality even on the most thrusting of battalions. 'Really it is quite impossible for anyone to attack anything in this winter's Somme mud,' was the comment of one infantry subaltern at this time. 'The men would be drowned before they could cross "no man's land".' The writer was Lieutenant B. L. Lawrence, a

Cambridge-educated volunteer officer serving with the 1/Grenadier Guards on the north-eastern edge of the area over which the five-month Battle of the Somme had just been fought. There was a further circumstance which made a relaxation of normal military behaviour almost mandatory; both sides had a perfect view of each other's positions. As Lawrence put it in a later letter, in February 1917:

> It was a curious situation as being so close to the Boche and so much above him, we looked down right into his trenches and could see every movement, while we for our part had to cross the sky line (only about 50 or 60 yards from him) to get to our front line. By common consent there was a sort of policy of live and let live and neither side was sniped. If either of us had begun to use our rifles, both front lines would have become untenable.

But the prevailing military ethos was as a rule utterly opposed to such accommodations. When at Kemmel in that same month, a brief armistice was offered by the Germans and accepted by the British, so that the latter could bring in their wounded following an unsuccessful raid, this evoked the severest condemnation from the Divisional Commander. His reaction was especially strong because the event had occurred immediately after the circulation of a memorandum on the subject of relations with the enemy, prompted by a similar incident elsewhere. Its keynote sentences stated:

> The Divisional Commander wishes it to be clearly understood by all ranks that any understanding of this or any other description is strictly forbidden.
>
> We have to deal with a treacherous and unscrupulous foe, who, from the commencement of the present war, has repeatedly proved himself unworthy of the slightest confidence. No

communication is to be held with him without definite instructions from Divisional Headquarters, and any attempt on his part to fraternize with our own troops is to be instantly repressed.

As it happened, Lieutenant-Colonel Rowland Feilding, CO of the battalion which had mounted the raid, 6/Connaught Rangers, had not seen the document in question when he agreed to the armistice. When he did so, his own reaction was as vigorous as his superior officer's, if bearing an entirely different stamp. In an eloquent letter to his wife, in which there are clear echoes of the appeal to 'sporting instincts' referred to by Beddington-Behrens, he quoted the memorandum at full length, then added angrily:

God knows whether I should have acted differently had I [seen it]. Anyway, a Court of Enquiry is to be convened, to decide whether we did fraternize or not, and orders still more stringent than that which I have quoted have been issued.

In future, if fifty of our wounded are lying in No Man's Land, they are (as before) to remain there till dark, when we may get them in if we can; but no assistance, tacit or otherwise, is to be accepted from the enemy. Ruthlessness is to be the order of the day. Frightfulness is to be our watchword. Sportsmanship, chivalry, pity – all the qualities which Englishmen used to pride themselves in possessing – are to be scrapped.

In short, our methods henceforth are to be strictly Prussian; those very methods to abolish which we claim to be fighting this war.

It is fair to add that Feilding makes no mention of any subsequent Court of Enquiry; it must be presumed that the threat was quietly dropped.

☆

There appears to have been no Christmas truce in 1917. That the commanders had not forgotten earlier events, however, is evident from the diary of a Captain R. C. G. Dartford, then serving as a liaison officer with an infantry brigade of the Portuguese Expeditionary Force near Laventie – a prime trucing area both in 1914 and 1915. The British were worried that the Germans might play the truce card to the unsuspecting Portuguese, who had arrived at the front only that year and had not gained the greatest of reputations for military ardour or effectiveness. Dartford wrote on Christmas Eve:

> Fear of fraternizing this evening so British officers have to go to the front line and report if there's anything unusual in the enemy's attitude. As a prevention there was a lot of harassing fire carried out during the night which annoyed everybody very much.

In fact there was little appetite for trucing on the Allied side. The year 1917 had been terrible. Mutinies in the French Army, Russia's defeat on the Eastern Front, and a widespread feeling among the British, following the sacrificial fighting at Passchendaele and the dashed hopes of Cambrai, that the conflict might go on indefinitely, made this fourth and, as it turned out, final wartime Christmas a grim one indeed. There had been altogether too much squalor and destruction, too much desperate glory, for friendly meetings in No Man's Land. Now it was a war without quarter and little chivalry, the exchanges of bully beef and cigars, the Anglo-German Bisleys all quite out of fashion. Yet the Germans had not entirely given up, as is evident from the following New Year's Day entry in the diary of Lieutenant-Colonel F. A. W. Armitage, CO of the 1/Hampshires:

> Enemy attempted to fraternize on our left, but were shot at by us, otherwise a quiet day.

Several days later there was a further offer of fraternization, in the area of the former battlefield of Cambrai. The episode is described in the diary of Captain Harold Horne of the 1/Royal Marines, a battalion of the 63rd Royal Naval Division. Conditions provided the basic cause, but there was also on the German side a hint of the old impulse to meet and relax between the lines:

6 January 1918. Frost broke. For some time there had been a keen frost and the trenches, usually wet, were frozen hard and like an 'ice palace'. When the frost broke the trenches collapsed and the mud rose and we had to get out of the trench. Fortunately the Germans were in the same plight. There we were, two lines of troops within hailing distance, walking about in the open, lighting fires to cook food and waiting till the trenches could be cleared. We had a Lewis gun post manned by two men some distance in front of our line in an old communication trench which connected our line with the German as ours was actually an old front line trench which had been captured during the Cambrai offensive in 1917. I noticed a German officer approaching our men and, as we had strict orders against fraternizing, I went across no man's land to intercept him. It took me some few minutes as the going was heavy and I had to get through our own barbed wire so that I was quite conscious of being watched by my own men and the Germans across the way. By the time I got there my two men and Jerry were trying to understand each other. It appeared that he had volunteered on behalf of a number of them who wanted to arrange a fraternal party with us. It took some time to convince him that we had to decline the invitation but eventually he accepted the situation. He gave each of my men a cigar, they gave him cigarettes which, apparently, he thought a good exchange; he saluted, I returned it, and we both went back to our lines.

☆

Were major truces unique to the Western Front in the First World War?

Evidence is patchy but undoubtedly there were occasions elsewhere when the sacredness of the season interrupted the normal routines of military activity. Nineteen sixteen witnessed such an occurrence on the Eastern Front in Galicia, where Austro-Hungarian and Russian forces confronted each other in entrenched positions not dissimilar to those that had long been endemic in France and Flanders. Friedrich Kohn, a young Jewish doctor serving as a medical officer with a Hungarian regiment, witnessed the event:

> The winter of 1915–16 was very severe and when I joined my regiment at the end of February the country was covered in deep snow. No military action was possible and the army lived in trenches, which were made as comfortable as possible. Nothing was to be seen in front of us and no shot was heard, only occasionally one saw a solitary human figure running about, who would then quickly disappear. Then thaw set in and the peace stopped and artillery duels between the Austrian and Russian armies started, sometimes by day, but more frequently during darkness.
>
> Then suddenly on Easter Sunday, about 5 o'clock in the morning, about twenty Russians came out of their trenches, waving white flags, carrying no weapons, but baskets and bottles. One of them came quite near and one of our soldiers went out to meet him and asked what he wanted. He asked whether we would not agree to stop the war for a day or two and, in view of Easter, meet between the lines and have a meal together. We told him that first we would have to ask the military authorities whether such a meeting would be possible. The Divisional Commander refused permission. Nevertheless at 12 noon the Russians came out of their trenches and brought with them their military band, who came playing at full

strength, and they brought baskets of food and bottles of wine and vodka, and we came out too and we had a meal with them. We also had wine and food to offer.

During the meeting both sides seemed to be embarrassed, but both sides were polite to each other and consumed the food and drinks which we offered to each other. After a few hours we all went quietly back to our trenches.

I talked with a Colonel who spoke perfect German and he told me that he had lived for several years in Vienna. When I asked him why he was always firing shrapnel at my first aid post – he told me he knew exactly where it was – he promised to leave me alone and he would send a rocket if he had to leave. For the next fourteen days I was left unmolested. Then he sent me a rocket, telling me that his unit was leaving.

There was for the next few weeks a lull in activities apart from a few skirmishes, until about the middle of May, when heavy artillery activities started which eventually led to the great Brusilov offensive which forced the Austro-Hungarians out of their trenches and made them retreat behind the river Dniester.

For Kohn this event was just one episode in a long life which would also include imprisonment under the Nazis and the dislocation of being a Jewish refugee, but it remained for him a major revelation about the paradoxes of war:

I have seen demonstrated in front of my own eyes that suddenly people who are trying to kill each other, and will try to kill again when the day is over, are still able to sit together and talk to each other.

☆

What of later wars?

The Second World War never saw anything on the scale, or

of the spirit, of the events of 1914. The conflicts with Nazi Germany and imperialist Japan were not of a kind to produce fraternizations or football matches. Quarter was rarely expected or given. There were, however, various minor instances of humanity between enemies, though Christmas was not part of the equation.

In the Desert War, during the siege of Tobruk in 1941, there was a brief interlude in the fighting which began in a somewhat curious manner, as described by a British artilleryman who witnessed the event from a forward Observation Post:

> Quite unexpectedly, one of the enemy climbed above ground, moved a few steps away from his trench and started to urinate. I waited for the Australians to open fire on him but, suddenly, there was a great laugh from someone on our side, then two or three of them climbed out and began to do the same.
>
> It was contagious. In a few minutes there must have been about fifty men, friend and foe alike, relieving themselves, shaking out their blankets, trying to toss cigarettes across the intervening space, and generally enjoying a holiday from hate. This must have gone on for about six or seven minutes before the whine of a shell sent everyone diving below ground again and the war was resumed.

Significantly, this episode occurred when the conditions of warfare approximated to a remarkable degree to those of the Western Front in the First World War, with opposing forces close to each other in entrenched positions. These conditions were repeated in Italy during the long struggles for Cassino in 1943–4, the defence of which for the Germans came to resemble that of the British at Ypres from 1914 to 1918 or the French at Verdun in 1916. In the words of a participant and subsequent chronicler of the Cassino battles, Fred Majdalany: 'It was a cause in its own right, a cause to die for.' There was, however, 'a more human side to the picture':

> The exceptional closeness of the combatants, together with the restriction it imposed on daylight movement, led gradually and spontaneously to the practice of openly evacuating wounded men in daylight under the Red Cross. Nothing was arranged officially. It was done sparingly. But it was done, and both sides respected the Red Cross. It was one of those strange situations in which front-line soldiers, separated by a hundred yards or less, seem to develop a strange kinship in extremity. In the mountains the stretcher-bearers of both sides made these occasional daytime excursions into the boulders and thickets of no man's land, and sometimes they exchanged words with each other . . .
>
> That was Cassino. A battlefield on which for weeks the dead could not be moved or buried: . . . which made survival, even at an animal level, an achievement in itself: yet on which the medical orderlies of both sides fell into the habit of wandering, almost at will, in a mute kinship that in its spontaneous charity was perhaps the most ironic witness of all to the folly that made it necessary.

The campaign in Western Europe also had its incidents of shared compassion. In September 1944 there was a day-long truce in Holland for the removal of the wounded; the initiative came from the Germans, their request being sent back via the chain of command on the British side and agreed by the Brigadier. A former Corporal who was present wrote: 'I cannot say if there is any official record of this incident but it certainly took place and we enjoyed the mental relaxation afforded by this quiet day.'

☆

There have been many conflicts since, with just the occasional echo of the truces of long ago. The Korean War was fought with an intensity exacerbated by ideological hatred yet when the cease-fire took effect in July 1953 former enemies were immediately out between the lines fraternizing, and, in the style of 1914, taking photographs of each other. In January 1969 in the Nigerian–Biafran war there was a forty-eight-hour truce during the visit to Nigeria of the Brazilian football team, Santos, which included the world-famous player Pelé. Reputedly, participants from both sides went to see the match while those remaining at the front listened to it on the radio. But there were other truces in this grim civil war which were honoured more in the breach than in the observance. A report in *The Times* only a few weeks later recorded that a much-publicized forty-eight-hour truce to mark the Muslim festival of Id-al-Kabir had been broken on its first day by an air raid in which 120 civilians had been killed; it added that this was not the first time such violations had occurred and that, notably, a Christmas truce arranged two months earlier had been marked by no fewer than four bombing-raids on Christmas Eve.

Yet it should be no surprise that such conflicts, like others closer to home such as the long struggle in Ireland, or more recent ones such as the war of ethnic cleansing in the former Yugoslavia, have regularly given rise, at the approach of December, to hopes of a Christmas truce. The concept has become part of the general culture, though regrettably it has tended to carry with it, as in the example given above, the assumption that, if agreed, it will either be of pathetically short duration, or be immediately and blatantly ignored.

'One human episode among the atrocities' was Conan Doyle's verdict on the Christmas truce of 1914, writing just two years later. From the perspective of several generations later, and a century which has been prolific in atrocities, its uniqueness still stands unchallenged. In view of the horrors which have followed, it would be easy to dismiss the events of that far-off Christmas as little more than a candle in the darkness. Yet they offer a light where no light might have been, and are thus a source of encouragement and hope that should not be overlooked and forgotten, rather acknowledged and, indeed, celebrated.

Appendix A

DOCUMENTS OF THE CHRISTMAS TRUCE

Official documentation of the events of Christmas 1914 can be found in the Army War Diaries held at the National Archives, Kew (class WO95), much of it of historical interest and value. Four reports are printed here, of which the common denominator is an attempt to show that the military intelligence gained justified the unconventional nature of what had taken place. This is especially true of Items 3 and 4, which form the report which Captain W. G. S. Kenny of the 1/39 Garhwal Rifles had 'the honour' to present in order to explain his actions and those of his fellow officer, Lieutenant J. C. St G. Welchman, when fraternizing with the enemy on Christmas Day. Despite his best efforts, Kenny failed to satisfy his superiors, with the consequences as described on pages 157–8.

1. Report to 11th Infantry Brigade by Captain J. D. M. Beckett 'on proceedings to the front of Hampshire Regt trench on Christmas Day'
(TNA WO95/1488: Appx 112 26.12.14)

The night 24/25 was particularly free from sniping; to our front the enemy were singing Christmas carols and their national songs. About 10 a.m. on Christmas morning I was making a sketch of the trench under cover of fog when I saw several of the enemy approaching from the trench north of our T piece. I shouted out for them to halt not firing as the enemy was without arms; this was complied with and I sent forward a patrol to state that they must approach no nearer and return to their trench or I should open fire. The enemy then returned to their trench. Soon after more of the enemy were seen approaching from their main trench to the East of our position. These men also were halted and a patrol sent forward. As the patrol seemed unable to induce enemy to return to their trenches and more were seen approaching I went forward, and asked to see an officer. An under-officer came forward, but failed to make him understand me; an interpreter however was soon produced and the enemy asked that there should be no shooting as it was Christmas day and that they should be allowed to bury their dead of which there were a considerable number a short way in front of their trench. This request I granted as by this time considerable numbers were walking about outside their trenches. A spot was indicated just by their foremost dead which I informed them if they passed I should be compelled to open fire on anyone outside the trench. The enemy agreed to these conditions and kept to them throughout the day. Towards evening what looked like a staff officer appeared and ordered all back to the trenches which order was immediately complied with.

To our right front a gathering of some two to three hundred men of both sides took place, the men exchanging gifts, handing over enemy's dead from near our trenches, and even exchanging rifles. Throughout the day I kept the garrison of my trench from contact with the enemy, the men not being allowed out of the trench on the enemy's side. I gained the following information as regards the enemy and his trenches and dispositions.

The men were well clothed and seemed well supplied; every man was wearing a pair of gum-boots.

The regiments represented were 132, 133 & 134 and some men with F.A. under a crown, the great majority belonging to the 133rd regiment. The men seemed in age to range between nineteen and forty-five.

They seemed very simple-minded creatures, and were much elated over alleged victories in Russia. They stated they wished the war would soon finish, but were confident of their success. The strength to our immediate front I estimated to be about one man to every two yards except on right front, where they appeared to be much stronger there being at least one man per yard looking over the parapet even after a considerable number had left the trench.

The wire in front of enemy's trenches was mounted on wooden frames with cross pieces at either end three foot high. The men appeared to have no difficulty in stepping over these, I could not see if there was trip wire in addition. The trenches seemed to be in good condition, the men jumped in from the parapet without water splashing about. The trenches are loop-holed about eighteen inches off the ground (in the front trench) these were about ten feet apart. Three lines of trenches were observed, the rear line being about six hundred yards from the front line, these were connected up by communication trenches. A fortified house about [will get this]* yards in rear of enemy's barricade on the north side of Le Gheer road was observed. I could see no Maxim guns or emplacements.

signed: J. D. M. Beckett
Capt ACC Coy Hampshire Regt

---

* In the event Captain Beckett was unable to provide this information.

2. Report to 12th Brigade by
Lieutenant-Colonel E. B. Cuthbertson,
Commanding Officer, 2/Monmouthshire
(TNA WO95/1501)

Observations 25th Dec. 1914

1. Opposite No 4 Trench Germans were burying their dead. Men were sent out to see that no trenches were dug or any ruse employed. Some Germans had 104 in red cloth letters on shoulder straps. Buttons on their tunics had crowns. A belt was picked up from one of the dead which had 104 Regt 2nd Brigade 5th Corps.

2. Other men were wearing either R.B. or R.P. it is not certain which. They had different Nos 3. 4. 5. 6. on buttons & their shoulder straps. These men were wearing buttons with crowns.

3. Others again had 107 & 108 on shoulder straps the latter also having a crown.

4. There were also some seen wearing 181 on shoulder straps & 10 on buttons.

5. One Officer was noticed wearing a cap similar to our Staff Officers cap, he was wearing spurs & had broad braid band on his cuff & 2 buttons.

6. Other Officers were hard to distinguish from the men but were pointed out by a German soldier from Nottingham who gave their character such as very hard on the men, another was 'snotty' and another 'grumpy'; he also asked why our Officers do not come out. This German also spoke about pay & said German soldiers were getting 3/- a week on Service & their navies were paid 8/-. He also said they were paid on the 1st, 11th & 21st.

He was sick of the war & stated that he had as many friends in England as in Germany.

7. Their NCOs carried torches on the buttons of their tunics & field glasses.

8. Signallers were seen with crossed flags.

9. Their uniforms were clean & their boots were very good.

10. They had plenty of tobacco & gave our men cigarettes & cigars & excellent socks. They offered them wine. It is interesting to note that one of our men being offered a glass of wine made the German sample it first.

11. They reported that the money was not much good to them as they stated the inhabitants had left behind them. [*sic*]

12. The unoccupied trench in front of No 4 was full of dead bodies, nearly all shot through the head. The trench was merely head cover.

13. Several were wearing short sling coats like oilskins.

14. Our men reported that Germans were of all ages from 14 or 15 to 40 & 50.

15. A large majority wore glasses.

16. When they came out to bury their dead a party doubled out of the reserve trench.

17. Opposite No 4 they zigzagged through the entanglements.

18. Opposite No 2 they stepped over the barbed wire coming out, but had more difficulty in getting back.

19. At no time were the Germans allowed to approach our trenches & it was to prevent them coming too near that our men were sent out.

20. Capt Watkins reports that they were strongest opposite communication trench between 2 & 3 where we have no men.

21. It was noticed that while the Germans would talk English, on German being spoken they took cover like rabbits.

22. They sent out to apologize for shooting one of our men.

26.12.1914   Lieut-Colonel E. B. Cuthbertson
                                                    2/Bn Monmouth Reg

3. Report by Captain W. G. S. Kenny,
1/39 Garhwal Rifles
(TNA WO95/3945)

To: The Adjutant 1/39th G

In compliance with your telephone message, I have the honour to submit the following report as regards the men of my section of defence leaving their trenches and approaching & fraternizing with the Germans this afternoon. At about 2.30 p.m. as far as I am aware, a Rifleman came and told me that many of the enemy were standing up on their parapet unarmed & shouting to us. I went to the Gap & there saw about 40 or 50 of the enemy as described. One or two called to us in English to come out & speak to them. Then one German came about 10 yards out of his trench & put a box of cigars on the ground. Lt Welchman was then with me & he gave Orders for all sentries to remain on the lookout at their posts.

A British cavalry soldier attached to 4th Cavy Machine-Guns, who was about 10 yards on my left, came out of the Gap trench & went towards the enemy. I then noticed that others on my left from the 2/39th Garhwalis were out of their trench & moving towards the enemy's trenches. On the impulse of the moment I also went out & Lt Welchman, Capt. Pearse 4' Cavy & some of the men came out too. About 12 or 15 Germans approached us & came up & shook hands with us & wished us the compliments of the Season. One or two spoke English. I ordered them not to come nearer our line than halfway. I then asked permission to bury the dead that were lying there: this was accorded & our men buried on the spot 1 Jemir & 4 Riflemen of the 2/3rd & Jemir Kushal Takuli & Rifleman Thepru F Coy. 1/39th G. Their identity discs were searched for but not found. One dead man was lying right at the foot of the German parapet & 3 men of H Coy were permitted to go right up to the German trench there.

One or two others of our men were given brand [*sic*] & cigrettes [*sic*] right close to the German trench.

Afterwards 2 German subalterns came out and spoke to us. The men were all of the 16th Saxon Regt. I asked them this (as I can talk a little German). They told me they were Saxons & not Prussians. I did not notice any other regiment amongst the men. Shortly after this I was told that Major Henderson was calling for me & I went back to him & he ordered me to bring all the men back into the trenches.

Unfortunately I then noticed that a party of 4 or 5 Germans had come up to about 10 yards from our trench. I had previously given orders for no one to approach us closer than halfway. But these men could not have seen into our trenches as our barbed wire would have prevented them. They could not have located our Machine-Guns as these are dismantled & hidden during the day.

Captain Burton 2/39th G told me that he found the body of Captain Robertson-Glasgow 2/39th G.

I wish to make it clear that a German first came up to halfway between the two trenches, & a British Cavalry soldier attached to 4th Cav. Machine-Guns then went up to him & shook hands, whereupon more Germans came out & then more of our men.

I attach herewith a report on the German trenches, seen by our men & corroborated by 2 British Cavalry soldiers who also went up to the German parapet & helped to bury a dead Gurkha.

Lt Welchman noticed a printed postal address on a box of cigarettes, which a German soldier had been handing round – on it was printed the man's name, Army Corps (7th), Division (14th) and Regt (16th).

Both the British Cavalry soldiers who helped to bury the dead Gurkha on the German parapet, state that at that time the Germans had completely evacuated their trenches, & were all outside & unarmed.

Lt Welchman & I estimate the numbers of the enemy we saw opposite the Gap & slightly to the left opposite the 2/39th as about 100.

(sd) W. G. S. Kenny Capt 1/39th G
25th December 1914

True copy (signed) J. Lumb Capt
for Acting Adjutant 1/39th Garhwal Rifles

4. Report on German Trenches Opposite 1/39th Left Section of Defence by Capt. W. G. S. Kenny
(TNA WO95/3945)

The German trenches in Depth, width, & general form resemble our own. The traverses seemed closer together, about 6 yards apart, but were not built right up to ground level. The parapet is very thick at least 5'. Loopholes very strong & well made some with strong wooden sides tops & bottoms, the side walls of such loopholes being in some instances 3" thick. Other loopholes were made of galvanized iron, sides, tops, & bottoms.

There are 2 Machine-Guns in epaulments opposite the centre of the Gap, 6' separating the two epaulments. There is another Machine-Gun opposite a point 20 yds from the Right Corner of the Gap.

The men's shelters are like ours & cut out underneath the parapet. It appeared that there were considerably more men than loopholes. The trenches were clean & dry. There were no wire entanglements anywhere. There is a *chevaux-de-frize* opposite the Left Centre of the Gap, but it is a good deal damaged. There were several ladders seen on the rear wall of the trench, but none on the front wall. But the ladders were movable & not fixed.

(sd) W. G. S. Kenny Capt. 1/39th G

25.12.14

True copy (signed) J. Lumb Captain
for Acting Adjutant 1/39th Garhwal Rifles

Appendix B

BRITISH INFANTRY BRIGADES IN THE LINE AT CHRISTMAS 1914

Battalions of which members are known to have truced are shown in *italic* type

Battalions of which members are known to have truced and fraternized are shown in ***bold italic*** type

{TF: Territorial Force battalion, with arrival date at front}

ATTACHED UNITS listed only if participated in the truce

Commander-in-Chief, British Expeditionary Force Field Marshal Sir J. D. P. French
GCB OM GCVO KCMG

II CORPS
(General Sir H. L. Smith-Dorrien GCB DSO)

3RD DIVISION
(Major-General J. A. L. Haldane CB DSO)

Kemmel facing Spanbroek Mill

7TH BRIGADE
1/Wiltshire   2/R. Irish Rifles   3/Worcestershire
1/Hon. Art. Coy (Inf.) {TF 9.11.14}   2/S. Lancashire

8TH BRIGADE
2/R. Scots (rl'd 3/Worcs & 2/RIR 27.12)
2/Suffolk (rl'd 1/HAC 27.12)   4/Middlesex (rl'd 1/Wilts 27.12)
1/Gordon Highlanders

9TH BRIGADE
1/Northumberland Fus.   4/Royal Fus.
1/Lincolnshire   1/R. Scots Fus.
10/King's (Liverpool) [TF 25.11.14] (in Bde reserve)

5TH DIVISION
(Major-General T. L. N. Morland CB)

Wulverghem–Messines Road

14TH BRIGADE
1/Devonshire   1/E. Surrey (billets until 29.12)
1/D. of Cornwall's LI (billets until 28.12)   *2/Manchester*

15TH BRIGADE
1/*Bedfordshire*   6/*Cheshire* [TF 11.12.14]
1/Cheshire (out of trenches)   1/Dorsetshire   *1/Norfolk*

III CORPS
(Lieutenant-General Sir W. P. Pulteney CB DSO)

4TH DIVISION
(Major-General H. F. M. Wilson CB)

St Yves/Ploegsteert Wood

10TH BRIGADE
2/Seaforth Highlanders   1/R. Warwickshire
2/R. Dublin Fus. (rl'd 1/R. Warwicks 28.12)
1/R. Irish Fus. (rl'd 2/Seaforths 27.12)

11TH BRIGADE

1/Hampshire   1/Rifle Brigade   1/Somerset LI 1/E. Lancashire
5/London (London Rifle Brigade) [TF 19.11.14]

12TH BRIGADE

2/Lancashire Fus.   2/Essex (rl'd 2/*Mons* 25.12, 8.30 p.m.)
2/Monmouthshire [TF 21.12.14] (rl'd by 2/*Essex* 25.12, 8.30 p.m.)
1/Kings Own (out of trenches)   2/Inniskilling Fus. (Bde reserve)

ATTACHED UNITS

XXXII Bde RFA · 135 Bty   31 Heavy Bty RGA
10 Field Ambulance

6TH DIVISION

(Major-General K. L. Keir CB)

Frelinghien/Houplines

19TH BRIGADE

2/R. Welch Fus. 2/Argyll & Sutherland Highlanders
5/Cameronians (Scottish Rifles) [TF 19.11.14]
1/Cameronians (Scottish Rifles)
1/Middlesex (billets – Div. reserve)

18TH BRIGADE (billets until 26.12)

1/E. Yorkshire (rl'd 1/Cameronians eve. 26.12)
1/W. Yorkshire (rl'd 2/Leinster 26.12)
2/Sherwood Foresters (rl'd 2/A & SH. 26.12)
2/Durham LI (rl'd 2/RWF eve. 26.12)

L'Epinette

17TH BRIGADE

2/Leinster 3/Rifle Brigade
16/London (Queen's Westminster Rifles) [TF 11.11.14]
(rejoined 18 Bde 26.12.14)
1/Royal Fus. (rl'd QWR 26.12)   *1/N. Staffordshire*

Rue du Bois to Grande Flamengrie

16TH BRIGADE

1/Leicestershire   1/The Buffs **(E. Kent)**   2/*York & Lancaster*
1/K. Shropshire LI (rl'd Buffs 26.12)

ATTACHED UNITS

XXXVIII Bde RFA 24 Bty   XII (HOW.) Bde RFA 87 Bty

IV CORPS

(Lieutenant-General Sir H. S. Rawlinson Bt KCB CVO)

7TH DIVISION

(Major-General T. Capper CB)

Bois Grenier

22ND BRIGADE

2/Queen's **(Royal West Surrey)** *8/R. Scots* [TF 11.11.14]
2/R. Warwickshire (billets)   1/R. Welch Fus. (billets)
1/S. Staffordshire (billets until 28.12)

La Boutillerie

21ST BRIGADE

2/Wiltshire   2/Bedfordshire
2/Yorkshire (rl'd 2/Beds 27.12)
2/R. Scots Fus. (rl'd 2/Wilts 27.12)

Sailly–Fromelles Road

20TH BRIGADE

2/Border   2/Gordon Highlanders
6/Gordon Highlanders [TF 5.12.14]   *2/Scots Gds*
1/*Grenadier Gds* (rl'd 2/Scots Gds 27.12)

ATTACHED UNITS
Northumberland Hussars [TF 6.10.14) (A & B Squadrons)
XXII Bde RFA 104 Bty   XIV Bde RHA F & T Bty
III Heavy Bde RGA 104, 111 & 112 Bty   55 Field Coy, RE

8TH DIVISION
(Major-General F. J. Davies CB)

Picantin/Fauquissart

25TH BRIGADE
13/London (Kensington) [TF 13.11.14]   *1/R. Irish Rifles*
2/Lincolnshire (rl'd 1/RIR 26.12)   *2/R. Berkshire*
2/*Rifle Brigade* (rl'd 2/R. Berks 26.12)

Chapigny

23RD BRIGADE
2/Devonshire 2/*W. Yorkshire*
2/Cameronians (Scottish Rifles) (rl'd 24.12 by 2/Devons)
2/Middlesex (rl'd 24.12 by W. Yorks)

La Bassée Rd, Neuve Chapelle

24TH BRIGADE
2/E. Lancashire   2/Northamptonshire
1/*Sherwood Foresters* (rl'd 2/E. Lancs eve. 25.12)
1/*Worcestershire* (rl'd 2/Northants eve. 25.12)
5/Black Watch [TF 13.11.14] (Coys in billets or reserve)

ATTACHED UNITS
2/Field Coy RE   XLV Bde RFA 5 Bty

INDIAN CORPS
(Lieutenant-General Sir J. Willcocks KCB KCSI KCMG DSO)

MEERUT DIVISION
(Lieutenant-General Sir C. A. Anderson KCB)

Richebourg L'Avoué

GARHWAL BRIGADE
2/39 Garhwal Rifles   *1/39 Garhwal Rifles*   *2/3 Gurkha Rifles*
2/Leicestershire (billets)

ATTACHED UNITS
18/Hussars att. *4/Cavalry MG*

I CORPS
(General Sir D. Haig KCB KCIE KCVO ADC Gen.)

2ND DIVISION
(Lieutenant-General Sir C. C. Monro CB)

Le Touret/Rue de L'Epinette

4TH (GUARDS) BRIGADE
1/Hertfordshire [TF 19.11.14]   2/Coldstream Gds
2/Grenadier Gds   3/Coldstream Gds (rl'd 2 Gren. Gds eve. 25.12)
1/Irish Gds

1ST DIVISION
(Major-General R. C. B. Haking CB)

Le Touret/Rue de L'Epinette

2ND BRIGADE
2/R. Sussex   1/Northamptonshire   2/KRRC (rl'd 1/King's 26.12)
1/Loyal N. Lancs (billets)

S. Festubert

3RD BRIGADE
4/R. Welch Fus. [TF 7.12.14]   2/R. Munster Fus.
1/S. Wales Bord. (billets)
1/Gloucestershire   2/Welch   4/Seaforth Highlanders (billets)

N. Givenchy

1ST (GUARDS) BRIGADE
1/Coldstream Gds
1/Cameron Highlanders (rl'd Bl. Watch eve. 25.12)
1/Scots Gds (½ billets / ½ into trenches eve. 25.12)
1/Black Watch   14 London (London Scottish) [TF 7.11.14]
(Reserve att. 2/Bde 28.12.14)

2ND DIVISION
(Lieutenant-General Sir C. C. Monro CB)

N.E. Cuinchy to Canal

6TH BRIGADE
2/S. Staffordshire (rl'd R. Berks 25.12)
1/R. Berkshire (rl'd 25.12, 1 p.m.)
1/KRRC (rl'd 25.12, 1 p.m.)
1/King's (Liverpool) (rl'd KRRC 25.12)

26 December 1914 BEF reorganized into two Armies:

FIRST ARMY
(under General Sir D. Haig)

I CORPS

IV CORPS

INDIAN CORPS

SECOND ARMY
(under General Sir H. L. Smith-Dorrien)

II CORPS

III CORPS

27TH DIVISION

Appendix C

GERMAN INFANTRY REGIMENTS OPPOSITE
THE BEF AT CHRISTMAS 1914

Regiments of which members are known to have truced
are shown in *italic* type

Regiments of which members are known to have truced and
fraternized are shown in ***bold italic*** type

SIXTH ARMY
(Crown Prince Rupprecht of Bavaria)

XIV RESERVE CORPS
(General von Loden)

6TH BAVARIAN RESERVE DIVISION

Kemmel

14TH BAVARIAN RES BDE
— 21st Bavarian Res. Regt, 20th Bavarian Res. Regt

12TH BAVARIAN RES BDE
— 16th Bavarian Res. Regt (some in billets),

17th Bavarian Res. Regt

XIX (SAXON) CORPS
(General von Laffert)
(Brigades and Regiments are split)

40TH DIVISION

Wulverghem

89TH BRIGADE – *134th Inf. Regt, 133rd Inf. Regt*

Ploegsteert Wood

48TH BRIGADE – *106th Inf. Regt*

88TH BRIGADE – *104th Inf. Regt*, 181st *Inf. Regt*

89TH BRIGADE – *134th Inf. Regt*

Frelinghien

133rd Inf. Regt

88TH BRIGADE – *104th Inf. Regt, 6th Jäger Bn*

24TH DIVISION

Railway Armentières–Lille

47TH BRIGADE – *139th Inf. Regt*

48TH BRIGADE – *107th Inf. Regt*

47TH BRIGADE – *179th Inf. Regt*

VII (WESTPHALIAN) CORPS
(General von Claer)

13TH DIVISION

Rue des Bois Blancs

26TH BRIGADE – *55th Inf. Regt, 15th Inf. Regt*

Fromelles

25TH BRIGADE – *158th Inf. Regt, 13th Inf. Regt, 11th Jäger Bn*

14TH DIVISION

Aubers

27TH BRIGADE – 53rd Inf. Regt, *16th Inf. Regt*

North of Festubert to canal

79TH BRIGADE – 57th Inf. Regt, 56th Inf. Regt

Notes and References

For sources of quotations by named soldiers see Index of Soldiers. For publication details of principal books quoted see Bibliography.

Preface 'One human episode amid all the atrocities . . .'

pp. xix–xx Soldiers' comments: Tilley, Sinkinson – See Index of Soldiers; German participant – anonymous soldier's letter quoted in *Vorwärts*, Berlin, translated and reproduced in *Daily Telegraph*, 9 January 1915.

p. xx Fraternizations in other wars: various sources, including 'Fraternizing on the Battlefield', from *The War, Nelson's Picture Weekly*, No. 24, 30 January 1915; 'Unofficial Armistice', E. Ashmead Bartlett, *Daily Telegraph*, 7 January 1915; *Four Years in the Stonewall Brigade*, John O. Casler, Morningside Press, Dayton, Ohio, 1971, originally published 1893.

p. xxi Kilvert reference: *Kilvert's Diary*, A Selection edited and introduced by William Plomer, Cape, 1944, Penguin, 1977.

pp. xxiii–xxiv Hall Caine – see Bibliography.

p. xxiv Conan Doyle history: *The British Campaign in France and Flanders 1914*.

One A Background of Hatred

p. 1 Richard Aldington quotation: from *Death of a Hero*, Chatto & Windus, 1928. Thomas Hardy quotation: from *In Time of 'The Breaking of Nations'* (written in 1915, but the reference is plainly to the cataclysm which began in 1914). C. E. Montague quotation: from *Disenchantment*.

p. 1 ff. Material on Anglo-German attitudes and propaganda, German atrocities, etc: from *Keep the Home Fires Burning*, Cate Haste, Allen Lane, 1977; *The Smoke and the Fire*, John Terraine.

p. 3 H. G. Wells quotations: from 1921 Introduction to *The World Set Free*, first published 1914. Harold Macmillan quotation: from *The Winds of Change*, Macmillan, 1966.

pp. 7–8 *Fire*, anti-English document: from album in the Regimental Museum of the Seaforth Highlanders, Inverness; also reproduced in contemporary newspapers.

pp. 8–9 Letter by Caroline Ethel Cooper: from *Behind the Lines, One Woman's War 1914–18*.

p. 11 Harold Macmillan quotation, op. cit.

Two 'Two huge armies sitting and watching each other'

p. 15 Sir John French's despatch to King George V: quoted in *The Little Field Marshal*, Richard Holmes.

p. 16 A captain of the Grenadier Guards: Captain E. J. L. Pike, quoted in *'Fifteen Rounds a Minute': The Grenadiers at War, 1914*, J.M. Craster (ed.).

pp. 16–17 British officer's account: letter by Captain H. M. Dillon, 2/ Oxford & Bucks Light Infantry, quoted in *The Old Contemptibles*, Keith Simpson.

p. 22 The Territorials were inevitably eager to show that they were as good as the Regulars. It has sometimes been assumed that, largely because they missed the bloody early battles, they were more prepared than the Regulars to fraternize with the Germans at Christmas 1914; and indeed not a few Regular battalions were proud that they had had no truck with the enemy at that time. On the other hand (see Appendix B) a considerable number of Regular battalions *did* fraternize, so there is no hard and fast rule. In any case it should be remembered that the Regular battalions of Christmas 1914 were by no means the same in complement as the ones which had marched in August, having been topped up with replacements as new to the Western Front as the Territorials themselves. If a generalization has to be made, it would probably be to the effect that new men were more prone to fraternize than hardened warriors – though even to this rule there would be numerous exceptions.

Three 'Pals by Xmas'

p. 34 'Live and let live' material, other than from sources indicated: from *Trench Warfare 1914–18: The Live and Let Live System*, Tony Ashworth.

p. 34 Liddell Hart quotation: from *The Memoirs of Captain Liddell Hart*, Vol. I, Cassell, 1965.

p. 36 A Trooper of the Scots Greys: quoted in *South Wales Echo*, 4 January 1915.

p. 37 Official History of 6/Gordon Highlanders: *The Sixth Gordons in France and Flanders*, Captain D. Mackenzie, 1921.

p. 37 'Nocturnal serenades': from *Twice in a Lifetime*, Leslie Walkinton – see Index of Soldiers.

p. 38 'Better entertainment': from letter by Second Lieutenant Dougan Chater – see Index of Soldiers.

p. 39 Armistice Day quotation from John E. Prescott, *In Flanders Fields, The Story of John McCrae*, The Boston Mills Press, Ontario, Canada, 1985, p. 130.

p. 41 Bavarian prince story: from *Vossische Zeitung*, quoted *The Times*, 8 January 1915.

p. 41 Visit of French President, hoax story: from Diary of General Sir Horace Smith-Dorrien – see Index of Soldiers.

p. 43 Document G. 507: TNA WO95/1560.

Four Pre-Christmas Initiatives

p. 46 Papal initiative: *New York Times*, December 1914; *Leslie Baily's BBC Scrapbooks for 1896–1914*; BBC Radio, *Scrapbook for 1914*; *Benedict XV: The Pope of Peace*, by Father H. E. G. Rope, Gifford, 1941.

It should be added that it has been claimed that whereas the Pope's plea did not win approval at national level it did have a major impact at the front among units from Catholic areas, such as the German Army's Bavarian regiments, and that in consequence much of the credit for the Christmas truce should be laid at their door. However, the argument that the Bavarians began an initiative which other regiments took up is difficult to sustain; trucing began simultaneously at many points of the line and the principal trucers in the British sector were the Protestant Saxons.

p. 46 'Senator Kenyon's initiative: *New York Times*, 11 December 1914.

p. 47 'The added comfort and protection . . .': from newspaper advertisement by Hope Brothers Complete Outfitters, Birmingham and London.

p. 48 An artillery officer: letter in *The Times*, 5 January 1915.

p. 50 Newspaper report (originating in Rotterdam): *New York Times*, 26 December 1916.

p. 51 Churchill quotation: from a memorandum of 29 December 1914, quoted in *Winston S. Churchill*, Martin Gilbert, Companion Part I (Documents) to Volume III, Heinemann, 1972.

p. 52 Comment on Sir John French: from *The Little Field Marshal*, Richard Holmes.

p. 54 2/Border diary: this half-illiterate but eloquent diary was recovered from a German trench in November 1915; its author has never been identified.

Five Christmas Eve

p. 58 Material on coastal bombardments: from *From the Dreadnought to Scapa Flow*, Arthur J. Marder, Oxford University Press, 1965.

p. 58 Commentator in *Illustrated London News*: Charles Lowe, 26 December 1914.

p. 63 Account by Vize-Feldwebel Lange: from *Behind the Lines*, C. E. Cooper, op. cit.

p. 64 'A relatively fine summer': The general assumption has always been that 1914 was one of the great hot summers, but in fact the Meteorological Office do not rate it as one of their top ten; temperatures did, however, reach the 80s and 90s in July and August, in time for the outbreak of the war and the first marches and battles. By contrast, December 1914 and January 1915 have always been thought of as particularly wet and unpleasant and the figures prove this, both months being noted for above average rainfall and flooding. French statistics, taken at Dunkirk, confirm that the weather was as bad on the Western Front, with 1·99 inches above average in December and 3·71 inches above average in January.

p. 66 First air raid on Dover: *Glasgow Herald*, 26 December 1914; *The First Battle of Britain*, Major Raymond H. Fredette USAF, Cassell, 1966.

p. 67 2/R. Welch Fusiliers' Christmas Eve: from *The War the Infantry Knew*, Captain J. C. Dunn; unpublished letter by Second Lieutenant M. S. Richardson (loose MS in Battalion War Diary, TNA WO 95/1365).

p. 67 An artillery officer: letter in *The Times*, 1 January 1915.

p. 68 Order from GHQ: TNA WO95/1440 and elsewhere.

p. 71 German soldier's letter: from *Reclams Universum* (illustrated magazine), Leipzig, 21 January 1915.

p. 79 Material on the Kensingtons (13/London): from *The Kensingtons*, O. F. Bailey and H. M. Hollier.

p. 82 They were in fact sent to Wittenberg POW camp, where conditions were harsh.

p. 84 Unnamed officer of Rifle Brigade: letter in *The Times*, 2 January 1915.

p. 86 2/Bedfordshire story: Battalion War Diary; *The Spice of Variety*, Charles Brewer – see Index of Soldiers.

p. 88 Belgian soldier's account: *The Times*, 2 January 1915.

p. 89 Account by Robert de Wilde: from *Mon Journal de Campagne*, published Paris, 1918.

p. 90 Account by Capitaine L. Rimbault: from *Journal de Campagne d'un Officier de la Ligne*, Librairie Militaire Berger-Lenroult, 1916.

p. 91ff. German regimental accounts: from appropriate Regimental Histories. See Bibliography.

pp. 96–98 Material on French attitudes: from monograph by the late Anthony Brett-James.

Six Christmas Day

p. 99 Officer of Queen's Westminster Rifles: letter in *Norfolk News*, 9 January 1915.

p. 100 Chaplain's account of Christmas service: from *With French in France & Flanders*, Owen Spencer Watkins, Charles A. Kelly, 1915.

p. 101 2/Devons story: letter by R. Loman, ex-soldier 2/Devons, *Daily Chronicle*, 24 November 1926.

p. 102 1/Leicester Tommy: Harold Startin – see Index of Soldiers.

p. 102 2/Border story: Diary of unknown soldier of the Border Regiment – see note to page 54 above.

p. 102 Queen's Westminster story: from Leslie Walkinton – see Index of Soldiers.

p. 102 2/Wiltshire story: from E. L. Francis – see Index of Soldiers.

p. 102 Another subaltern: A. P. Sinkinson – see Index of Soldiers.

p. 102 Old Contemptible: Harold Startin, 1/Leicester, as above – see Index of Soldiers.

p. 103 German soldiers' letters: from *Vorwärts*, Berlin, January 1915, quoted the *Daily Telegraph*, 9 January 1915; and *Reclams Universum*, Leipzig, 21 January 1915.

p. 104 Officer of the Rifle Brigade (as p. 84): letter in *The Times*, 2 January 1915.

p. 105 A subaltern: letter in *Manchester Guardian*, 6 January 1915.

p. 106ff. Material on joint burial service, etc.: from *The 6th Gordons in France & Flanders*, op. cit.; *Letters* by Sir Edward Hulse – see Index of Soldiers; 20th Brigade War Diary (TNA WO95/1650); 2/Scots Guards War Diary. (TNA WO95/1657).

p. 115 German soldiers' letters: from *Reclams Universum*, op. cit.

p. 117 A piper in the Scots Guards: letter in *The Times*, 11 January 1915.

p. 117 A junior officer of the 6th Cheshires: letter in *Cornish Guardian*, 8 January 1915.

p. 120 Material on the Kensingtons: as p. 79.

p. 120 An LRB man: from 'Christmas 1914', Frank & Maurice Wray, *The Army Quarterly*, October 1968.

p. 122 A soldier from the same battalion: letter in *Birkenhead News*, 4 January 1915.

p. 123 A British subaltern: letter in *Daily Telegraph*, 31 December 1914.

p. 123 Officer of the Queen's Westminster Rifles: letter in *Norfolk News*, 9 January 1915.

p. 124 Dum-dum bullets: Soft-nosed bullets which spread on impact, causing particularly unpleasant injuries. Developed by the British (Dum Dum was the British arsenal in Calcutta), they were subsequently prohibited under the Hague Convention of 1902. A dum-dum effect could be achieved, however, by adapting bullets in general use, and this was almost certainly done in some instances by both the British and Germans during the First World War.

p. 125 2/Border account: anonymous diary: see note to p. 54.

p. 126 Rifleman of the Queen's Westminster Rifles: letter in *Daily News*, 30 December 1914.

p. 129 Prussians and Saxons: It seems that hard-line battalions on the German side were referred to automatically as Prussians whether they were in the strict sense of the term Prussians or not. The corps opposite Captain Jack's Cameronians was a Saxon one, but as in the British army some units, even individuals, were more 'thrusting' than others. It seems also that soldiers from Saxony or Bavaria were prone to use the term Prussian to denote troops from any other state.

p. 130 Lieutenant of *Landwehr*: letter in *The Times*, 28 January 1915.

p. 137 Barber from Holborn story: from 'The Last Days of Chivalry', J. A. Maxtone Graham, *The Kiwanis Magazine*, December 1964–January 1965.

p. 140 Christmas menu of soldiers of Honourable Artillery company: *Evening News*, 4 January 1915.

p. 141 Account by former transport driver: C. W. Howe, 1963 letter, Imperial War Museum.

p. 143–144 Material on Berlin and Germany: *New York Times*, 26 December 1914; *The Times*, 30 January 1915; C. E. Cooper, *Behind the Lines*, op. cit.

p. 144 English resident in Paris: from *Paris Waits*, M. E. Clarke, Smith Elder, 1915.

p. 144 British correspondent in Paris: *The Graphic*, 2 January 1915.

p. 144 London material: *New York Times*, 26 December 1914; *In London during the Great War*, Michael MacDonagh, Eyre & Spottiswoode, 1935; *Dear Old Blighty*, E. S. Turner, Michael Joseph, 1980.

p. 145 Sandringham menu: *Daily Sketch*, 24 December 1914.

p. 146 Kaiser's speech: *The Times*, 30 December 1914.

p. 147 Material on gifts from Princess Mary's Fund: from *HRH The Princess Mary's Fund Report*, May 1920. Other variations were: for the nurses, chocolate instead of tobacco; and for ships' boys – likewise not to be encouraged in the smoker's art – a bullet pencil case. Everybody received a gift box and a card. This was the only year of the war in which such a gift was distributed. The only British parallel from other wars appears to have been a gift of a box of chocolates by Queen Victoria to all soldiers serving in South Africa to celebrate the New Year 1900.

p. 156 Iron Cross references: The Iron Cross was a decoration only given in wartime. There were two versions during the First World War: for combatants, First Class, and for non-combatants, Second Class, of which five million were awarded throughout the war. Already, by Christmas 1914, there were those who deplored their indiscriminate distribution.

p. 158 Royal Artilleryman: from account by a Chelsea pensioner first printed in *The Gunner*, reprinted *The Stafford Knot*, April 1980.

p. 161 An officer of a Glasgow Regiment: letter in *Glasgow Herald*, 1 January 1915.

pp. 162–163 An officer of the RAMC: letter in *The Times*, 1 January 1915.

p. 164 *Landstürmers*, visit to British trenches: from report by Harold Ashton, Special Correspondent of *Daily News*, 31 December 1914.

p. 164 A British subaltern: letter in *Daily Telegraph*, 6 January 1915.

p. 165 'My captain etc. . .': letter by a junior officer, *Cornish Guardian*, 8 January 1915.

p. 165 'Some Uhlan officers. . .': from *History of The 1st and 2nd Battalions The North Staffordshire Regiment (The Prince of Wales's) 1914–1923*.

p. 166ff. Football games in billets: soldier's letter, courtesy The Queen's Regimental Museum, Clandon Park.

p. 167 Footballs tied to knapsacks: *The Sphere*, 9 January 1915.

p. 167 Officer of a Highland Regiment: letter in *Morning Post*, 2 January 1915.

pp. 169–70 The fact that two scores of 3–2 occur in the accounts of Christmas Day football must be assigned either to a curious coincidence or to mistaken memory. The two matches referred to could not have been the same one, in that the units concerned were separated not only by geographical distance but also by the river Lys.

p. 175 'A good sing-song': anonymous diary, see note to p. 54.

p. 176 German 143rd Infantry Regiment truce account: since it is unlikely that Lieutenant Meinicke and his comrades would confuse French opponents for British, it would seem apparent that some British unit or units must still have been in the area relinquished to the French during the reorganization of sectors which followed the closing down of the First Battle of Ypres. This was a very early stage in the Western Front war when the orderly disposition of forces on maps was not necessarily reflected in actual practice on the ground. At the same time there seems no obvious contender for the role of British partner in this fraternization and it should be pointed out that the nearest known British units, those of Major-General Haldane's 3rd Division (which reached as far north as Wytschaete), were not involved in the Christmas truce at all; see p. 199.

p. 178 Belgian soldier's letter: as p. 88.

pp. 178–9 Account by Robert de Wilde: as p. 89.

p. 179 French Infantry Brigade War Diaries: *Journals des Marches et Opérations de la 139e et de la 56e Brigades d'Infanterie*, courtesy *Service Historique de l'Armée de Terre*, Vincennes.

p. 180 French joint burial: account by Emile Barraud of 29th Regiment in *The Graphic*, 30 January 1915.

Seven Boxing Day

p. 183 'One soldier on Boxing Day': letter in *Manchester Guardian*, 1 January 1915.

p. 185 Story told to Ethel Cooper: *Behind the Lines*, op. cit.

p. 186 Boxing Day burial: War Diary of 2/Queen's Regiment, TNA WO95/1664.

p. 190 Cameron Highlanders under sniper fire: *Historical Records of the Cameron Highlanders*, Vol III, W. Blackwood & Sons, 1931.

p. 191 Smith-Dorrien memorandum, 25 December 1914: TNA WO95/1560.

p. 191 Smith-Dorrien memorandum, 27 December 1914: TNA WO157/262.

Eight 'The Long Truce is Broken'

p. 198 *1914*, Field Marshal Viscount French of Ypres.

p. 203 *History of the Great War*, John Buchan.

p. 203 Order of 1 January 1915 from Second Army: TNA WO95/1441 and elsewhere.

The fact that so few orders relating to the Christmas truce have survived should not cause surprise. So many orders and signals were despatched to all units by all staffs at all times that it was rare for them to be carefully preserved for the enlightenment of future historians. Indeed, since the majority of them were written or typed on small pieces of flimsy paper, they tended to finish their brief career pressed into further service to the nation in that most humble but vital of areas, the trench latrine. Who knows what fascinating fragments of history were, as one might put it, 'wiped' in this way? As corroboration of the potential value of such documents, it is worth citing the experience of Colonel Richard Meinertzhagen in the East African campaign, who arranged that paper used by German officers in their necessary moments should be salvaged for the assistance it might give to his intelligence reports. See Richard Meinertzhagen, *Army Diary 1899–1920*, Oliver & Boyd, 1960.

pp. 210–11 Signals from Saxons opposite 11th Brigade: TNA WO95/1488.

p. 217 'The Wonderful Day': Headline, *Evening News*, 2 January 1915.

p. 233 War Diary of 8/Sherwood Foresters: TNA WO95/2695.

p. 234 War diary of 1/Welch Regiment: TNA WO95/2277.

p. 238 RAF flying officer's diary: R. J. Fairhead, unpublished MS, Imperial War Museum.

p. 243 Old Contemptible: Harold Startin, 1/Leicester – see Index of Soldiers.

p. 243 Comment by G. H. Perris: from *The Campaign in France & Belgium*, Hodder & Stoughton, 1915.

Nine Christmas 1915

p. 244 A. J. P. Taylor quotation: from *The First World War, an Illustrated History*.

p. 247 Orders forbidding unauthorized truces: 140th Infantry Brigade papers, TNA WO95/2731.

p. 249 German anti-fraternization order: TNA WO/157/4.

p. 255 Report by Lord Cavan: TNA WO95/1190.

Postscript

p. 266 L. E. Tutt: MS memoir, Imperial War Museum, also quoted in Adrian Gilbert, *Imperial War Museum Book of the Desert War*, Sidgwick & Jackson, 1992, pp. 23–4.

pp. 267 A former Corporal, September 1944: Mr A. Roberts, letter to authors 1983.

pp. 267–8 Korean War fraternization: the review of the first edition of this book in the *Journal of the Royal Artillery* in March 1985 ended with the following comment: 'The reviewer was glad of the opportunity to read it since he too had been a party to an informal meeting of former combatants on the narrow deck of land between "The Hook" and "Renown" in Korea on the day the war ended there.'

p. 268 Nigerian–Biafran truce for football game: Pelé, with Martin L. Fish, *My Life and the Beautiful Game*, New English Library, 1977.

p. 268 Broken truces in Nigerian–Biafran war: report in *The Times* from Winston S. Churchill, published 27 February 1969.

Bibliography

Ashworth, Tony *Trench Warfare 1914–18: The Live and Let Live System*, Macmillan, 1980

Baily, Leslie *Leslie Baily's BBC Scrapbooks for 1896–1914*, Allen & Unwin, 1966

Bairnsfather, Bruce *Bullets and Billets*, Grant Richards, 1916

Binding, Rudolph, Morrow, Ian F. D. (translator) *A Fatalist at War*, Allen & Unwin, 1929

Blake, Robert (ed.) *The Private Papers of Douglas Haig 1914–1919*, Eyre & Spottiswoode, 1952

Bloem, Walter, Wynne, G. C. (translator) *The Advance from Mons 1914*, 1930

Brewer, Charles *The Spice of Variety*, Muller, 1948

Buchan, John *History of the Great War*, Nelson, 1915–19

Caine, Hall *The Drama of 365 Days*, Heinemann, 1915

Chapman, Guy *Vain Glory*, Cassell, 1968

Charteris, Brigadier-General Sir John *At GHQ*, Cassell, 1931

Cooper, Caroline Ethel *Behind the Lines, One Woman's War 1914–18*, edited by Decie Denholm, Jill Norman & Hobhouse, 1982

Craster, J. M. (ed.) *Fifteen Rounds a Minute: The Grenadiers at War, 1914*, Macmillan, 1976

Doyle, A. Conan *The British Campaign in France and Flanders 1914*, Hodder & Stoughton, 1916

Drage, Charles *The Amiable Prussian*, Blond, 1958

Dunn, Capt, J. C. *The War the Infantry Knew*, P. S. King, 1938; Jane's, 1987

Eksteins, Modris *Rites of Spring: The Great War and the Birth of the Modern Age*, Bantam Press, 1989

French, Field Marshal Viscount John of Ypres *1914*, Constable, 1919

Griffith, Ll. Wyn *Up to Mametz*, Faber & Faber, 1931

Holmes, Richard *The Little Field Marshal*, Cape, 1981

Housman, Laurence (ed.) *War Letters of Fallen Englishmen*, Gollancz, 1930

Hulse, Captain Sir Edward *Letters*, privately printed, 1916

Jolliffe, John (ed.) *Raymond Asquith, Life and Letters*, Collins, 1980

Jünger, Ernst *The Storm of Steel*, Chatto & Windus, 1929

Miquel, Pierre *La Grande Guerre*, Fayard, Paris, 1983

Montague, C. E. *Disenchantment*, Chatto & Windus, 1922

Norman, Terry (ed.) *Armageddon Road, A VC's Diary 1914–1916*, Kimber, 1982

Perris, G. H. *The Campaign in France & Belgium*, Hodder & Stoughton, 1915

Richards, Frank *Old Soldiers Never Die*, Faber & Faber, 1933

Simpson, Keith *The Old Contemptibles*, Allen & Unwin, 1981

Taylor, A. J. P. *The First World War, an Illustrated History*, Hamish Hamilton, 1963; Penguin, 1966

Terraine, John *The Smoke and the Fire*, Sidgwick & Jackson, 1980

Terraine, John (ed.) *General Jack's Diary*, Eyre & Spottiswoode, 1964

Thornton, Lt-Col L. H. CMG DSO and Fraser, Pamela *The Congreves: Father and Son*, Murray, 1930

Walkinton, Leslie *Twice in a Lifetime*, Samson Books, 1980

Williamson, Henry *A Fox under my Cloak*, (fiction) Macdonald 1958; Chivers Press, Bath, 1983

Witkop, Philipp (ed. 1928), Wedd, A. F. (translator) *German Students' War Letters*, Methuen, 1929

OFFICIAL AND REGIMENTAL HISTORIES

BRITISH

History of the Great War: Military Operations, France and Belgium (1914–15) compiled by Brigadier-General J. E. Edmonds and Captain G. C. Wynne, Macmillan, 1927

Anon. *History of 1st and 2nd Battalions of the North Staffordshire Regiment (The Prince of Wales's) 1914–1923*, Hughes & Harper, 1932

Bailey, O. F. & Hollier, H. M. *The Kensingtons*, Regimental Old Comrades Association, 1936

Berkeley, R. *The History of the Rifle Brigade in the War of 1914–18*, 1927

Drake-Brockman, Brigadier-General D. H. *With the Royal Garhwal Rifles in the Great War from August 1914 to November 1917*, 1934

Evatt, J. *Historical Record of the 39th Royal Garhwal Rifles*, Vol. I, 1922

Falls, Cyril *The History of the First Seven Battalions, the Royal Irish Rifles in the Great War, Vol II*, 1925

Henriques, T. Q. *The War History of the 1st Battalion the Queen's Westminster Rifles 1914–1918*, 1923

Latter, J. C. *The History of the Lancashire Fusiliers 1914–1918, Vol. I*, 1949

Mackenzie, Captain D. *The Sixth Gordons in France and Flanders*, 1921

Maurice, F. *The History of the London Rifle Brigade 1859–1919*, Constable, 1921

Petre, F. Loraine *The History of the Norfolk Regiment 1685–1918, Vol. II*, 1925

Petre, F. Loraine & Ewart, W. *The Scots Guards in the Great War 1914–1918*, Murray, 1925

Smith, C. *War History of the Sixth Battalion the Cheshire Regiment*, 1932

Stacke, H. FitzM. *The Worcestershire Regiment in the Great War*, 1928

Story, H. H. *History of the Cameronians (Scottish Rifles) 1910–1933*, 1961

Verney, Colonel W. *The Rifle Brigade Chronicle 1914*, John Bale, 1915

Ward, C. H. Dudley *Regimental Records of the Royal Welch Fusiliers Vol. III*, London, 1928

Willcocks, General Sir James *With the Indians in France*, Constable, 1920

GERMAN

Anon. *History of the 133rd Infantry Regt*, Hamburg, 1969

Appel, Dr Friedrich, *History of Reserve Infantry Regiment No. 205*, Berlin, 1937

Baldenstein, R. von, & others *Das Infanterie-Regiment Freiherr von Sparr* (History of the 3rd Westphalian Infantry Regiment), Berlin, 1927

Bossert, Capt. Hans *We of the 143rd: The (4th Lower Alsace) Infantry Regiment No. 143 in Peace and in War*, Vol. I, Berlin, 1935

Crusius, Baumgarten, *History of the 139th (11th Royal Saxon) Infantry Regt*, Dresden, 1927

Goldammer, A. *History of the 179th Infantry Regt*, Leipzig, 1931

Masoben, Ernst *History of Reserve Infantry Regiment No. 212*, Oldenburg, 1933

Orgeldinger, Louis *History of Württembergische Reserve Infantry Regiment No. 246*, Stuttgart, 1931

Pflugbeil, H. *History of the 181st Infantry Regt*, Dresden, 1923

Reinhardt, G. H., & others *History of the 107th Infantry Regt*, Dresden, 1928

Riebensahm, G. *History of the 15th (2nd Westphalian) Infantry Regt*, Minden, 1931

Note: German Regimental Histories available in German only

MAGAZINE ARTICLES, PART WORKS, etc.

'Christmas 1914', A. J. Peacock, *Gun Fire*, Vol. 1, No. 2, York Educational Settlement, 1984, and later numbers

'Christman 1914, and After', John Terraine, *History Today*, December 1979

'Christmas 1914', Frank & Maurice Wray, *The Army Quarterly*, October 1968

'Christmas Day in Plugstreet', Peter T. Scott, *Stand To!*, No. 12, Winter 1984

The Great World War, Frank H. Mumby (ed.), Gresham, Vol. II, 1915

The Great War . . . I Was There!, Sir John Hammerton (ed.), Amalgamated Press, 1938, Parts 7 and 12

'The Last Days of Chivalry', J. A. Maxtone Graham, *The Kiwanis Magazine*, December 1964–January 1965

The Times History of the War, Vol. IV, 1915

'Time off from Conflict: Christmas 1914', David Winter, *Royal United Service Institution Journal*, December 1970

Twenty Years After Vol. I, Sir Ernest Swinton (ed.), Newnes, 1938

The War Illustrated 1914–1918, Vol. I, Nos. 20 & 22, Vol. III, No. 71

Index of Soldiers

Sources of quotations are listed at the end of each entry. Ranks as at the time of the events described.

1914 NAMES

BRITISH

GERMAN

SOLDIERS QUOTED IN POSTSCRIPT

Index